The Essential Guide to
Flatsharing

The Essential Guide to
Flatsharing

Rupert Hunt and Matt Hutchinson

A HOW TO BOOK

ROBINSON

ROBINSON

First published in Great Britain by How to Books, 2009

This edition published in Great Britain by Robinson in 2016

Copyright © Rupert Hunt and Matt Hutchinson 2009, 2011, 2013, 2016

1 3 5 7 9 8 6 4 2

The moral right of the author has been asserted.

A CIP catalogue record for this book is available from the British Library.

ISBN 978-1-84528-548-7

Printed and bound in Great Britain by Bell & Bain Ltd, Glasgow, G46 7UQ
Papers used by Robinson are from well-managed forests
and other responsible sources

Robinson
is an imprint of
Little, Brown Book Group
Carmelite House, 50 Victoria Embankment, London EC4Y 0DZ

An Hachette UK Company
www.hachette.co.uk

www.littlebrown.co.uk

How To Books are published by Robinson, an imprint of Little, Brown Book
Group. We welcome proposals from authors who have first-hand experience of
their subjects. Please set out the aims of your book, its target market and its
suggested contents in an email to Nikki.Read@howtobooks.co.uk

Contents

Chapter 4: Lodgers (LIL) 46

Chapter 5: The Language of Flatsharing 72

Preface

When we wrote the preface to the first edition of *The Essential Guide to Flatsharing* we talked about how the Internet changed the way people look for flatshares. Now, seven years later, that seems outdated. Everyone looks for everything online these days – we just take it for granted.

The real story today is the rise of flatsharing itself. Sharing is on the up for a whole host of social and economic reasons. We won't bore you with them (and you probably know them all anyway), but, in a nutshell, most of us are feeling the pinch when it comes to money and that's reflected in the way we're living.

So why are we sharing more?

There are a whole host of reasons people flatshare, but the simple fact is it's cheaper than living on your own. Much cheaper.

There are other benefits too, though. Some are obvious, others you may not have considered at all.

Sharing is ...

Affordable – Renting on your own is, on average, 121% more expensive than flatsharing.

Flexible – You're not tied down so you can move as and when you need to.

Sociable – There's always something going on in a flatshare. Living on your own can be lonely.

Less hassle – If the boiler breaks in the middle of winter, or the roof leaks, it's your landlord's problem, not yours

Green – Sharers have significantly smaller carbon footprints than those who live alone. Just sharing a two bed flat means a 40% carbon saving per person. This rises to 59% if you share a five-bed house.

A few facts about flatsharing that may surprise you

- Someone finds a room or flatmate on SpareRoom every 3 minutes

- The over 50s are the fastest growing group living in shared accommodation

- Almost 15,000 people attended Speed Flatmating events in London in 2015

- The average UK homeowner could earn £6,500 a year by renting out their spare room. The first £4,250 is completely tax free. That amount is rising to £7,500 a year from April 2016, thanks to Spare Room's six-year 'Raise the Roof' campaign

- 53% of flatsharers would be happy to rent long term if there wasn't such pressure to buy in the UK

- 19% of sharers think it will take them more than 10 years to buy a property

- A further 19% say they never expect to be able to buy

- The number of people looking for lodgers in the UK has doubled in the past 5 years

- In 2015 more than 750,000 new people signed up to SpareRoom to find a room to rent

Whatever your reasons for reading this book, rest assured you're not on your own. Sharing is fast becoming a way of life for millions of people in the UK. Whether you need somewhere affordable to live, want to find a new flatmate or are thinking about renting your spare room out to make a bit of cash, everything you need to know is in this book.

How to Use this Book

This aim of this book is to provide you with all the information you need to identify, find and live in any type of shared accommodation. Whether you need a room in a shared house, someone to replace a departing flatmate or a lodger for your spare room, all the information you need is here.

As the book caters for several types of reader, with different needs, not all the information will be immediately relevant to everyone so there are three main ways of using this book:

Read it straight through

If you're new to the world of sharing you could do worse than to read the book straight through. This will give you a good idea of the different types of share and a sense of what living in each is like, followed by advice on finding the right place to live and what to do once you're in. Having found out a bit about all the options, you can re-read the chapters you think are particularly relevant to help you find the best accommodation to suit your needs.

Chapters of interest

If you've got a more specific idea of what you're looking for then you'll probably want to read the most pertinent chapters first. To help you do this we'll point out on the contents page which groups it will be most useful to. The following abbreviations will be used:

SH – Chapters particularly suitable for sharers and flatmates.
RS – This indicates content aimed primarily at those looking for a room (often known as room seekers).

LIL – If you're looking for a lodger then chapters marked LIL (short for live-in landlord) will be the place to start.

You shouldn't just read the chapters you think are aimed at you, if you're thinking of becoming a lodger (for example) reading the chapter aimed at those looking to take in a lodger will give you some insight into their thought processes and should ultimately help you understand each other when it comes to living together.

Some chapters are of interest to more than one group and are marked accordingly; anything without a specific marking is general information, which will be of use to everyone.

On one or two occasions (most notably the chapters on finding a flatshare and finding a flatmate) information is relevant to more than one group. If we feel there's a possibility you might miss it (for example you might be looking for a flatshare and skip the chapter on looking for a flatmate) we've kept it in both relevant sections. In most cases we'll mention the topic briefly and point you to the chapter where you'll find the information in full.

Index

At the back of the book you'll find an index so, if there's a particular topic you need information on, you'll be able to navigate to it quickly.

There's also a glossary (Chapter 5, *The Language of Flatsharing*) you can refer to if there are any terms you aren't familiar with.

FLATMATES OR HOUSEMATES?

Rather than stick to one or the other throughout the book, we decided that (as both are commonly used and fairly interchangeable) we'd use whichever seemed to fit in a certain situation or, failing that, whichever sprang to mind first. Technically whichever you use depends on whether you live in a flat or house but usage tends not to be so strict in practice.

FURTHER RESOURCES

At the back of the book you'll find a list of useful resources for handy reference. Most of these will be mentioned in the relevant chapters but we've collected them all together for ease of use. Additionally there are several links to sections of the book (such as checklists) that are also available online. These are mentioned alongside the relevant information as it occurs in the text.

Introduction:
Flatsharing – The Basics

What is flatsharing?

Simply put, flatsharing is a group of (generally unrelated) people joining together to rent a property. If it's a flat it's known as a flatshare and if it's a house (you guessed it) a houseshare – the people you share with are your flatmates or housemates. These terms have all become pretty interchangeable so don't worry about which you use, we generally refer to SpareRoom.co.uk as a flatshare site even though many of the rooms listed are in houses.

Why flatshare?

There are many reasons why people choose to live in a flatshare and most of them fall under the broad categories of funds, flexibility and friendship.

FUNDS

Flatsharing is an affordable way to live (much more so than renting somewhere on your own) so, for many people, it's the perfect option. Whether they're on a budget, paying off student debt, saving for a deposit or just making their money go as far as possible, thousands of people in the UK choose flatsharing as the best option. Despite interest rates remaining low, most young people are struggling to buy a property as saving for a deposit is proving difficult and mortgages are harder to get. This means more people are sharing for longer. With house prices still rising in many parts of the country, home ownership is shifting further out of reach for many. At the same time, many people are simply finding that sharing suits them at this stage in their lives.

FLEXIBILITY

Sharing with other people gives you so many options for how and where you want to live. You can choose how large a property you live in and how many people you share it with and whether you want a quiet retreat or a vibrant party house. Often you'll find that areas that are way out of your price range on your own become affordable if you share. This is also the case with the type and quality of property you'll find in many cases.

Sharing doesn't usually tie you into long contracts or require you to commit large sums of money so it's the perfect option if you're not sure where you'll be in a year's time. This isn't just the case for younger people, we're seeing more and more older sharers taking advantage of the flexibility offered by sharing, whether they're recently divorced or separated and need somewhere to live while they sort themselves out or needing to move for work but don't want to buy and settle long term in an area. We're also seeing an increasing number of people who rent somewhere near their work whilst keeping a permanent property elsewhere.

This flexibility, and its appeal to all age groups, is evident at the Speed Flatmating events we run in Central London. A recent event spanned all ages from late teens to early 60s and the variety of rooms on offer (in terms of price, location and type of property) had something to suit most (if not all) situations.

FRIENDSHIP

The final F-factor, friendship, is not one to be overlooked lightly. We've spoken to thousands of sharers over the years that choose their lifestyle based of the other Fs (funds and flexibility) but cite friendship as one of the things they've gained most from by sharing. One successful young professional (in her early 30s) we spoke to recently revealed that she was looking for a lodger for her spare room not because she needed the money but because she just wanted someone else around the house.

We constantly hear from sharers who have found some of their best friends through sharing. We've even had a few weddings as a result of people meeting on SpareRoom!

Who lives in flatshares?

The simple answer to this is 'pretty much anyone'. SpareRoom's five million plus users range in age from school leavers to pensioners and include couples as well as single people. The main body of our users are young professionals (the breakdown on the site at the moment is around 70% professional to 30% student) but flatsharing is popular with all sorts of people looking for somewhere to live.

You'll find ads on SpareRoom from:

- students
- graduates
- young professionals
- immigrant workers
- families renting out a room
- live-in landlords looking for a lodger
- recently divorced or separated people
- retirees
- people relocating for work
- those looking for a room Monday to Friday only
- people visiting the UK from overseas
- couples.

Whatever your situation, there will be a flatshare out there to suit you or the perfect flatmate or lodger. With so many on offer, it can be daunting knowing where to begin looking so we've filled this book with as much advice as we can based on our ten years of running flatshare websites. We hope it will help you in your search, whatever you're looking for.

Matt and Rupert

CHAPTER ONE

Types of Let

The term flatshare is widely used in the UK to describe any shared accommodation, not just flats. Similarly the term 'flatmate' is the most commonly used word to describe someone you share with ('room-mate', a commonly used term in the United States, is only generally used in the UK to denote someone you actually share a room with – see below).

Regardless of the terms used to describe them, there are a few basic types of share you'll come across, and each will be discussed in detail in the following pages. Knowing which type of share is the right one for you will be vital when it comes to looking for somewhere to live (see Chapter 2, *Find a Flatshare*) so consider each carefully and how it meets your needs. Different types of tenancy suit different people and have their own characteristics. Certain types of share are more common in some parts of the country than others (although you'll probably find every type of share there is in London – see Chapter 9, *Flatshare in London*).

Flat or house share

This is one of the most common forms of share and is usually the first one which springs to mind when people think of living together. The property is rented out as whole by a group of (two or more) sharers under a joint tenancy. In most cases each sharer has their own room and facilities such as kitchen, bathroom and living room are shared. It's not uncommon for living rooms to be used as extra bedrooms to help keep individuals' rents down as the monthly rent is for the whole property, not by the room. It's also common for sharers to pay different amounts (usually mutually agreed between them) based on the size of their room and any extra benefits such as en-suite bathrooms. This can be a convenient way for groups of friends with different income levels to share a property.

Generally flatshares of this type are great for groups of people who already know each other. Similarly, you'll often find situations where two smaller groups, maybe two pairs of friends, join together to rent a property. This can work well as larger properties are often better value for money than smaller ones. This makes sense if you think about it; two people still need a kitchen, bathroom and living room. A four or five bed house may well have an extra bathroom or toilet but will still generally only have one kitchen and living room so the cost of these 'extra' rooms is split between more people.

Renting by the property rather than the room can have drawbacks. Tenants are often 'jointly and severally liable', which means that anyone (or all tenants) can be held responsible for the rent payments and any other obligations of the contract, such as utility bills or council tax. Things can also get tricky if one flatmate wants to leave before the others, as their notice has the effect of ending the tenancy for everyone and a replacement contract (with a replacement flatmate) is not an automatic right. However, landlords (or their agents) generally allow a replacement flatmate to be found and the contract to be re-signed. See Chapter 8, *Contracts, Rights and Agreements* for more on tenancy agreements.

There is an unwritten code that says a departing flatmate must do all he or she can to find a replacement so as to cause the other flatmates as little inconvenience and expense as possible. As a result you'll see room offered adverts placed by a departing flatmate trying to fill their room before they move out. You'll also find rooms advertised by the existing flatmates as, after all, it is they who will be living with the new flatmate so they'll be keen to be involved with choosing who moves in.

If you're renting a whole property between you the chances are you'll have an 'assured shorthold' tenancy. This is the most common form of tenancy agreement in the UK and the good news is it's covered under the recent Tenancy Deposit Scheme laws (see Chapter 8, *Contracts, Rights and Agreements*). If you're moving into a property to replace a departing tenant it's important to check you're covered by an agreement of some kind as, if the paperwork isn't amended and the old flatmate is still named, you may find yourself in a tricky situation and discover you have no rights.

PROS
✓ Bigger properties are usually better value per room than smaller ones.
✓ You don't have your landlord living with you.
✓ Often the most sociable way to live.

CONS
✗ Lack of privacy.
✗ Sharing facilities with several people.
✗ You may be jointly responsible for rent and bills, which can cause problems if one member of the house falls behind or doesn't pay up.

Rooms for rent (live-in landlord)

Lodging, where a homeowner rents out a spare room to a lodger while living in the property themselves, is one of the oldest forms of shared accommodation as we know it. Thanks to the government's Rent a Room Scheme allowing owners to earn up to £4,250 per year tax free by taking in a lodger (rising to £7,500 from April 2016), this arrangement has become extremely popular again. Over half the 'rooms offered' listings on SpareRoom now come from people taking in lodgers.

In the past it was common for live-in landlords to take in several lodgers and often provide extra services such as laundry and meals. Women often depended on this for an income and, more often than not, lodgers were male.

Today you're just as likely to find a young professional (or couple) renting out the spare room(s) in their flat to help cover the mortgage. In cases like these the living arrangements can be far more like living in a flatshare than the traditional image associated with lodgers. For example, it's not standard practice for meals to be included with your rent today (although some landlords will still offer this service). It's also not uncommon to find older couples or families renting out a room in their family house, perhaps the room of an older child who has left home.

Living with your landlord can be very different from living in a standard flatshare (especially if you're the only lodger) but can be the perfect arrangement for many sharers. If you're living as a lodger in a two-bed flat then it becomes even more important to make sure you find the right person to share with. Similarly, for a landlord, it's vital to choose the right lodger to minimize hassle. It's rare to find a two-bed flatshare made up of strangers (unless one is the landlord) for the very reason that it's an unusual way to live. Add to that the fact that one of you is the landlord and the need for caution is obvious.

A lodger's dodgy experience

'My landlord lived on the top floor and he didn't have a door to his room but had a staircase. My room was at the bottom of the staircase and I could hear his girlfriend telling him "don't be shy!" I was hysterical!'

Amy

Advice for landlords on taking in a lodger can be found in Chapter 4, *Lodgers* and tips on choosing the best lodger can be found in Chapter 3, *Find a Flatmate*.

The landlord's experience

Owen is an actor in his 30s living in South-East London. He bought a flat just under two years ago with the intention of renting out the second room to help with the mortgage. 'Acting is a notoriously insecure career' he says. 'I'd inherited a small amount of money and just been paid for an advert I'd been in. Between the two I managed to get a deposit together which was enough to buy a two-bed rather than a one-bed. By renting out the second room I can cover the difference in mortgage repayments and know I've got some security. I didn't know about the Rent a Room scheme until recently and that's made things much more affordable.'

PROS

✔ Often better quality accommodation as the landlord has to live there too.

✔ Can feel more like a home for the same reason.
✔ If anything goes wrong the landlord is on hand to sort it out.

CONS
✗ Can feel like you're a guest in someone else's house so can be more difficult to invite people back after the pub or have your partner stay over.
✗ If you get on well financial issues can get in the way of your friendship.
✗ Generally sharing with fewer people (often just your landlord) so can be uncomfortable if you don't get on.

Rooms for rent (live-out landlord)

Some landlords prefer to rent their properties by the room. This basically means that each tenant (or couple if they're sharing a room) has an individual contract for their room and all other facilities are shared. The benefit to landlords is that, if one person moves out, it doesn't necessarily mean the whole property will become vacant. Landlords also usually make more renting by the room than renting their property as a whole.

For sharers, there's the bonus of having your own contract and not being responsible for anyone else's rent or share of bills. It also makes for a convenient way for someone on their own to become part of a houseshare without moving in with an already established group and feeling like the odd one out. On the other hand, you may well be sharing with a group of people who don't know each other that well so, if you prefer a social house, it may not be the best option for you.

Traditionally this type of let catered to the lower end of the housing market but, increasingly, landlords are targeting the professional market. Professional landlords and specialist companies have started to offer properties, often new builds, in areas designed to appeal to young professionals. The properties are let by the room and generally furnished to a higher standard than average.

If you're part of a group and are renting rooms in a property without filling it, be aware that the landlord will probably have the right to fill any vacant rooms without telling you first or giving you any say in the matter.

Sharer's view

'A few years ago I was sharing a four-bed house with two other friends. We each had separate contracts and all was fine for six months. Then one day, while I was in the kitchen washing up, the front door opened and someone came in. He said "Hi, I'm Tony, your new housemate". Turns out the agent had let the other room and hadn't even warned us so a complete stranger just let himself in with his own key and we had no idea whatsoever.'

Tim

PROS

✔ Great if you don't already have people to share with.

✔ Means you're not responsible for anyone else's bills or rent if they fail to pay.

✔ Often a choice of differently priced rooms within one property so you can work to budget very effectively.

CONS

✗ Not always the most sociable way to live.

✗ Can have a higher turnover of flatmates, leading to a less settled flatshare.

Bedsits

Bedsit is short for 'bed sitting room' and is exactly that – a room which functions as a bedroom and living space in one. Essentially it's like living in a shared house, rented by the room but you have your own (lockable) room, which will typically have more space than a basic bedroom. Bedsits may have cooking facilities but this can involve nothing more than a microwave and kettle. Most bedsits were created by subdividing larger properties into small, cheap units without too much expense in conversion costs, therefore bedsits tend to be towards the lower end of the housing ladder.

Initially bedsits satisfied a demand created in the years after the Second World War. As people began to feel the need for more personal independence there was a shift away from the traditional boarding house towards more self-contained accommodation, without communal dining and relying on your landlady for meals. This didn't lead to totally isolated living conditions, however, as you'd still be likely to run into your neighbours on a regular basis. In fact the sitcom *Rising Damp* was born out of a situation such as this (see Interlude: *Fighting Over the Remote – Flatshare on the Box* for more on this and other flatshare inspired films and TV shows).

Bedsits have a reputation for being somewhere near the bottom end of the housing market and conjure up images of miserable Smiths fans gazing out of the window at the gasworks, writing poetry and contemplating suicide. And the Moody Blues referenced this perception of bedsits in the song *Nights in White Satin*.

In truth there's a wide range of bedsit accommodation out there and it can provide an affordable option for those on a low budget and new to an area. In many respects bedsits aren't strictly 'shared' accommodation in the same sense as most flatshares, as you won't necessarily have a communal living area, but they are an extension of lets 'by the room'.

PROS
✓ Cheap.
✓ Self-contained up to a point so more privacy than a typical flatshare.

CONS
✗ Can feel isolated.
✗ Not generally the most comfortable places to live.

Room shares

A room share takes things that one step further, meaning you share your bedroom with someone. Generally, this option is taken up by students and overseas visitors staying in London on a tight budget (though, let's face it, most visitors to London are on a fairly tight budget!) and is usually only survived for short periods. Certainly not to be recommended with anyone you don't know extremely well (or aren't prepared to get to know extremely well).

PROS
✔ Generally the cheapest of all the options.

CONS
✗ Sharing a room with someone!

Mon–Fri lets

One trend which has increased in recent years, particularly (although by no means exclusively) in London, is the Monday to Friday let. Basically, this works the same as a standard let but the room is only rented during the week and the tenant is elsewhere at weekends. This can work well for both parties as the landlord (usually a live-in landlord in this case) gets their weekends to themselves and can use the room for visiting friends and family whilst still earning a regular income from it. The lodger gets the flexibility of having somewhere to stay near work during the week at a reduced price and can go home for the weekend. We even heard of one person who lived with his family on the Costa Del Sol and flew back to London on Sunday nights for work on Monday morning. He'd leave a bit early on Friday and be at the beach bar in time for an evening drink!

These lets are often used by people who have a home and family life in one place, but are required by work to spend a lot of time in another location. London is the largest market for this type of let (see Chapter 9, *Flatshare in London*) but anywhere with a large employer (airports, hospitals, universities) can create a demand for this type of room.

The landlord's view

'I must admit that it is for financial reasons rather than social and I am out so much during the week it seems crazy not to earn some pounds on my rather lovely spare room. I tend to be around more at the weekends and want the flexibility to have family or friends to stay. It helps towards the mortgage and gives you the flexibility to either have folk to stay at the weekends or just be on your own – because, let's face it, we don't always feel like making small talk or closing the bathroom door! It seems that there are a growing number of people who just work in town during the week and don't want to pay for a full-time rent so it's a win-win for everyone as far as I can see!'

Rachel

PROS
✔ Flexible and often cost effective if you need to be in two places.
✔ Can save hours of travelling time.

CONS
✗ Hard to feel settled during the week.
✗ Can put a strain on home life if you're leaving behind a partner and/ or children during the week.

A few thoughts on sublets

Subletting isn't exactly a type of let, more a let within a let – hence the name. In basic terms, if two people rent a three-bed property under a standard assured shorthold tenancy then rent out the third room, collecting the rent themselves, this is called subletting. This is not permitted under most standard tenancy agreements. It does, however, go on and there will be cases where the landlord has agreed (perhaps off the record) for it to happen. It can also suit people in certain situations where neither party wants any commitment as there are no contracts involved. Such a casual arrangement obviously has its risks, the primary of these being your rights. If you return home one day to find your flatmates have changed the locks and won't let you back in you won't have much recourse. On the other hand, without any form of agreement, your flatmates can do very little about it if you decide not to pay your rent. In general we'd advise you to steel clear of sublets as they are a grey and difficult area. If you have three friends with a spare room, you need somewhere to stay and you feel confident the situation is safe then go for it but be wary of sublet arrangements if you're dealing with people you don't know.

CHAPTER TWO

Find a Flatshare

Finding somewhere to live and moving house can be one of the most stressful things you do. Luckily, the finding somewhere part is easier than ever now thanks to the Internet. Rooms in flatshares of all types all across the UK are easy to find, and right now there's a great choice as plenty of people are renting out a room to bring in a bit of extra cash.

Taking a bit of time to work out what it is you're looking for before you start your search will make it much easier to find the right room (and save you a lot of time aimlessly clicking through lists). The basic questions you'll need to answer when looking for a room are 'Where, What and How'. Firstly though you'll need to sort out your budget.

Budget

The factor that will most determine what you look for, and where you look, will be your budget, so it's vital to get this sorted before you do anything else. All this boils down to is working out exactly how much you can afford to spend each month on rent and bills.

Top Tip Don't forget, some rooms will have bills included in the rent and some won't, make sure you check. If your monthly budget is £400 and you're expecting to pay bills on top of that, then a £450 room with bills included could be a great deal. Without bills included it's simply £50 over budget.

Bear in mind how much you spend every month on travel too. It may well be that you can afford to pay a little more in rent if you're going to be living nearer where you need to be every day and your travel costs will be lower.

Once you've got your budget it'll help narrow down your choices and save some legwork and maybe a little heartache (there's no point viewing and falling in love with a £500 a month room if your maximum budget is £375). It's worth viewing a few slightly above budget, as the perfect place may be worth a little financial hardship (and you can sometimes haggle the rent down a bit) but, in general, stick to searching for places you can afford.

If you need help working out your budget try using an online budget calculator such as the one at: https://www.moneyadviceservice.org.uk/en/tools/budget-planner.

Got your budget sorted? Right, here's what's next . . .

What to look for

The first thing you need to decide is what type of property you want to live in. Would you prefer a busy shared house with four or five flatmates or maybe a smaller flat with just one or two other people? Have you considered living as a lodger? Chapter 1, *Types of Let*, will give you all the information you need on the different types of shared accommodation so you should read that to get an idea of your options. In busy areas like London you'll have the choice of all types, but some smaller towns or quieter areas might give you fewer options.

WHAT TYPE OF PROPERTY ARE YOU LOOKING FOR?

What are you looking for? The type and size of property will make a difference to what you can afford and where you can live. As with areas, it's worth thinking about these things first so you can really target your search to find the best place.

Does it matter to you whether you live in a house or a flat? Do you mind living in a tower block and having to use lifts? Often the type of property isn't as important as the features it has so look through this list first and decide which are important to you.

Features

Number of floors

This may seem like a strange one but lots of people don't like sleeping on the ground floor of a building. A house will generally have more than one floor (unless it's a bungalow of course) but flats often have all the rooms on one level.

Outside space

Do you need a garden, balcony or roof terrace? Outside space is great in the summer and is really useful for hanging out washing. In areas with lots of flats and converted houses there will always be more flats without gardens than with (as there's only one ground floor to a building) so you might find something better or cheaper if a garden isn't essential. Often flats will have a communal garden you can use, otherwise is there a park nearby you can use instead?

Parking/bike storage

If you drive you'll need somewhere to park your car. Do you need somewhere off street to park or will you be happy parking wherever you can nearby? In the case of a house converted into flats there are usually more people than parking spaces so always check who gets to use the ones there are, don't just presume that because there is one you'll be able to use it. If you ride a bike you'll need somewhere to keep it that's safe.

Washing machine

Unless you want to cart your laundry to a launderette every week you'll definitely want a washing machine.

Broadband/wi-fi

Most people want Internet access these days and having wi-fi means you can check your emails from your own room, which is always a bonus.

Bathrooms

If you want your own en-suite then it will narrow down the number of rooms available to you and will probably cost a bit more as well. On the upside, you won't need to queue to use the toilet or bath so it may well be worth finding an en-suite if you can. This may be something that falls into the 'preferable but not essential' category.

Own front door

If you live in a converted house you may well have one communal front door leading to an internal hallway with individual entrances. This could mean everyone's post comes through the main door and you all have to sort through it to find your own.

These are some of the more obvious points that will help you refine your search, for a list of points to bear in mind whilst actually looking round a specific property see our checklist below.

Size

The other important factor to consider is how large a property you want to live in. Basically this means 'how many people do you want to share with'. If you want a fairly quiet place to live you might want to share a smaller two or three-bed flat. This can put a bit more pressure on the relationship, if you live with just one other person and there's a conflict, there's nobody else to help mediate.

If you like a lot of people around then you'll probably want to live in a bigger, shared house. Larger properties are often cheaper per person than smaller ones but bear in mind you'll have more of a battle to use the bathroom or kitchen if there are several of you.

If you're not too concerned with this point then just search by budget and area and see what comes up.

WHERE DO YOU WANT TO LIVE?

We asked users of SpareRoom what the most important factor in choosing a room was. Fifty-seven per cent said location, twice as many as those who said cost (in second place with 25%).

'I live in a houseshare with four other people. You're probably thinking it sounds noisy, a little bit hectic and that personal space is but a dream. However, the house is large enough to take us, our creative pursuits and our crazy adventures.

With the right mix of people, and a big enough house to accommodate you, the advantages of a large house share far outweigh the negatives. Rent and utilities are more manageable and I have found that you can get better value for your money without compromising personal space. Financial savings are not the only benefits; this style of community living also affords you a friendship network rich in support and fun.

The day-to-day boring bits of managing a large house share can be a potential source of conflict and you're right to presume that there will be times when some housemates feel taken advantage of. In my house we try to avoid this bubbling cauldron of resentment through a cleaning rota and a house kitty that we all share responsibility for. If we have any big decisions to make, we usually cook a house meal, pour a glass of wine (optional), have a natter and then reach a majority decision. From time to time there is the usual flare of temper when somebody hasn't done their weekly clean, a few sarcastic comments about the toilet roll fairy and milk fairy (which I sometimes think are one being), and then there's always the moment when the boredom of compromise sets in – but all in all, this is the general wear and tear of family life and most of the time things run smoothly.

I would best describe my house share as like *Friends* but without the affairs and television cameras, because when it works, it really works. However, if you have a housemate that doesn't quite work with the mix, or, the house isn't big enough to accommodate your individual and group space, then the house can become a challenge.

My housemates and myself have reached that fashionable age of thirty-something, and yes you're right, the birthday parties were great; a big house does equal a big party. I only mention age to indicate that a large house share is not the exclusive property of the twenty-something. Perhaps your measure should be, that as long as you are happy to be part of a community and don't mind sharing the responsibility of a large house share, then I would say dust off that welcome mat and let the fun begin.'

Louise

Where you live will be decided by many factors including:

Budget

No matter how much you love a particular area there's no point looking there if prices are too expensive. You may as well be realistic with your budget from the outset as it's unlikely to change just to suit you.

'A couple of years ago I lived in a small, two-bedroom, ex-housing association flat in North London with a friend. When I say small, I mean very small. Space was limited; he left his bike in the lounge for about eight months once because there was nowhere else to put it. On the upside, bills were cheap and there was never a queue for the bathroom. He would spend most nights at his girlfriend's place so I had the flat to myself, which was difficult at first.

Gradually I came to enjoy the extra space. I taught myself to cook, I could watch what I fancied on TV and have friends to stay whenever I liked. When he was around it was great too, I had a great year, we didn't see much of each other but then again we didn't get in each other's way either.'

John

Work/study

Where do you need to be every day? It makes sense either to look close by or within easy reach of direct transport links as the less time and money you need to spend commuting the better.

Friends/family

Do you want to be near people you spend time with? If so do they live in areas you can afford and like?

Facilities

If you need to be able to get to a gym regularly check if there's one in the area you want to live in. Similarly, look for local shops, bars, restaurants etc, especially if you want to be able to go out locally.

Transport

If you need to use public transport then check what the options are. Is there a good bus service or a tube/train station nearby that goes to where you need to be on a regular basis?

Security

Will you feel safe walking home at night? Will your car be safe on the streets? How safe will you feel in the property?

Matt says:

'I lived in a beautiful flat a few years ago that was just perfect as a property. The trouble was it was in an area I really didn't feel safe living in and it just wasn't a pleasant place to be. The flat I live in now is smaller and doesn't have the same wow factor but I wouldn't swap in a million years.'

Working out the areas you want to live in before you start looking will help define your search and save time in the long run. If you're really not sure you can always start with a fairly wide search area and see which specific areas seem to fit your needs and budget. It would be worth spending a day or two looking round these areas, if you have the time, to see how you feel about them. Take a friend and look round the local shops, see what the transport is like and have a drink in the local pub. This won't always steer you towards one area but it may well help you discount one or two.

If you're moving to a completely new town or city you know nothing about then try a little bit of Googling to see what you come up with (I Googled the area I live in as a test and was rewarded with three different local forums, some information on local schools, several articles on local property, and a fascinating Wikipedia entry which I spent half an hour engrossed in when I should have been writing this – Matt).

A note on postcodes

In your search for somewhere to live (wherever in the UK you are) you'll find yourself dealing with postcodes as a means of describing where a property is. If you're new to the UK, or don't fully understand the system, here's what you need to know.

UK postcodes have two parts, the first half includes information on the post town and location within it, and the second contains more detailed information of the street and specific location of the property. The first half is the bit that tells you most of what you'll need to know when flat hunting.

The first letter (or two letters) tells you which town the property is in the region of, and the number usually denotes how far from the town centre it is. For example, PR is the code for Preston, Lancashire. PR1 is the first half of the postcode for the city centre, whereas PR6 covers an area of villages a few miles away.

WHO DO YOU WANT TO LIVE WITH?

Note – Some of this information is repeated in Chapter 3, Find a Flatmate, in a slightly modified form – aimed at those looking for a flatmate but not a room.

It's also worth thinking about who you want to live with. It can often be easier to share with strangers than friends but it really depends on you and what works best. We asked users of SpareRoom who they thought made the best flatmate – existing friends came in at 28%, with someone you don't already know well ahead at 55%.

There are no hard and fast rules so consider all the options.

Points to bear in mind are:

Age range
Do you mind sharing with people much older or younger than you?

Couples
Would you be prepared to share with a couple? Couples can affect the overall dynamic of a shared house (especially if they have a tendency to argue – see below).

Gender
Some people prefer to live in a single-sex household and some prefer a mix. This one is entirely about what works for you, although in larger flatshares it can be a bit much if you have only male or female flatmates.

Occupation
Does it matter to you whether you live with professionals, students or a mixture of both? Bear in mind a mix can affect your council tax bill (see Chapter 7, *Finance and Bills* for more on this).

Pets
Do you want to share with just people or are their animals okay too?

Smokers

Would living with smokers bother you? How about smokers who only smoke outside? (SpareRoom's research has shown that we're becoming increasingly less tolerant when it comes to living with smokers).

Landlords

Living as a lodger, whilst in many ways no different from living as a flatmate, can have a slightly different dynamic due to the fact you're living with your landlord. See Chapter 1, *Types of Let* for more on what to expect from living as a lodger.

Beware the couple

'I don't generally have a problem living with couples but, when one half of the pairing is perfectly normal and the other half is a complete nightmare it can get tricky.

The couple I lived with recently personified the "opposites attract" cliché. He was laid back and fun, whilst she was anal and completely insecure.

She also had a real problem with laundry – just touching a freshly ironed, perfectly folded pile of sheets would provoke a guaranteed screaming hissy fit, a slamming door and half an hour's manic driving around the streets. As for taking her dry washing off the radiators so you could use them . . .

On another occasion he was home late and she was getting progressively wound up. When he finally rocked up at the insanely late hour of 11.45, I was already in bed. I heard him creeping up the stairs but I was nearly deafened by her cry of "Will you be quiet, you're waking up the whole house!"

So, my advice is that living with a couple is risky. Simply put – any housemate carries a certain possibility of disaster but a couple comes as a unit so the odds immediately go up. Tread carefully.'

Sally

THE PERFECT FLATMATE

Choosing the perfect room is the easy bit, choosing the perfect people to share with can be less straightforward, especially if you only have a few minutes during a viewing to get to know people.

There are a few key points to consider, however, to get you moving in the right direction and discount a few obvious mismatches.

Decide what you want from a flatmate

For example, if you are new to the area, you may be flatsharing as a way to create a new social circle and will be looking for someone who shares similar interests and is open to going on the odd night out. On the other hand, you may already have a wide circle of friends in the area and just want somewhere to rest your head, so the age and interests of your flatmate are irrelevant. It's generally best not to expect your flatmates to become your new best friends, if it happens great but don't try and force the issue.

Work out whether your lifestyles will be compatible

If you have to be up early in the morning for work and like to go to bed at 10pm, you won't enjoy living with someone who works late and gets home around 1pm with half the local pub in tow . . . and vice versa!

Be honest about how houseproud you're likely to be

You'll get a sense of how clean the existing housemates are from the viewing (although bear in mind, they've – hopefully – tidied up a bit before showing you round). Be honest with yourself, if you view an absolutely spotless flat and you're a bit of a slob then chances are you'll have problems somewhere down the line.

Make sure you meet all of the flatmates before agreeing to move in

Even if you've met two out of three and get on really well with them, you could still find you hate the third person once you're in and it's too late.

Find out about any house rules and regulations

Be honest with yourself about whether you will be able to stick to house rules. In the interests of harmony, most households will have at least some written or unwritten rules and expectations; however, there will be households where the list is extensive. If you don't like any of the rules on the list, or are unsure you can stick to them all, it's probably better that you don't move in, for your own sake as well as the rest of the household.

Finally, don't move in with someone you are sexually attracted to

If you are attracted to a potential flatmate invite them out for a drink instead; if it doesn't work out at least you won't be stuck living with them.

A cautionary tale

'Be wary of moving into a house purely because the housemate is beautiful. I did and ended up with great sex for two weeks, but, when that cooled off, it was unbearable living in the house. DO NOT sleep with flatmates!'

Benji

HousemateHeaven.com has a fun tool for working out what type of housemate you are and who you'll be compatible with, see: http://www.housemateheaven.com/lifestyles.php.

WHAT AM I LOOKING FOR?

We've prepared a short questionnaire for you to fill in to help you narrow down your search and work out what's most important to you. You can fill this one out, photocopy it so you can use it more than once or print and edit a copy from: www.SpareRoom.co.uk/essentialguide/checklist.

	Definitely not	Don't mind	Preferable	Essential
Budget £				
Preferred areas				
Property has/is . . .				
Outside space				
Parking/bike storage				
Washing machine				
En-suite				
Own front door				
Bills included				
Near a bus stop				
Near a tube/train station				
Wi-fi				
Happy to share with . . .				
Couples				
Pets				
Students				
Landlord				
Single sex				
Mixed household				
Smokers				

Where to look

Now you've got a clearer picture of the type of flatshare you're looking for you'll need to start looking for it.

LOCAL RESOURCES vs ONLINE

Local papers, notice boards and shop windows can be a good way of finding accommodation but it'll be a bit hit and miss regarding quantity and quality of rooms on offer. By far the easiest way to search is online using one of the many dedicated flatshare sites. Not only will you be able to see photos and even video of the rooms on offer, the selection online is greater and bang up to date so you can be sure you're seeing rooms that are actually available.

If you're moving to a totally new area you'll be able to start your search from a distance using the Internet and do your homework before you get there. This also means you can line up several viewings in a day or two so you can make the most of the time you have if you can only get to the new area for a short time before you move.

Online flatshare listings will also have maps showing exactly where the properties are and have access to a lot more info than you can fit in a print advert or a card in a shop window. It's preferable to use a specialist flatshare site as opposed to a general listings site for several reasons, the most important of these is security.

WHY DEDICATED FLATSHARE SITES?

With so many general classified listings sites around why should you bother with a dedicated flatshare site? General classifieds sites are appealing as they can be used without having to register and are a simple way of reaching a lot of people. The downside is that your chances of encountering a scam advert or a fraudulent advertiser are far higher than if you use a reputable site which checks all ads for any scam attempts. At SpareRoom we also require users to register in order to contact you so we have a record of who everyone is. This means that, if a listing does turn out to be fraudulent, we can notify anyone who has been in contact with the advertiser and warn them.

For more information on staying safe using the Internet to find a flatshare, see Chapter 10, *Staying Safe*.

How to look

The best way to search is online and, now you've decided what you're looking for, you'll be able to search far more effectively. If you go to www.SpareRoom.co.uk you'll see a search box on the home page. This will let you search by town or postcode. Try clicking on 'advanced search' as this will give you the option to specify other criteria (such as budget) which will give you better results, especially in areas with a lot of rooms advertised.

If you're in London and need to live near a particular tube line you can search using the Tube Line Tool, which will only show rooms near stations on the line you need. For more on looking in London, see Chapter 9.

By creating a profile on the site you can also sign up for free email alerts, letting you know about any new rooms advertised in your area. This helps you keep on top of your search by having the effect of looking for you while you're busy doing something else.

PLACE A 'WANTED' AD

To make sure you cover all bases you should consider placing a 'room wanted' ad; this will allow people who need to fill a room to find you on the site. Most landlords don't just advertise their room and wait for the emails to flood in, they also search the wanted ads to see who's looking in their area. Placing a wanted ad will also get your details emailed out in alerts to anyone advertising a room in your area and, as most contact on the site comes through room wanted ads, you'll increase your chances of finding the room you're looking for.

Make your ad personal by including some information about yourself so prospective flatmates get some sense of what you're like. Adding a photo to your ad will make people much more likely to click on it – you can even add a short video of yourself.

By giving prospective flatmates a chance to find out a bit about you you'll be more likely to attract the right people. Take these as examples:

Double room wanted

Double room needed in Clapham, near tube. Budget is £500pcm – no smokers.

Outgoing guy looking for a room in a friendly, fun flatshare

Hi, I'm Adam and I need a room (preferably a double) in the Clapham area as I'm moving there to be nearer to work (which is graphic design for the web). I'm hoping to share with a friendly, relaxed bunch who aren't averse to the odd glass of wine, trip to the pub or summer BBQ.

My budget's around £500 a month but a bit more might be possible for the right room with the right people. If you've got a room and think we might get on then get in touch. I'd prefer not to live in a smoking house but smoking outside is fine.
Cheers!

Which gives you a better sense of what Adam might be like as a flatmate? Would you even click on the first one?

BUDDY UP

It's also possible to 'buddy up' online and find other room seekers to share with. Maybe you've found a great three-bed flat that you really want to live in but have nobody to share with – by Buddying Up you can find other people in your situation who'd like to share and form a flatshare of your own. This can also be great if you're a little intimidated by the idea of moving into an existing share where everyone knows each other already. Look out for the blue 'buddy up' links on SpareRoom ads.

SPEED FLATMATING

If you live in London then Speed Flatmating is a great way to meet potential flatmates. It gives you the chance to meet several people in one go in a relaxed and informal setting plus places the importance on the people rather than the property, which can often help you decide which room to go for.

For more information, see Chapter 9.

Professional house shares

A new type of rental accommodation is starting to appear in some of the larger UK cities. These consist of clean modern (often new build) properties managed to a high standard by a professional landlord and regularly include benefits such as a cleaner and Sky TV as part of the package. They're generally only let to professionals and managed to a high standard. Alistair Lawes runs Rooms in Birmingham:

'I choose to rent my four-bedroom houses as multi-let house shares for up to four single professionals. My room rates are fixed and rent includes all bills, maintenance and cleaning; tenants can easily manage their budget and relax in the knowledge that I take care of everything, so it's hassle free for them. This allows me to take control of the bills to make sure they are paid, keep the houses properly maintained and managed and provide the highest standard of cleaning for my tenants – which they obviously appreciate. They enjoy Sky TV with all channels (including Movies and Sports), ultra-high speed wireless Internet, modern appliances and furnishings. The houses are cleaned weekly with carpet cleaning, gardening and window cleaning also taken care of.

My rooms are aimed squarely at single professionals in full-time employment. Single professionals in part-time employment, couples, families including children and those with pets are not accepted. I interview all prospective tenants personally to gauge their suitability as a future tenant of mine.

This way of renting gives tenants the flexibility to move with their career and change direction quickly if job redundancy or relocation occurs. Being able to budget their accommodation costs for up to six months in advance allows them to plan ahead to stay financially afloat. Living in one of my house shares is a fun and sociable way to meet new people, make new friends and relax in a secure environment.'

Alistair Lawes

SPAREROOM MOBILE APP
SpareRoom.co.uk has free mobile apps that makes it easy to find a flatshare wherever you are. You can browse room offered ads, contact other users and manage your account, all from within the app. Just search foor SpareRoom on Apple's App Store or Google Play.

Viewings

Now you've found a few rooms to go and see, it's time to think about viewings. It's important to make sure you ask all your questions while you're there rather than sitting on the bus home thinking 'does the rent include bills – I forgot to ask!'

The first things you'll need to know will most likely be covered by the advert you replied to so, before you arrive, you should hopefully know:

- How much the rent is.
- Exactly where the property is.
- How many other people live there.
- If a deposit is required.

If possible you should make sure all the other flatmates will be there when you go to look round as the people you'll live with will make as much difference (if not more) as the room itself. If there are five rooms but you only meet two housemates when you go to view, then you might not get a chance to meet the others 'til you move in, by which time it's too late if there's a problem of any kind.

ASKING THE RIGHT QUESTIONS
The viewing is the ideal time to ask all the questions you have. Some of these (is there a double bed or a single, is there a washing machine) will be obvious from looking round the property, others you'll have to ask.

Here's a list of things you might need to know. It's far from exhaustive and not all of these will apply to you so pick the ones you think you need and add any of your own to the list:

Are bills included in the rent?

If so, which ones? Will you have to pay for council tax, water rates, electricity, gas, phone, broadband? 'Bills included' is fine but very non-specific.

Will I have to pay a deposit?

Most landlords will ask for a deposit along with a month's rent in advance. The typical deposit is a month's rent but it can go up to six weeks (or occasionally higher) so make sure you know. For more information on deposits, see Chapter 8.

Are there any other costs?

It's not unusual for agents to charge admin fees and costs for checking references. Generally, you'll be dealing with an agent in this case rather than the existing flatmates, so they will have all the details. It's worth asking this question anyway, whoever you're dealing with, just so you can be certain.

Will I need to sign a contract?

Whether you're renting from an agent, a landlord, a flatmate or a friend, it's generally a good idea to have a written contract of some kind. Agents and landlords will generally always expect you to sign a contract but it's not always the case if you're going to be living as a lodger. Contracts aren't just there to protect the landlord, they also secure your rights so, if you're not asked to sign anything, don't immediately think 'great!'. See Chapter 8 for information on the kinds of contract you'll be faced with and what they're for.

Is the furniture that's in the room staying or does it belong to the current flatmate?

This may seem unnecessary but you really don't want to find out you don't have a bed on the day you move in. Most rooms will be offered furnished but you need to know if not.

Is any contents insurance included?

You'll need to make sure your possessions are protected so find out if that's something you'll need to sort out or if there's already insurance for the flat as a whole.

Is there a parking space or somewhere safe to put my bike?

Some residential streets operate residents' parking permit schemes so, even if there's space on the street, you may have to pay and/or apply for a permit. If this is the case there will be signs on the street so have a quick look when you're on your way in or out.

Is there a washing machine?

This should be fairly obvious from your viewing but, if you can't see one, don't just presume there is one.

How often and when is the rent due?

If you get paid monthly then it'll be easier for you to pay your rent monthly. It'll also help to be able to pay soon after your wages come through so you can budget for the month.

Does the flat have access to the garden?

Just because there is a garden doesn't mean your flat has the right to use it. The garden may be communal or solely for the use of the ground floor flat so it's best to ask if outside space is high on your list.

Are there any existing house rules I need to know about?

Some houses have rules and some don't but it's probably a good idea to ask although, generally, the existing flatmates will let you know in advance if there are rules you'll be expected to follow.

Is it okay if my other half stays over occasionally?

If your boyfriend or girlfriend tends to stay with you on a regular basis you should check if this is okay as sharing with one person who turns out to be two can be a problem for some people. In most instances it won't be a problem but there may be an agreement between the flatmates that limits the number of times a week people can stay, so ask.

You can print this list (or copy it so you can edit your own version) at: www.SpareRoom.co.uk/essentialguide/checklist, along with a 'viewing notes' sheet you can print out to keep track of what you've seen – this can be especially useful if you're seeing several properties in one day.

Setting up your own flatshare

You may find, once you start looking for somewhere to live, that you come across friends, colleagues or friends of friends who are also looking for somewhere to live. Maybe you've Buddied Up through SpareRoom or a Speed Flatmating event. If this is the case, and you now have a group of people, it might be easier to set up your own flatshare than try and find one with several rooms available.

All this really amounts to is finding a suitable property and coming to an agreement between you about how you'll divide the rent. All the advice you'll find in Chapter 6, *Living Together* is still relevant as is the information in other chapters such as Chapter 8, *Contracts, Rights and Agreements* and Chapter 7, *Finance and Bills*.

FINDING THE PROPERTY

If you're looking for a whole property then you can still search SpareRoom.co.uk as there are whole flats and houses available. It would make more sense, however, to search: www.FindaFlat.com as this site specializes in whole properties rather than rooms.

You should also check your local estate agents to see which ones also deal with lettings. You'll be able to register your details with them in the same way you would if you were looking to buy, they'll then let you know what they have that would be suitable and arrange viewings for you.

You should be aware that lettings agents, although paid by the landlord not the tenants, will usually charge additional fees to cover certain admin costs (such as checking references).

CHAPTER THREE

Find a Flatmate

Where you live is one of the most important everyday factors that affect your happiness (along with things like relationships and work) and, if there's a problem, it can be hard to focus on anything else. If you live somewhere you don't want to go back to after you've finished work (or don't feel you can relax in), then your chances of being content in your day-to-day life are fairly slim.

Finding the right property can be difficult enough in itself but it's finding the right people to share with that's the real trick to successful flatshares. An okay property with great flatmates can make for the perfect flatshare, but if you live with people you either don't like or get on with, no amount of lovely hardwood flooring and posh kitchen appliances can make up for it.

Sometimes it can be difficult to share a space with people you're really close to, let alone with strangers, so, how do you go about finding a new flatmate? Looking in the right place is a good start but how you look and what you look for are just as important.

Who do you want to live with?

Note – Part of this advice also appears in Chapter 2, Find a Flatshare, in a slightly different form, aimed at those looking for a place as well as people to share with.

FRIENDS AND COLLEAGUES

There are several choices available to you when it comes to finding a flatmate. The first, and most obvious, is to look amongst people you already know. Do you have a friend who needs somewhere to live or a work colleague perhaps? It's worth bearing in mind that sometimes you can have too much of a good thing, it can be easier to live with people you don't spend all your time with!

Matt says:

'The first flat I shared in London was with my three best friends. We were all in a band together and rehearsed, recorded and stored all our gear in the flat (which had no living room). By the end of the year we were pretty much all ready to kill each other. Luckily we didn't and, once we'd moved into different flatshares, life became much easier! We're all great friends and three of us are still in a band together (the other guy lives abroad now – not because of us I hasten to add). In hindsight we just spent too much time together!'

FRIENDS OF FRIENDS

You may not have any friends looking for somewhere to live (or any friends you want to live with) but your friends and colleagues may well know someone who needs a room. Sometimes the extra distance of knowing someone without being in each other's pockets makes it easier to live together.

STRANGERS

The word strangers makes this option sound far harsher than it is; sometimes people you don't know make the best flatmates. We asked SpareRoom users and 55% said that someone you didn't already know would make the best flatmate (with existing friends scoring 28% of the vote).

Points to bear in mind are:

Age range
Do you mind sharing with people much older or younger than you?

Couples
Would you be prepared to share with a couple? Couples can affect the overall dynamic of a shared house (especially if they have a tendency to argue – see page 37).

Gender

Some people prefer to live in a single-sex household and some prefer a mix. This one is entirely about what works for you, although in larger flatshares it can be a bit much if you have only male or female flatmates.

Occupation

Does it matter to you whether you live with professionals, students or a mixture of both? Bear in mind a mix can affect your council tax bill (see Chapter 7, *Finance and Bills* for more on this).

Pets

Do you want to share with just people or are their animals okay too?

Smokers

Would living with smokers bother you? How about smokers who only smoke outside? (SpareRoom's research has shown that we're becoming increasingly less tolerant when it comes to living with smokers).

THE PERFECT FLATMATE

Choosing the perfect room is the easy bit, choosing the perfect people to share with can be less straightforward, especially if you only have a few minutes during a viewing to get to know people.

There are a few key points to consider, however, to get you moving in the right direction and discount a few obvious mismatches.

Decide what you want from a flatmate

For example, you may be looking for someone who shares similar interests and is open to going on the odd night out. On the other hand, you may already have a wide circle of friends and just want someone to fill the room, so the age and interests of your flatmate are irrelevant. It's generally best not to expect your flatmates to become your new best friends, if it happens great but don't try and force the issue.

Work out whether your lifestyles will be compatible

If you have to be up early in the morning for work and like to go to bed at 10pm, you won't enjoy living with someone who works late and gets home around 1pm with half the local pub in tow . . . and vice versa!

How houseproud are you?

Be honest with yourself, if you like an absolutely spotless flat you're unlikely to see eye to eye with someone who cleans only when absolutely necessary.

Finally, don't give the room to someone you are sexually attracted to

If you are attracted to a potential flatmate invite them out for a drink instead, if it doesn't all work out at least you won't be stuck living with them.

A cautionary tale

'Be wary of moving into a house purely because the housemate is beautiful. I did and ended up with great sex for two weeks, but, when that cooled off, it was unbearable living in the house. DO NOT sleep with flatmates!'

Benji

A WORD ABOUT LIVING WITH COUPLES

Living with couples can drastically alter the dynamic of a flatshare. If they don't get on then it can be extremely difficult, if they do they're likely to take the same side in any house discussions and outnumber you. Additionally, if you let a double room to a couple then there's one more person needing to use the kitchen and bathroom than there would be if you let to a single person (on the other hand, there's an extra person contributing to bills).

We're certainly not trying to put you off living with couples, just consider how it might be different and affect the house as a whole first.

Beware the couple

'I don't generally have a problem living with couples but, when one half of the pairing is perfectly normal and the other half is a complete nightmare, it can get tricky.

The couple I lived with recently personified the "opposites attract" cliché. He was laid back and fun whilst she was anal and completely insecure.

She also had a real problem with laundry – just touching a freshly ironed, perfectly folded pile of sheets would provoke a guaranteed screaming hissy fit, a slamming door and half an hour's manic driving around the streets. As for taking her dry washing off the radiators so you could use them . . .

On another occasion he was home late and she was getting progressively wound up.

When he finally rocked up at the insanely late hour of 11.45 I was already in bed. I heard him creeping up the stairs but I was nearly deafened by her cry of "Will you be quiet, you're waking up the whole house!"

So, my advice is that living with a couple is risky. Simply put – any housemate carries a certain possibility of disaster but a couple comes as a unit so the odds immediately go up. Tread carefully.'

Sally

Where to look

LOCAL RESOURCES vs ONLINE

Local papers, notice boards and shop windows can be a good way of advertising your room but it'll be a bit hit and miss regarding the number of people who will see your ad. By far the easiest way to advertise is online using one of the many dedicated flatshare sites.

FLATSHARE WEBSITES

Not so long ago you had to rely on local papers and Loot to find somewhere to live. It can be almost impossible to get any real sense of what to expect from an ad that's short, e.g:

Tooting Bec – Dbl rm in 3-bed flat nr tube. GCH, fitted kitchen, share w/2 guys in 20s. £450 pcm plus bills.

These days it's much easier as online listings allow you to see photos and video of each property along with detailed information on what the room and facilities are like and maps showing the exact location.

Why dedicated flatshare sites?

With so many general classified listings sites around why should you bother with a dedicated flatshare site? General classifieds sites are appealing as they can be used without having to register and are a simple way of reaching a lot of people. The downside is that your chances of encountering a scam advert or a fraudulent advertiser are far higher than if you use a reputable site. At SpareRoom.co.uk, we check all our ads thoroughly for any scam attempts. We also require users to register in order to contact you so we have a record of who everyone is. This means that, if a listing does turn out to be fraudulent, we can notify anyone who has been in contact with the advertiser and warn them.

For more information on staying safe using the Internet to find a flatmate, see Chapter 10, *Staying Safe*.

PLACING AN AD

Advertising your room on one of these sites is easy to do and can reach a huge number of potential flatmates (at the time of writing SpareRoom. co.uk has over a million registered users across the UK and overseas). It's worth taking a little time to make the most of your advert to help it stand out from the others and attract the right flatmate for you. Here are a few tips to get your ad in shape.

Browse some other ads

This should be first on your list. Try doing a search on SpareRoom.co.uk for other rooms in your town, area or postcode. This will help you with several things:

- Checking prices to make sure you're not over- or under-charging.
- Getting an idea of the quantity and standard of other rooms on offer near you.
- Becoming familiar with how ads are laid out and what information you should put in yours.

It'll also help you when it comes to writing your ad. Have a look at some other listings and see which you'd be interested in if you were looking for a room, you can then use these as a starting point. Think why you liked the look of them (good information on local facilities, lots of good photos of the room and flat, a friendly tone of voice etc.) and incorporate that into your own listing.

Take your time

It's important to remember to **take your time** when you write your listing. It'll be tempting to knock something out in five minutes during a break at work but resist – the more time you spend on your ad, the better it will be. At the moment, there are more people looking for someone to fill an empty room than ever so you'll need to stand out from the others.

Give your ad a catchy title

'Double room' says what you've got but 'Bright double in friendly and spacious garden flat' says so much more. If you're advertising in a busy area your ad may have to compete with hundreds of others, so give room seekers a reason to click on yours first.

Price your room to the best effect

Once you've seen what others are charging you should have a good idea of where your room falls in the price scale. Don't forget you'll need to make it clear whether or not bills are included. If they are it's worth mentioning this in the title (e.g. 'Large double in cosy 2-bed flat – BILLS INC'). Otherwise seekers might just glance at the price and think it's a bit steep, not realizing that it's all inclusive.

Know your local market

If you've got a large employer near you (hospitals, airports and universities all fall into this category but there are plenty of others too) then you're likely to find it easier to fill your room. Have a scout around and see what there is nearby; if it's the kind of area a lot of people commute to you might get more responses by offering the room all week or just Monday to Friday (at a reduced rate). This has the added bonus of giving you most weekends free. Universities are always great as they not only employ hundreds of people but also have a steady (and self-renewing) supply of students. Don't forget, not all students want a party house, often final year or post-graduate students will want to retreat somewhere quiet to work when deadlines loom.

Don't just sell the room . . .

A great room is a good starting point but the property as a whole can be just as important so make the most of it. Include photos of the best rooms and mention anything you think might sway people, for example:

- A garden, roof terrace or balcony.
- Multiple bathrooms (always a bonus in a flatshare!).
- Newly fitted kitchen or bathroom.
- Wi-fi
- Big flat screen TVs and cable or satellite packages.
- Great views if you're on the top floor of a tall building.

Mention the area too

If there's anything in the area that you think will help sell your room then mention that too. Some examples of things people look out for when they're moving are:

- Great local bars or pubs.
- Good restaurants or takeaways.
- A handy supermarket or local shops.
- A gym.
- Parks.
- Proximity to public transport.
- Cinema.

The more you can convince someone that where you live is a good place to be, the easier it will be for them to imagine themselves living there. Tell them what you like about living where you are.

You get the idea, as always, a quick browse through some of the ads on SpareRoom will give you a good idea of what's considered desirable.

Have a look at these two listings as examples. Which tells you most about the room and what it would be like living there and which would you click on first?

Double room, E3

Double room available in Bow. Has own shower room and flat has a garden. Near tube and shops. £450 pcm.

Lovely bright en-suite double in quiet Bow garden flat

Recently re-decorated double room with its own en-suite shower room (with power shower and underfloor heating). The flat is in a quiet residential road just 4 mins walk from the tube and handy for a great range of shops and bars. There's a garden for sitting out with a glass of wine in the summer and a parking space out front that we don't use (so it's all yours if you need it).

You'll be sharing with 3 young professionals (ages 25–31) who like to share the occasional bottle of wine and cook dinner together sometimes. Rent is £450 a month and this includes council tax. If this sounds like what you're looking for give us a shout!

The second is clearly more interesting (both the headline and the ad text). A real listing has space for much more information than this (and the general information you fill in will also be displayed as well as a map of where you are), but this should give you an idea how much difference it makes if you spend a little time on your listing.

Preparing the room and making the most of photo and video advertising

If you're taking photos and video to upload to your ad then make a little effort. Treat it like a viewing and tidy up first; photos of a nice clean room (and flat) will look better and the room itself will seem bigger if it's not full of clutter.

A quick video tour of the house or flat will help give people a good sense of the layout and what's available. You don't need to be Steven Spielberg to do this, even a quick video shot on your mobile can be uploaded to give potential flatmates a sense of the space.

How to look

BE PRO-ACTIVE

It's not just a case of placing your ad then waiting for the perfect flatmate to call you. Be pro-active and look for people who need a room in your area. Check the 'room wanted' ads to see who's looking for something near you and contact any who look good. You can also sign up to receive alerts from SpareRoom letting you know of any new room seekers in your neck of the woods; by doing this you might just come across someone who missed your ad on the site or hasn't got round to searching yet.

SPEED FLATMATING

If you live in London then Speed Flatmating is a great way of meeting several potential flatmates in one go. The bonus of this method is that you get to spend a little time with people in a relaxed, social setting so you're far more likely to get a sense of what they're like than you would from a five-minute viewing after work.

Chapter 9 is the place to look for information on Speed Flatmating.

SPAREROOM MOBILE APPS

SpareRoom.co.uk has free apps for iPhone, iPad and Android, making it simple to find a flatshare wherever you are. You can browse room offered ads, place ads and manage your account, all from within the app. Just search for SpareRoom on Apple's App store or Google Play.

Viewings and interviews

If you've seen the beginning of *Shallow Grave* (see Interlude: Fighting Over the Remote – *Flatshare on the Box*), you'll know that the flatmate interview can be a strange process for both parties. It's tricky to get a sense of someone from such a short process. However, it's often the only chance you get to assess someone's suitability to live with you so make the most of it.

A FEW THOUGHTS ON VIEWINGS

Firstly, make a bit of an effort when someone's coming round to see the room. I wouldn't suggest resorting to levels of preparation some of the property shows go to (light a fire, make a pot of fresh coffee, have some fresh bread just out of the oven, and so on), but a bit of a tidy up should be the least you do. If there's still someone in the room that's being offered get them to declutter as much as possible so the person thinking of moving in doesn't just see their stuff and not notice the room itself.

Secondly, it may not always be possible but, whenever you can, try and have all the flatmates available when you do viewings. That doesn't mean you all have to open the door together and follow your prospective flatmate round while they take the tour but they'll want to meet everyone they might be living with. On top of this, if you're going to share your flat with someone for the next 12 months, you probably want to check them out, don't you?

Thirdly, try not to rush people. You can look round a three-bed flat in five minutes and that's not necessarily enough time to decide if you want to live there so give people a bit longer if they look like they need it and let them ask any questions they may have about the flat, the rent, the area, whatever.

Obviously some people just won't be right for your flatshare and that will be obvious, so don't spend ages with people you think are wrong but don't just shove them out of the door!

You may get the occasional odd viewer as did one of our users a couple of years ago (luckily we don't hear too may of these):

'When interviewing for a flatmate I had a bloke come to see the flat. Before he even got up the stairs he told me that he had a long journey and could he use the loo (fair enough). Twenty-five minutes later he was still in there, after thirty-five minutes he opened the door, said thank you very much and left. Needless to say I bleached everything!'

Charlie

Additionally . . . see as many people as you can. Don't just accept the first person who shows up and is prepared to take the room; this is someone you'll be sharing with for months (if not years) and you may well end up seeing them more than you see your friends. The more people you see, the better your chances of finding someone great.

If someone comes for a viewing and you think they could be good then you could suggest going for a quick drink before they head off. It'll give you a chance to see each other in a more relaxed setting and get a sense of what spending an evening with them would be like.

If someone comes round to see the room and you really fancy them it's probably a better idea to ask them out than let them move in. If you have expectations of what will happen and they're not interested then it'll make things awkward for both of you (especially when they want to bring someone else back with them!). Even if the best were to happen and you fell in love, would you really want to live with your boyfriend or girlfriend from day one of your relationship? Ask them out to the pub and tell them why you're doing it!

Interview notes

We've prepared a simple viewings sheet for you so you can take notes to help you remember each person. It can be downloaded and printed at: www.SpareRoom.co.uk/essentialguide/viewingnotes.

CHAPTER FOUR
Lodgers

'I shall never, Master Copperfield', said Mrs. Micawber,
'revert to the period when Mr. Micawber was in difficulties,
without thinking of you. Your conduct has always been of the
most delicate and obliging description. You have never been a
lodger. You have been a friend.'
David Copperfield – Charles Dickens

Background

RIGSBY & CO – GONE BUT NOT FORGOTTEN

When you hear the word 'lodger' what springs to mind? Rigsby from Rising Damp; cheap rooms to let; formidable landladies; an album by David Bowie? Although lodgers seem like an old fashioned concept they've been making a huge comeback in recent years – people advertising a room in their own home now account for over half the ads on SpareRoom (it was only a third a few years ago), so why the big increase?

LODGERS TODAY

There are several reasons why people take in a lodger. In these times of financial difficulty there are plenty of people who need a little extra income as well as plenty more who need somewhere affordable to live but don't necessarily want to live in a big shared house. Taking in a lodger can go a long way to helping with mortgage payments, especially with the government's Rent a Room Scheme allowing you to earn up to £4,250 tax free by renting out a room. That's going up to £7,500 from April 2016 thanks to SpareRoom's six-year Raise the Roof campaign. Read the full story at www.spareroom.co.uk/raisetheroof

Taking in a lodger can provide an easy source of additional income and is enabling thousands of people to stay in their homes. It's also a flexible solution as you can take a lodger in for three months, six months, a year or however long you need to (and you can have breaks between lodgers if you want) so you're not committing to a permanent change in your lifestyle. Many people also take in a lodger for company as well as money – see Melanie's story below.

WHO TAKES IN A LODGER?

Traditionally we think of lodgers in terms of an older landlord (as often as not a landlady) who rents out several rooms in their house and provides meals for lodgers. While this group still exists there are plenty of other people taking in lodgers today.

People who take in lodgers can be roughly broken down into three groups:

- families and couples;
- young professionals;
- more traditional landlords and landladies.

Families

Often a family with children (perhaps young children or older children who have left for university) has a spare room in their home and decides to let it out for a little extra income. In these cases the situation is very much like living in a family house rather than a flatshare. Meals are sometimes provided, especially if you're likely to be around when the family eats. This type of lodging can be perfect for students who want to live in a family situation rather than a noisy shared house (especially if they have a lot of course work to get through). This type of lodging can also suit younger people looking for a room in a property with a family feel – especially if it's their first experience of living away from home.

How long have you been taking in lodgers and how many have you had?
We took in our first lodger nine months ago and she's still with us now. She's the only lodger we've had.

What have been the best and worst parts of the experience?
Best: Our lodger joining in our family Christmas; having a babysitter on hand.
Worst: My son calling her 'Mummy'!

How has taking in a lodger benefited you?
It has been a huge financial help and has meant we get to stay in our home during these hard financial times. Also, we have made a friend and our children simply love her, which means we feel comfortable going out for an evening and leaving her in charge.

What advice would you give to anyone thinking of taking in a lodger in terms of preparation?
Always conduct a relaxed interview. People will be on their best behaviour when they come to see you but you need to know the real person. Also, don't assume their personal problems (divorce/recent break up etc) will impinge on your life, give people a chance. Make sure the person fits in with your lifestyle (e.g., if you are a 20 something who likes to party, don't have a 50 year old lodger who wants to go to bed at 9pm!).

Can you explain the process you go through when you advertise for a lodger?
We advertised on SpareRoom, then invited people who responded to our home for a cup of tea and a chat, then talked it over in private before advising of our decision.

What kind of questions do you ask prospective lodgers?
What hours do they keep re their job; will there be a boyfriend/girlfriend visiting; do they smoke; do they mind cats; do they like children; are they prone to coming in late ALL the time; where are they coming from (another house? in which case are references available).

How has it been for you overall?
We have been very lucky with our lodger and she fits in with the family fantastically. I think, at the interview, you usually know if you are comfortable with someone, and that's what it's all about. You need to be able to relax in front of that person – if you don't feel like you could veg out in your pyjamas, watching a bad film in front of them then they aren't right to be living with you!

Alex

Young professionals

This type of lodging generally consists of a young professional (or a couple) who has bought a two- or three-bed flat on their own and wants to rent out their spare room. It's far more likely to feel like a flatshare, even if one of you does own the flat, so don't expect your meals and laundry done for you.

'I had lived by myself for a long time and needed to get a lodger. I am the kind of person that enjoys my own company a lot but, if I spend too much time alone, I am in danger of developing strange, anti-social habits. I think it's important to have people in place to keep you in check.

I have had bad experiences in the past with flat mates so it was crucial for me to select the right one. I would always ask a friend for a second opinion but, generally, I would make sure the person is friendly, relaxed and they don't smell bad! In a short space of time you can only go on what feels right – trust your instinct even if you can't articulate it'.

Melanie

Traditional landlords and landladies

This is what we think of when people mention lodgers. Usually it will consist of an older landlord or couple who rent out several rooms in their home, often to students. You're more likely to get meals included in this type of share but it won't always be the case.

'My wife & I are 68 years old and love having paying guests in the house. My wife is a Scottish Tourist Guide and I started a small charity, which keeps me out of trouble. I feed the guests whenever possible so we all eat our evening meal together. When we decided to have paying guests, I took over the cooking and looking after the house – cooking had been a hobby of mine but doing it regularly is very pleasant therapy. Most of my experiences have been quite delightful. When they are not delightful, it is usually my fault – I have not explained the terms of taking the rooms clearly enough, although they were clear enough to me!'

Mark

Did you know . . . ?

LODGER FACTS

We recently conducted a survey of almost 3,000 people in the UK who take in lodgers – here's what we found:

- 62% of those who have taken in a lodger are female
- The biggest age group taking in lodgers are the over 50s at 30%. The overall age breakdown is:
  - 18-24   7%
  - 25-29   13%
  - 30-34   14%
  - 35-39   12%
  - 40-49   24%
  - 50+   30%
- 56% of live in landlords are educated to degree level or higher
- 43% don't have a written agreement with their lodger
- 64% only started taking in lodgers in the past two years
- 15% have been taking in lodgers for five years or more
- 8% have had more than 10 lodgers
- 41% couldn't afford their mortgage without a lodger
- Just 10% have an existing friend as their only lodger

LODGER EXPERIENCES

- 93% said it had been a positive experience
- 94% said they'd do it again
- 60% said they regarded their lodger as a friend

Lodgers – the basics

If you're thinking of taking in a lodger there are a few things you'll need to consider. Some of it's just plain common sense but there are a few things you might not have thought about so, starting with the basics, here's our guide to taking in a lodger.

WHAT IS A LODGER?

A lodger is someone who rents a room in your home without having exclusive rights to any part of the property. Lodgers can have extra services (such as cleaning, laundry or meals) included by agreement but they're not compulsory.

WHAT'S THE DIFFERENCE BETWEEN A LODGER AND A TENANT?

'Lodger' isn't a legal term – strictly speaking your lodger is a licensee. This means they have the right to live in your home but don't have exclusive access to any of it. Tenants, on the other hand, have more rights than lodgers and you, as a landlord, have more obligations, so it's important you don't take someone in as a tenant when they should really be a lodger. The simple rule is not to have a lock on your lodger's bedroom door. This doesn't mean you can wander in and out of their room at will though (not if you want them to keep living with you and paying rent).

WHO CAN TAKE IN A LODGER?

Most homeowners and local authority tenants can take in a lodger but there are several factors to consider before you go ahead. You will need to inform your mortgage lender or local authority and you'll almost definitely need to alert your insurance provider. If you claim any benefits these will probably be affected if you take in a lodger. If you rent you need to check with your landlord to see if your tenancy allows for sub-letting. Most don't automatically but your landlord may be fine with you having a lodger, especially if it stops you falling behind on the rent. You shouldn't need a new tenancy agreement in this instance, a letter of permission from your landlord will be enough.

WHAT WILL I NEED TO PROVIDE?

In the simplest terms you'll provide a furnished room plus use of communal areas and facilities. Other benefits such as cleaning and meals are up to you.

HOW MUCH CAN I CHARGE?

That all depends on where you live and what your property is like. Have a look on: www.SpareRoom.co.uk at other rooms available in your area to get an idea what the going rate is likely to be. At the time of writing, the national monthly average earned in the UK by taking in a lodger is around £548, this equates to £6,576 a year. In London the average is £708 per month or £8,496 per year.

CAN I EVICT SOMEONE IF IT DOESN'T WORK OUT OR I NEED MY ROOM BACK?

The law recognises that, as a live-in landlord, you're more vulnerable if your relationship with your tenant breaks down. That's why, generally speaking, it's easier to evict a lodger than a tenant (you will need to give 'reasonable notice' if you intend to evict).

We strongly recommend a written agreement between you and your lodger(s) so the conditions are agreed upon in advance. The contract should include the following information at minimum:

- The amount of rent you're charging.
- How long the let is for.
- What notice either of you must give if you want to end the agreement.

If you find you have a dispute with your lodger some councils have a Tenancy Relations Officer you can turn to. They can't tell either of you what to do but can mediate to help resolve a situation. See Chapter 8, *Contracts, Rights and Agreements*, for more on evicting a lodger.

WHAT'S SO GOOD ABOUT TAKING IN A LODGER?

The obvious benefit is money; that's why most people take in a lodger. The other positives can be company (especially if you live on your own) and – crucially – flexibility. The great thing about taking in lodgers is that it's entirely up to you how long you do it for. You can rent out a room for six months then have a break, take a few months off whenever your lodger decides to move on, rent Monday to Friday to give yourself weekends free or just take a lodger for a fixed period to help you through a specific financial low point.

WHAT ARE THE DOWNSIDES?

Inviting someone else into your home is always a bit of a risk. The one thing you will certainly lose is a bit of your privacy although, as one cash strapped SpareRoom user said to us recently, it's better to lose a little privacy than to lose your home. By taking a few simple precautions you can minimise the risks and take much of the anxiety out of the process (more on this later in the chapter).

It doesn't always work straight away, but when it does . . .

'In the last year alone I have had some dreadful experiences with renting out my spare room. One guy totally took over my lounge and wouldn't let me watch TV or listen to music as he was watching Top Gear re-runs all the time – he left owing me about £300. Since then I have had better luck, and in the past have met some lovely people through renting out my spare room, some of whom are my closest friends now and one of whom is now my boyfriend! So it's not all bad!'

Helen

HOW CAN I FIND A LODGER, IS IT DIFFICULT?

The advent of online flatshare listings has made finding a lodger easier than ever. With an online listing on sites such as: www.SpareRoom.co.uk you can include photos and a video of your room so prospective lodgers can see what's on offer. You can also check out who's looking for a room in your area.

WILL I BE TAXED ON MY INCOME AND DO I HAVE TO DECLARE IT?

Under the government's Rent a Room Scheme you can earn up to £7,500 tax free by taking in a lodger and, provided you don't earn more than this, you won't need to declare it. There's more info on this later in the chapter.

DO I NEED TO COMPLY WITH THE NEW TENANCY DEPOSIT LAWS?

So far the law only applies to assured shorthold tenancies so you can take a deposit (and we recommend you always do) without having to use the scheme.

WHAT ABOUT GAS SAFETY CHECKS AND FIRE REGULATIONS?

If you rent out a room in your home you must make sure that all gas appliances are maintained in good order and that an annual safety check is carried out by someone who is registered with the Gas Safe Register.

Fire Safety Regulations only apply if the property isn't your main residence and is considered primarily as a source of income. You should fit (and regularly test) smoke alarms as a matter of common sense.

SHOULD I WORRY ABOUT HMO?

HMO (or House in Multiple Occupation) refers to a property that's rented by a group of unrelated people. Most flatshares are HMOs. As a live-in landlord your property will only be classed as an HMO if you take in more than two lodgers. Lodgers that are related to you don't count as they're counted as part of your family (the same is true of any domestic staff that live with you, e.g. a nanny or au pair). If you plan to take in more than two lodgers you should look into HMO regulations and whether you will need a licence. A free introductory guide to HMO regulations is available at http://www.spareroom.co.uk/hmo_licensing_ guide. For more information you should speak to your local authority planning office as the rules are implemented differently by different local authorities.

One landlord's experiences

Highs of house sharing from a live-in landlord's perspective:

Extra income. I can't stress this enough! Thanks to the tax break I can earn £350 each month without worrying about tax, which is a huge bonus. It effectively doubled my disposable income after all my outgoings. Without it I wouldn't have been able to get on the property ladder.

Flatmates can bring additional skills to the table that you can get at a knock down rate. In the past three years I've have electricians stay (and repair wiring, run in outside lights, wire in power to the garage); a builder (handy van to do tip runs) and an IT engineer . . . very handy for when the laptop crashes!

Lows

Inevitably the burden of sharing space. No tenant will ever treat the house with as much respect as you (as the owner) do.

Past girlfriends have felt threatened by other girls renting a space in the house.

You'll always feel you're tidying up more than just your own mess. No cleaning rotas ever get stuck to.

Awkward if you've got your mum and dad coming to stay and your drunk flatmate has sex with his latest one night stand one floor above them!

... and the lodgers themselves

The first guy that moved in was a bodybuilder. On arrival at home after work I found him fully oiled up wearing speedos sun bathing on the pavement outside the front of the house – on day 1! Also everything he ever touched seemed to have a fine coating of protein powder on it.

I put up a commuter for six months, who was going through a messy divorce. He seemed the perfect tenant, as he was likely to be away at the weekends with his kids. Best thing was, in the first week of his new job, he met a new girl and shortly after moved in with her. In the next five months I only saw him 10 times, so he stayed at my place for less than one night a week, but was happy to pay full rent! Result.

James

The process of taking in a lodger

Okay, so that's the basics covered – now let's look at the process in a little more detail.

Having decided you want to take in a lodger it's important to do your preparation and make sure you've thought everything through. Whilst you can get rid of a lodger if you find out they (or just having a lodger at all) won't work for you, you can put yourself in a strong position to start with, which should eliminate most of the worry. This section of this chapter guides you through the process of taking in a lodger, including how to prepare, interviews, agreements and what to do when your lodger moves out. There's a handy checklist at the end of the chapter to remind you of the main points and some good advice from people who have been through the process themselves.

PREPARING TO TAKE IN A LODGER

Before you take anyone in you should do your homework and make sure you know what's involved in the whole process. Not only does this give you a chance to reflect and decide whether you're ready to get a lodger, eans you'll be aware of some of the more important stumbling blocks and therefore better prepared to avoid them.

Check you're allowed to take in a lodger

You must inform your mortgage lender before you take in a lodger. If you rent then it all depends on the agreement you have with your landlord. Most will prevent you from sub-letting a room as a matter of course but your landlord may well be fine with you taking in a lodger, especially if it means you're more likely to be able to afford the rent on an ongoing basis. Check your tenancy agreement and speak to your landlord – if he gives you permission make sure you get it in writing. It shouldn't be necessary to sign a new contract, a simple letter of permission will be fine.

Local authority tenants should always check before taking in a lodger. It may well be okay for you to do so but it could affect your benefits, leaving you no better off than without a lodger, so make sure you understand the regulations before you do anything.

Inform your insurance provider

There are two main reasons for doing this: to make sure you're still covered and so you can let your lodger know if they'll need their own insurance. Some insurance companies are fine with you taking in a lodger, as long as you let them know in advance, but, in some cases, it will invalidate your insurance agreement. *Always* check first to avoid any nasty surprises further down the line. You may need to change your contents insurance provider in order to get cover with a lodger.

If you own your own home you're required to have buildings insurance, but you're not obliged to include your lodger on your contents insurance. There are plenty of 'room contents' policies your lodger can use to cover their belongings.

Right to rent checks

As of February 2016 anyone taking in a lodger is required to check their lodger's eligibility to live in the UK. Visit www.SpareRoom.co.uk for details.

Inform your local benefits agency

If you receive any benefits it's almost certain they will be affected by taking in a lodger so find out in advance what the result will be.

Let the council know if you're paying reduced council tax for single occupancy

If you pay reduced council tax then your lodger will affect this and you'll almost certainly be liable for the full amount. You can pass this on to your lodger in the rent of course, or as part of the bills they pay. If your lodger is in full-time education or on a government youth training scheme they may be exempt from council tax liability, so double-check with your local authority. Also, if you rent your room on a Monday to Friday basis, and your lodger has another home where they already pay council tax, then your discount should remain the same. You will need to inform your council tax office and you may be required to provide some documentation as proof (such as your lodger's council tax bill from their other property).

Get the room ready

Make sure you have all the furniture you need and everything is ready for a lodger. Remember, if you're going to use the Rent a Room Scheme to earn tax-free income, you *must* provide a furnished room. The minimum we'd recommend is a bed (double if possible), a wardrobe and chest of drawers, a bedside table and a lamp. Most lodgers will appreciate some desk space if there's room but it's not absolutely essential.

Make sure all your own clutter is cleared away as your lodger won't want to live in a room full of your junk. Do this before you have anyone round for viewings.

Most people today have their own mobile phone so you shouldn't have to worry about a phone socket in the room. If you have broadband (and it will be useful if you do) then wi-fi will mean your lodger can access the internet from their room.

Decide in advance what the terms and conditions will be

It may seem unnecessary at first but will avoid most nasty problems before they occur and give you a clear point of reference if you run into any difficulties. This includes you deciding in advance which bills are included in the rent and what else your lodger will pay for.

In addition to financial terms relating to the agreement you should also think about what other expectations you have. Just because you understand what you expect from a lodger it doesn't necessarily follow that they'll presume the same things you do. The more you discuss things up front the less chance there will be of a misunderstanding. Most of the live-in landlords we've spoken to who have had difficulties with a lodger say a lack of communication initially was part of the problem, so make sure you cover as much as possible. Not only does this create a set of expectations you're both aware of, it also gives you a chance to find out what a prospective lodger is like as they may not react as you'd expect them to when you're having the conversation.

Some points to consider:

House rules

This is a broad subject and can cover all sorts of things from who does the washing up to how you buy necessities such as toilet roll and cleaning products. Lodgers may expect you as the landlord to be responsible for these things, whereas in reality, many live-in landlords expect things to be run more along the lines of a traditional flatshare. It doesn't matter how you agree these things but it's always essential to have a frank conversation before you agree to someone moving in to make sure you're both expecting the same things.

Bills

Will your rent include bills or are you going to charge an extra amount for these? If so which bills are included: council tax, water rates, utilities, TV licence, broadband, satellite TV? Don't forget, the amount you can earn tax free under the Rent a Room Scheme includes whatever you charge for bills (if they're included in the rent).

Insurance

Your lodger's belongings won't automatically be covered by your policy – make sure they know this and tell them they'll need their own room contents cover for their possessions to be insured properly.

Guests

Standard lodger agreements usually include a clause stating that overnight guests aren't allowed without your permission. It's reasonable for your lodger to want their partner to be able to stay over occasionally but, if you're not careful, you may find yourself living with a couple and outnumbered in your own home. Make sure you're clear about the rules before someone moves in. If you're happy for their partner to visit and stay over you may want to limit it to one or two nights per week. One live-in landlord we spoke to recently told us he thinks it's fair for his lodger's girlfriend to stay as many nights a week as he stays at hers. Whatever you decide, don't wait till your lodger has moved in to have this conversation.

Pets

Are you happy for your lodger to have a pet? What if they move in and then get a pet once they're in? Make sure you're clear about this from the start.

Smoking

If you're not happy for your lodger to smoke in the house would it be okay for them to smoke outside?

Get a Lodger Agreement

Signing an agreement in advance, so you're both covered, is not a legal requirement but is nevertheless essential. Despite this 43% of live-in landlords don't have a written agreement with their lodger. A lodger contract doesn't need to be a lengthy or complicated document but should set out the basic terms and conditions, including what either of you will need to do to terminate the agreement. The essentials for any lodger agreement are:

- Both your full names.
- The address of the property.
- How much the rent is and whether it's to be paid weekly or monthly (and on what date).
- What deposit is required or has been taken.
- How long the agreement lasts and what needs to be done in order to terminate it.

You can find links to online agreements at http://www.spareroom.co.uk/content/info-landlords/lodger-agreement.

Check local rents

You need to know what your room is worth so you can set a fair rent that makes it worth your while without pricing yourself out of the market – there's no point in overpricing your room and struggling to find a lodger. Use: www.SpareRoom.co.uk to search in your area and see what other people are asking for similar rooms.

Get your gas appliances checked by a Gas Safe registered professional

You need to get your gas appliances checked before you take in a lodger (and once a year after that). They must be checked by a Gas Safe registered engineer – you can find one at www.gassaferegister.co.uk.

Advertise your room

Go to: www.SpareRoom.co.uk and place your listing. Don't forget to check the 'room wanted' ads and sign up for alerts so you'll be aware of anyone looking for a room in your area. For advice on placing the best advert see Chapter 3.

Viewings

This is one of the most important steps in the process and one you absolutely shouldn't rush through, however desperate your financial situation is. Take your time with viewings. This gives your potential lodger a chance to ask any questions but also gives you a little more time in their company to see what you think of them. It's important not to just accept the first person who wants and can afford the room – you're not selling a car, you're inviting someone to live in your home. If someone looks round and says 'yes' you can reasonably tell them you've got a few other people coming to see the room and you'll let them know. As you're going to be letting a stranger into your home it's worth taking as much time as you feel you need. Tell them when you'll let them know by (and make sure you follow up on this).

Trust your instincts – if you're not sure about someone you can always wait and advertise your room for a little longer. The extra time it takes to find the right person will be worth it in the long run. Why not ask a friend to sit in on the meeting and ask their opinion when the potential lodger has left – another perspective may well help.

One tip we got from a live-in landlord who uses SpareRoom regularly is to invite anyone you get on with to the local pub for a quick drink after the viewing. It'll give you chance to get to know them a bit in a more relaxed situation and see if you think you're compatible. This is a particularly useful technique if you're renting out a room and there will be just two of you in the property as it becomes even more important to find the right lodger.

Have a look at the advice from live-in landlords at the end of this chapter for some great tips on taking in a lodger from those who've done it before.

Holding deposits

If someone wants to take your room but can't move in immediately, then one option is to ask for a holding deposit. This isn't the same thing as a security deposit (see below), it's simply a sum of money given to you by the lodger in order to keep the room for them. Providing everything goes according to plan and the lodger moves in then the holding deposit can be returned or (more commonly) used towards the security deposit or the first month's rent. If the lodger decides not to move in then you don't have to return a holding deposit (although, if your lodger has to pull out due to unforeseen personal circumstances, you may choose to return the deposit if you think that's reasonable). A holding deposit won't be as much as a security deposit as a rule.

Credit checks

Once you've found a prospective lodger you may want to use a credit checking facility. Not everyone does this with lodgers but there are plenty of services available should you wish to. For links to tenant checking resources, have a look at: www.spareroom.co.uk/essentialguide/lodger.

Security deposits

A security deposit is an amount taken by a landlord as a guarantee against damages or unpaid rent at the end of the term. The standard amount taken is one month's rent (although six weeks is also becoming common). As a live-in landlord you don't need to use a tenancy deposit scheme as it only applies to ASTs (assured shorthold tenancies). Unless you have good reason, the deposit should be fully refunded at the end of the term, so you should make sure it's available whenever your lodger wants to move out (so don't spend it thinking you'll replace it at a later date – it's not your money).

It is also standard practice to take a month's rent up front, so your lodger should pay one month's rent plus a security deposit before you let them move in.

Signing contracts and agreeing terms and conditions

Setting out the details of who is responsible for what in advance is highly advisable to avoid any later problems. You should have prepared for this already, so all that remains is going over the agreement with your lodger, making sure you're both comfortable with the terms, and signing it.

Inventory

At this point your lodger should also sign an inventory. This is a list of all the furniture, fixtures and fittings in the room. The inventory is used when your lodger moves out to establish that everything is as it should be and nothing is damaged before you return the security deposit. For full details of inventories, see Chapter 8.

Getting your lodger to set up a standing order for the rent

This takes the personal element out of collecting the rent, which allows you to avoid having to ask for it every month if your lodger is a little disorganised. It also provides a record of all the money the lodger has paid to you, which will be invaluable in the event of any disputes.

Right to rent checks

Check your lodger's eligibility to live in the UK. Visit www.SpareRoom.co.uk for details.

Lodger moves in

It's a good idea to be available for your lodger on the day they move in – don't just give them a key and go out. They're bound to have questions on the first day so make it easier for them to move in and feel settled –

don't stand around and watch them unpack but make sure they know your door is open if they need you.

Inform your tax office if you earn over £7,500 a year from your lodger

The Rent a Room Scheme allows you to earn up to £7,500 a year by taking in a lodger without paying any tax. If you earn more than this you'll need to declare it.

How does the scheme work?

You let out a room or part of your main property

This can be a whole floor but not a self-contained flat.

It must be furnished

Unfurnished rooms don't qualify under the terms of the scheme.

You don't have to be a homeowner

As long as you have your landlord's consent you can take advantage of the scheme as a tenant. Check your tenancy agreement first or, if in doubt, ask your landlord.

Nothing to declare

If you don't normally fill out a tax return and the income is below £7,500 (around £625 a month) you don't even have to do anything, the exemption is automatic. If the amount you earn is above just let the tax office know.

If you're not PAYE

If you usually fill out a tax return you should consider whether you're better off in the scheme or not. Under the scheme you can't claim expenses for wear and tear, insurance and so on, so you may be better paying tax under the rules for residential lettings. This will enable you to offset certain expenses incurred against income. If you usually fill out a tax return and have an accountant, you should check with them to see whether you'd be better off under the scheme or not.

If you charge your lodger extra for meals or laundry services this all counts towards your £7,500 so bear this in mind. In addition, if you take in a lodger and co-own your property (with your partner, for example) then the allowance is split between the two of you – you can't earn £7,500 each without paying tax.

For full details of the scheme, see: Direct.gov.uk.

Social tenants and taking in lodgers

New government legislation came into place in 2013 to deal with 'under-occupancy' in social housing. The changes essentially mean anyone with a spare bedroom will get less housing benefit. The common name for this is The Bedroom Tax.

Tenants will need to cover the shortfall through existing income or benefits - one option for some is to take in a lodger. Most social tenants can take in a lodger if they want but there are other things to consider, such as how this can affect any other benefits they get. For more on the ins and outs of taking in a lodger for social tenants download SpareRoom's free guide at http://www.spareroom.co.uk/bedroomtax

---

When your lodger moves out
WHAT HAPPENS NOW?
Sooner or later you or your lodger will decide it's time for them to leave. In most cases the relationship will end amicably but there are still a few things you'll need to know.

ENDING THE AGREEMENT
Your agreement with your lodger should contain details of what needs to happen in order for either party to terminate the arrangement. Standard procedure is to have a notice period of four weeks – this will give your lodger time to find somewhere else to live. It's possible to insert a clause that gives a shorter period (say two weeks) so either party can end the agreement early if they need to. Otherwise you'll find yourself at the end of the agreed term and you'll need to decide whether your lodger wants to stay (and sign another agreement) or leave. It's worth having a conversation about this before the end of the term so you both know what the other's plans are.

RETURNING THE DEPOSIT

When your lodger moves out you should return the security deposit paid to you when they moved in. The only reasons you should withhold money are if there is damage to the room, property or contents, or any unpaid rent. If there has been any damage (beyond the expected wear and tear of someone living in a property) you will need to deduct a suitable amount to cover it. If you're not sure how much this will cost then say you'll find out and let them know – you should aim to do this within a week if possible.

UNPAID RENT

If your lodger owes you any rent when they move out you can deduct this from the deposit before returning it. Don't be tempted to let your lodger off the last month's rent and just keep the deposit – while this may seem like a good idea it doesn't leave you with any security if anything should happen in the last month.

PROBLEMS WITH YOUR LODGER

In the unlikely event you run into problems with your lodger you should try (in the first instance) to talk to them. Chapter 6 *Living Together* includes plenty of advice (including some specific to living with a lodger). Most problems are the result of misunderstandings or a lack of communication and can be dealt with by talking to each other.

If problems persist then you, as the owner of the property (or the tenant if you rent), have more rights than your lodger. Your first resort should be to put everything in writing so there's a record of what the issues are and when you attempted to speak to the lodger about them. If you can't resolve your differences then you should give your lodger notice to leave (again in writing as well as verbally), as set out in your agreement. If things aren't working out your lodger will probably be as happy to move out as you are to see them go. The standard notice period is 28 days. In extreme circumstances (such as abusive or violent behaviour, drug taking or other criminal activity) you can give a shorter notice period.

EVICTION

In the worst case scenario you could end up with a lodger to whom you have given notice but refuses to leave. This is an extremely difficult situation and should be handled carefully – luckily this rarely happens. After giving your lodger the required notice period (after which they still haven't left) you will need to change the locks once they're out and not allow them entry into the property. This is an extreme course of action and should only be taken where absolutely necessary. We'd recommend seeking some legal advice before you attempt this – in part to protect yourself against any comeback if you fail to follow all the necessary legal procedures. Contact Shelter to talk things through before you attempt a forcible eviction.

Checklist

Having decided to take in a lodger you'll need to plan ahead, so here's our step by step guide to help you work your way through the process with minimal fuss and make sure you've got everything covered in advance.

Points marked with an asterisk (*) are absolutely essential – you shouldn't ignore any of these. Those with the 'recommended' symbol ® are points we'd strongly advise you to consider.

This list can be downloaded and printed from: www.SpareRoom.co.uk/essentialguide/lodger.

1*   Check with your mortgage lender, landlord or local authority

2*   Inform your insurance provider

3*   Inform your local benefits agency

4*   Let the council know if you're paying reduced council tax for single occupancy.

5®   Get the room ready

6®   Decide in advance what the terms and conditions will be

7®   Get a lodger agreement

8® Check local rents

9* Get your gas appliances checked by a Gas Safe registered professional

10® Advertise your room

11® Viewings

12® Credit checks

13® Carry out Right to Rent checks

14® Signing contracts, deposit and agreeing terms and conditions

15® Getting your lodger to set up a standing order for the rent

16® Lodger moves in

17* Inform your tax office if you earn over £7,500

From one live-in landlord to another

Most people find taking in a lodger a positive experience. Even those who have had difficulties with a lodger often put it down to bad luck and try again, usually with better results. Don't forget, it's not just about how good the lodger is, it's also about how you are as a landlord and that's something you'll become better at as you progress.

We asked a selection of live-in landlords who use SpareRoom to give us their tips for anyone new to taking in lodgers. Here's a selection of their experiences and advice.

'I have had four lodgers and all have been totally different. None of them have really integrated as I thought but, as time has gone on, I actually preferred it that way. I find the best lodger is one that has a job and hobbies so they don't feel caged in the house. My only tip would be don't believe everything they tell you (e.g "I'm really clean and tidy"). Speak to previous landlords to check.'

'I have had two lodgers now. The requirements of the first were very different to the second so you can't prepare totally for what you think a person will need. Be flexible. Also treat your lodger as part of the family: trust and respect hopefully will be returned.'

'I have had good and bad experiences and have learned to trust my instinct about a person and be upfront about expectations.'

'I recommend the "boyfriend" rule that overnight guests can stay for as many nights as the lodger stays at theirs.'

'Set the ground rules from the outset – we could have failed miserably as housemates because neither of us had been in this position before. However, we agreed to start again, established the ground rules and things have been good ever since.'

'I have realised that lots of my preconceptions about the type of lodger I thought I would like were wrong. As it turns out, I'm not sure that friendship is the key, but rather that there are clear boundaries that are respected in each direction. My current lodger is someone whom I like very much and have a great deal of respect for, and am more than happy to share my home with, but with whom I have no personal relationship at all. After all, it is a business arrangement. My first lodger and I shared a lot in common in terms of interests, as I had advertised in this way. But in fact this caused quite a strain as it was then hard to keep the right distance.'

'I have found it much easier to have a lodger live with me than I thought it would be. It's best to lay out what you expect of them right from the start – if there is anything you are unhappy with bring it up straight away but in a calm and reasonable way. I have only had one difficulty, quickly resolved, and would consider another lodger should my current lodger decide to move on.'

'I have always had great people from SpareRoom – with one exception. My own fault – I allowed myself to be rushed into saying he could take the room, even though I had lots of reservations. My advice to everyone is, don't be rushed into a decision.'

'Getting a random person in is completely different to living with a friend and, unless you're exceptionally chilled-out, small things will bug you, it's only human. The key is to be tolerant and understanding and just talk – don't rely on emails or texts to communicate. Make sure you share out the household chores too, or get a (good) cleaner, as this can be the cause of so many little bug-bears that needn't be there.'

'Our lodgers generally do Monday to Friday and that works well for us as we are a family with two young boys. I wouldn't say that the lodgers become friends but we usually have a relaxed, friendly relationship with our lodgers. At the end of the day they are paying for a room so it is a commercial relationship, but we have usually found that is it quite amicable and if it doesn't work then we ask them to move out.'

'It took three attempts but have finally found someone I get on with and we both seem to get on living together. It can be difficult and is a lot to get used to but I don't regret it.'

'Don't take anything for granted. If you haven't shared for a while you forget that other people can live in very different ways! Don't assume anything. Everything needs to be communicated, whether you prefer to do this verbally or on paper, even down to who puts the rubbish out and locking the back door. I have a lovely lodger and think I have been rather lucky. I would communicate more the next time – we are quite relaxed but it could have been very different.'

'Most lodgers are very good. In 28 years of letting my rooms I have only had to ask two to leave – one was very weird and the other one was just smelly. I must have had hundreds by now so thats a very good percentage – about a quarter became good friends.'

'Having done this for a few years I would say that a combination of trustworthiness and a good personality are the most important things. Always go with your instincts and you'll be fine. If there's any doubt then there is no doubt.'

'I just make sure I meet and really feel out the prospective tenant before agreeing. I never "close" on the first impression, saying I have a couple more people to see still, then review my feelings afterwards. If they're negative I politely decline the guest. I saw three or four people each time before taking my lodgers.'

'Most have been okay but one did not pay his rent. He kept saying there had been some problem at the bank. Stupidly I believed him and then he disappeared, having paid one month's rent out of three. Don't let this put you off though – my current lodger has become a true friend.'

'It has been a good experience for me, apart from the odd blip which was quickly sorted out. I have always been straight with people and ask them to regard the house as their home, treat it with respect, and just do things off their own back if they see something needs doing rather than have a list of "duties". On the whole they have been more responsible if they know it is up to them. I just have to mention a few points occasionally and I try to lead by example (e.g. always leave the kitchen clean and put everything in the dishwasher or wash and put it away after cooking my meal or empty the dishwasher when it is finished). The lodgers are responsible for keeping their bathroom clean – they share a bathroom and have their rooms on the same floor. It has been a good experience for me on the whole but when there are problems you just have to make it clear that it is not acceptable. I can be authoritative if I need to be but usually we chat comfortably, get on well, they tell me their problems sometimes but I still think it is good to keep a little distance.'

'I have had seven lodgers in the last few years, one for over three years who had already been a friend. Personally I think it's easier on the finance side to have people you do not know, however, on the comfort side, knowing your lodgers can be a great deal more fun and relaxing. Your choice depends how you live and how well you think you can integrate a stranger into your home.'

'Know what kind of person you want and then interview prospective lodgers thoroughly to ensure you get a good match. We've had several and, as we've got better at interviewing them, the experience has got more comfortable.'

CHAPTER FIVE

The Language of Flatsharing

Flatshare adverts have their own language and terminology so it's important to know what it all means, especially if you're new to the UK. Some terms that are widely used in one country may mean something slightly different in another (see 'Room mate' for an example of this).

In the days of rooms being advertised in local newspapers, jargon and abbreviations such as GCH (gas central heating) were invented to make it easier to fit more words into an advert. Some of these still exist today but there are also plenty more terms you'll come across in your search.

Here's a list of the more commonly used ones.

Administration fee

This is a fee, usually payable to an agent (see below), to cover the drawing up of contracts or the checking of references.

Agent

An agent manages part or all of the process of finding tenants for a landlord in exchange for a fee. This may mean simply finding tenants but could also extend to conducting viewings, arranging contracts and even managing the property during the tenancy.

Assured short-hold tenancy (AST)

This is the most common form of tenancy in the UK and is similar to an assured tenancy but lasts for a fixed period of at least six months. ASTs are more popular as they make it easier for the landlord to give notice and end the agreement.

Assured tenancy

An assured tenancy gives you the right to remain in a property unless the landlord can convince the court there are good reasons to evict you (such as rent arrears, damage etc.).

Bedsit

Bedsit (an abbreviation of 'bed sitting room') refers to single room accommodation that serves as both a bedroom and living space in one. Generally, you'll be sharing a bathroom and/or kitchen with others.

Bills included

This means utilities such as gas, electricity and water are included in the rent. Council tax and other bills such as phone or broadband may be included but check in advance which bills are covered, as 'bills included' is fairly non-specific.

Buddy up

Buddy Ups are a feature found on sites like SpareRoom.co.uk and at Speed Flatmating events. They allow individual room seekers (or groups of seekers) to join together to find a property.

Bungalow

A bungalow is a single-storey house with all the rooms on the ground floor.

Buy-to-let

This term is used to describe buying a property with the specific intention of renting it out rather than living in it.

Co-buying

Co-buying refers to buying with another person who isn't your partner, generally in order to be able to buy property you couldn't otherwise afford.

Contents insurance

A policy covering your personal possessions, clothes, furniture and other belongings as opposed to buildings insurance, which covers the structure itself. Generally, if you're renting or sharing you'll need to get your own contents insurance as it won't be included in the rent. See also 'Room contents insurance'.

Contract

A contract, in the world of flatsharing, refers to a written agreement between the tenant(s) and landlord, signed by both parties, setting out the terms of the tenancy. It's always a good idea to have an agreement of some kind as it protects both the tenant and the landlord. See also 'Tenancy agreement'. For information on the main types of contract see Chapter 8, *Contracts, Rights and Agreements*.

Conversion

A conversion is a house that has been divided to make two or more flats. Often there will be a communal entrance with individual front doors off the main hallway. Victorian conversions are amongst the most popular flats in the UK, especially for buyers.

Cottage

The term cottage generally refers to smaller rural properties, although it can be used for other properties (usually if the person describing the property wants to convey a sense of quaintness or cosiness).

Council tax

Council tax is a form of property tax based on the value of a property and (to some extent) who lives in it. Council tax raises around 25% of local government revenue in Great Britain.

Credit check

Landlords and agents may carry out a credit check to satisfy themselves that you can afford to pay your rent before allowing you to move in. This may involve contacting your bank or employer to verify your income.

Deposit

A deposit is a fixed sum taken by landlords or letting agents at the start of a tenancy to cover reasonable losses (such as rent arrears or damage beyond the normal wear and tear of living in a property). Whether you're renting or lodging, you should expect to pay a deposit before moving in; the standard amount is one month's rent. Providing you don't owe any rent at the end of your tenancy, and haven't caused any damage, your deposit should be refunded in full by your landlord. See also 'Tenancy deposit scheme' below.

Detached

A detached house is one that is completely separate from its neighbours, as opposed to terraced or semi-detached houses, which are connected by a shared wall.

Double room

This applies to the size of the room and means a room that has, or can fit, a double bed. In practical terms, the size of double rooms offered varies a great deal – some have just enough space for a double bed and for you to squeeze round it while others will have plenty of space.

DSS

DSS refers to anyone who relies on state benefits to pay their rent. The term comes from the abbreviation of 'Department for Social Security'. You will often see room adverts with the term 'no DSS', meaning the room isn't available to those on benefits.

En-suite

An en-suite room is one that has its own bathroom or toilet, for sole use of that room's occupant.

Eviction

Eviction refers to the process of a landlord expelling a tenant from a property before the end of an agreed term. This is governed by strict rules dependent on the kind of tenancy in place. For information on eviction, see Chapter 8.

Ex-local authority

This refers to a property formerly owned (and usually built) by the council. Often, especially in London, this refers to purpose built blocks of flats.

Fixed term

This refers to the length of an assured shorthold tenancy. If, at the end of the period, you remain in the property without signing a new fixed term agreement, the tenancy becomes periodic (see page 82).

Flat

A flat is usually a property occupying only part of a building – known as an apartment in the US. Blocks of flats can be purpose built or in converted houses.

Flatmate

Flatmate is a term mainly used in the UK and Australia to describe someone who shares a flat or apartment with you. Generally, housemate is used when the property is a house but both terms are fairly interchangeable.

Flatshare

This describes a property (usually a flat) shared by one or more (generally unrelated) people when each person (or couple) has their own bedroom. See also 'Houseshare'.

Fractional letting

Fractional letting is a term used to describe ongoing lettings that don't cover the whole week. The most common example is Monday–Friday lets where the tenant is elsewhere for weekends. Fractional lets are a good way of taking in a lodger without them being there all the time and provide a useful solution for those who commute long distances to work but want to maintain a home elsewhere.

Garden flat

Literally a flat with a garden.

Granny flat

A granny flat is a smaller, self-contained flat at the back or on an upper floor of the main property, usually with its own front door. The term comes from people creating a separate space for an older relative to live with the family without being in the main house.

HMO

HMO is the new buzzword in property rental. It stands for Home in Multiple Occupation and is a system used by local authorities to regulate the quality and safety of shared accommodation. Rules apply to determine what is and isn't an HMO and only certain properties require a licence. If you're renting out a room to a single lodger then you needn't worry about this but for more information, see Chapter 8 or have a look at: http://www.spareroom.co.uk/content/info-faq/HMOs.

House

This usually refers to a whole property on more than one level. One house can contain several flats.

Houseboat

A houseboat is a floating house usually, but not always, converted from a boat.

House rules

The house rules are a set of written or verbal terms agreed upon by all housemates and designed to divide responsibility. They can range from essentials, such as how much rent each housemate pays, to things like who is responsible for cleaning what and how often. House rules aren't essential but can help everyone understand what's expected and minimize conflict.

Houseshare, house share

This describes a property (usually a house) shared by one or more (generally unrelated) people when each person (or couple) has their own bedroom. See also 'Flatshare'.

Inter-sharer agreement

This is similar in some ways to the house rules (see above). An inter-sharer agreement is a contract between housemates which (usually) deals with the more important aspects of the share, such as rent and bills.

Inventory

Some landlords/agents ask tenants to sign an inventory at the same time as their contract. This is a list of all the fixtures and fittings (including furniture) in the room and their current condition. Always check carefully and report any mistakes or omissions BEFORE signing. Once signed, this document provides proof to protect both the tenant and the landlord when inspecting the room on moving out. The inventory will usually be consulted before you get your deposit returned in full so, while it may seem like just another piece of paper when you move in, it's important to check it thoroughly. For more on inventories, see Chapter 8.

Joint and several

A joint and several agreement is one which holds all parties liable. This means if one housemate fails to pay, the landlord can chase any one of the tenants to recover the money. For more information, see Chapter 8.

Key (or card) meter

In rental properties it is common for gas and electricity to be supplied via a key or card meter. This works as a 'pay as you go' system that prevents tenants from running up big utility bills before leaving a property. The downside is generally higher energy prices for key meter customers. For more on this, see Chapter 7.

Landlord's insurance

This is a specific type of insurance offered by certain companies to cover the needs of landlords and can cover anything from rent losses and damage to re-housing tenants in the case of emergencies.

Live-in landlord

A homeowner who rents out one or more rooms in their property whilst living there themselves (i.e. has one or more lodgers) is referred to as a live-in landlord.

Live-out landlord

This refers to a landlord who rents a property they do not live in themselves.

Lodger

A lodger is a tenant who rents a room (or rooms) in another person's house, usually from a live-in landlord (see above). Lodgers' arrangements vary greatly from simply sharing the property with the landlord to living with a family and having meals provided. For more on this, see Chapter 4.

Loft apartment

Generally in former industrial premises, and often open plan in layout, loft apartments have high ceilings and lots of natural light. New York is famous for its loft apartments, popular with artists in the 1960s and 70s and highly desirable (and therefore expensive) now.

Maisonette

A flat on two levels with internal stairs and/or it's own street-level front door is known as a maisonette. These can be purpose built or converted by dividing an existing house.

Mansion

A mansion is usually a very large or expensive house. The term is also used in London to describe a particular style of purpose built flats which generally have high ceilings.

Master bedroom

The biggest bedroom in a property is usually referred to as the master bedroom.

Mews

Mews are traditionally rows of former stables now converted into residential properties. The original ground floor stable area is usually a garage and the living quarters (which would have housed the ostler) are above. Traditional mews houses in London were built behind larger houses so the owners could have their horses (and staff) close by, as a result they're nearly always found in wealthier areas. The term is also used to describe rows of modern properties that mimic the mews style of construction (and is generally used to add desirability to the properties, as mews houses are highly sought after).

Mon–Fri renting

This is a arrangement where the room to let is only available Monday to Friday. This can be a good option for commuters who stay in the city during the week but go home for weekends as rent is reduced accordingly. It can also a good option for the person renting out the room as they get the property to themselves at weekends. See also 'Fractional letting', page 77.

No DSS

This means that the room is not available to those reliant on state benefits to pay their rent.

Party wall

The wall shared by two connected properties, for example terraced houses, is referred to as a party wall.

PCM

This stands for per calendar month so means the rent is calculated as a monthly amount, usually payable at the start of each month.

Penthouse

The penthouse is the top floor of a multi-storey building and is generally the most desirable flat in taller buildings due to improved views, no upstairs neighbours and a greater distance from street noise.

Periodic tenancy

A periodic tenancy is one without a fixed term, usually the result of a fixed-term tenancy that has expired. If you have a periodic tenancy your landlord may not need a reason to ask you to leave.

Postcode

The system used by the Royal Mail in the UK to condense address information into a simple formula (as the US postal service does with zip codes). For more information, see Chapter 2, *Find a Flatshare* – for information on London postcodes, see Chapter 9.

Purpose built

This refers to a collection of flats built as such rather than those converted from an existing building.

PW

PW stands for per week, meaning the rent is payable every seven days.

References

References are a set of documents recommending you as a suitable tenant. The most common form is a letter of recommendation from your previous landlord but you may also be asked for references from your bank and employer. It's common to see the phrase 'references required' in room listings.

Rent a Room Scheme

The Rent a Room Scheme is a government incentive that allows you to earn up to £7,500 a year tax-free by taking in a lodger. The scheme is becoming very popular as more people look to take in lodgers to help with their mortgage payments.

Re-signing fee

Some agents and landlords are happy to extend your contract at the end of the agreed term or amend a contract to include a new flatmate, but you'll usually have to sign a new agreement. Many agents charge a fee for this.

Room contents insurance

Room contents insurance is a specific policy to cover those who rent a room within a property. The policy will insure all your personal belongings without you having to have shared contents insurance for the whole property (for more information and links to insurance providers, see Chapter 7, *Finance and Bills*).

Roommate

Roommate is an American term, now used internationally due to the influence of American film and TV. As the name suggests it can be use to describe someone who shares a room with you but is often used as we would use 'flatmate', to describe people who share a flat or house with you (i.e. they don't have to be in the same room to be described as a roommate). In the UK 'roommate' would generally mean someone you share a room with.

Room seeker

Room seeker is the term used to describe someone who is looking for accommodation in a shared property or with a live-in landlord.

Seasonal lettings

Seasonal lets are short-term lets covering a particular time of year (such as summer or the duration of a particular event). For example, many people in Edinburgh rent out a room during the annual Edinburgh Festival as thousands of people visit the city every year either to attend or perform at the festival, so it's a good chance to make some money without having a permanent lodger.

Semi or semi-detached

This refers to two houses joined together by a connecting wall (as opposed to detached houses).

Sharers

Sharers is the term used to describe those living in shared accommodation together. Usually sharers is used to refer to people renting a whole property between them but can apply to any group of people who share accommodation.

Short-term let

A short-term let is one that lasts for three months or less. Standard tenancies are usually six months and above so anything under that could be considered short term.

Single room

This denotes a room with space for a single bed rather than a double.

Speed Flatmating®

Speed Flatmating is a social event, run by SpareRoom.co.uk, and is popular in London as a way to meet several potential flatmates in one evening. See Chapter 9 or: www.speedflatmating.co.uk for more information.

Studio or studio flat

A single room for cooking, living and sleeping with its own bathroom is called a studio flat. The room is usually divided into a cooking area and a living/sleeping area and is, in basic terms, a one-bed flat without the bedroom.

Sub-let

A sub-let is an arrangement whereby the existing tenant lets all or part of the property to another. This is a complicated issue and one we usually advise people to avoid – see Chapter 1, *Types of Let*, for more information on this subject.

Tenancy agreement

A tenancy agreement is a contract (verbal or written but usually written) between landlord and tenant. The contract outlines the rights both parties have (for example, your right to occupy the property and the landlord's right to receive rent from you). The contract is designed to protect both the tenant and the landlord and will contain information on issues such as whether you can keep pets in the property and how much notice you need to give if you want to leave. See also 'Contract', or, for further information, see Chapter 8, *Contracts, Rights and Agreements*.

Tenancy Deposit Scheme

The Tenancy Deposit Scheme was introduced by the government in 2007 to safeguard deposits taken by landlords. So far the scheme only applies to assured shorthold tenancies (see above) and requires the landlord to place the deposit in one of a choice of schemes to be returned in full at the end of the tenancy (provided there's no unpaid rent or damage to be paid for). If there's a dispute about the amount of deposit to be returned then there's help available to sort out the problem in a fair manner. See Chapter 8 for more on the scheme.

Tenant

Someone who rents and occupies a property from another is known as a tenant (unless they live with their landlord, in which case they become a lodger).

Terraced house

A terraced house is one in a row of (usually) identical properties connected to each other by shared (or 'party') walls.

Townhouse

This term is used to describe a style of (originally) upper class house (generally in London), often with three or more floors.

Viewing

This is the term for showing someone round (or being shown round) a property.

Walk-up flat

Walk-up refers to a block of flats (mostly low rise) that have individual front doors externally, usually off a shared walkway (as opposed to off a communal internal hallway).

Interlude: Fighting Over the Remote – Flatshare on the Box

Over the years there have been many memorable films and TV shows based around flatshares and lodgers. Some of these are classics and some not so great, but all recognize that there's a wealth of humour, fun, sadness, conflict and drama (all the things we need for a good story) in any shared house or flat.

Here are a few of our favourites.

Film

SHALLOW GRAVE

Set in Edinburgh, the film opens with a group of friends interviewing potential candidates to fill their spare room, in what is probably the most memorable flatshare scene ever written. If you've ever been to look round a shared flat then this is the interview you least want.

The high (or possibly low) point – certainly the funniest – comes when Alex Law (played by Ewan McGregor in his first main feature role) asks one hopeful:

So tell me, Cameron, just tell me because I'd like to know, what on earth could make you think that we would want to share a flat like this with someone like you? I mean, my first impression, and they're rarely wrong, is that you have none of the qualities that we normally seek in a prospective flatmate.

The plot begins to unfold once chosen flatmate Hugo (Keith Allen) moves in and promptly dies, at which point the flatmates discover a huge amount of cash in his room. Should you ever find yourself in this situation (and we hope you don't), we'd suggest you go to the police rather than following their example!

SINGLE WHITE FEMALE

This 1992 thriller starring Jennifer Jason Leigh and Bridget Fonda takes us to the extremes of what can go wrong when you let a stranger into your home. Allie Jones needs a new flatmate to replace the fiancé she's kicked out but starts to despair after a string of unsuitable candidates apply. Then along comes Hedy Carlson, who Allie decides is perfect and gives the room to. As the film unfolds, and Hedy starts becoming unnervingly like Allie, we discover the truth about her background and she turns out to be far from the ideal flatmate.

The film's tagline, 'Allie's new roommate is about to borrow a few things without asking. Her clothes. Her boyfriend. Her life' sums up all that people worry about when they have to find a new flatmate. Luckily it generally doesn't end like this!

THE ODD COUPLE

Felix (Jack Lemon) has split up with his wife and decides to kill himself but is saved by Oscar (Walter Matthau). Oscar persuades Felix to move in with him but it turns out they have very different ideas of how they'd like to live. Neil Simon was nominated for an Oscar for the screenplay, based on his own Broadway play. A TV series based on the play was also a hit in the 70s.

TV

THE YOUNG ONES

This classic sitcom, based on four very different characters sharing student digs in 1980s Britain, made stars of actors Rik Mayall (who also co-wrote the series), Adrian Edmonson and Nigel Planer (and co-writer Ben Elton). The students' slapstick, violent and often downright surreal adventures were a breath of fresh air when they first hit UK TV screens and helped give rise to the wave of 'alternative comedy' which swept Britain in the 1980s.

The show was far more violent, dirty and anarchic than anything previously seen in a prime time comedy slot on the BBC and, at times, it seemed like the plot was non-existent, but the show was a huge hit with audiences and ran for 26 episodes between 1982 and 1985.

RISING DAMP

Another all-time classic UK sitcom, this time set in a seedy bedsit house run by thoroughly unpleasant landlord Rigsby (played by Leonard Rossiter). The series (which later spawned a film) was based on Eric Chappell's play *The Banana Box*, which originally starred Wilfred Bramble as the landlord (who was called Rooksby, later changed to Rigsby after complaints from a real life Mr Rooksby) before Rossiter took over. Bramble is best known for playing another cantankerous old miser Albert Steptoe in the classic sitcom *Steptoe and Son*, as well as Paul McCartney's grandfather ('he's very clean') in *A Hard Day's Night*. In fact, of the show's regular cast, only Richard Beckinsale hadn't already played his part in the stage version.

Rigsby remains, for many, the stereotypical image of the money-grabbing landlord, presiding over a kingdon of shabby little bedsits, long after the world of bedsits and lodgers has moved on.

MEN BEHAVING BADLY

After the alternative comedy of *The Young Ones* in the 1980s, we had the laddism of *Men Behaving Badly* in the 1990s. The show, which was a huge hit for the BBC, actually started on ITV with Harry Enfield starring alongside Martin Clunes. Enfield quit after the first series and was replaced by Neil Morrissey but ITV lost faith, possibly feeling the show needed a star such as Enfield to guarantee ratings.

The BBC picked up the series in 1994 and took the decision to broadcast it after the 9 o'clock watershed, allowing the show to embrace its subject matter (and its humour, based on 'boobs, belching and booze') a little more directly.

Men Behaving Badly, whether the embracing lad culture of magazines such as *Loaded* or simply a backlash against the 90s caring, sharing 'new man' (as has been suggested), allowed audiences a glimpse into the life of two men struggling to grow up (and, often, failing to see why they should).

FRIENDS

The one where a group of six friends hang out in a New York coffee shop (and all seem to live with each other at some point).

Friends is probably the best loved (and most successful) sitcom of all time. Over the space of ten years (and ten seasons), the ups and downs of the relationships between Rachel, Ross, Monica, Joey, Chandler and Phoebe kept millions tuning in every week and made household names of the actors who portrayed them. It also spawned spin-off series *Joey* in which Matt Le Blanc's character moves to Hollywood in search of an acting career.

Friends shows a more contemporary view of flatsharing than either *The Young Ones* or *Rising Damp*. This type of shared accommodation, with groups of young professionals living together, is becoming far more common today (although most of us can't afford flats quite as nice as theirs).

The show won a whole host of awards, including several Emmys (most surprisingly one for Bruce Willis – Outstanding Guest Actor in a Comedy Series!).

PEEP SHOW

From the glamour of Manhattan to Apollo House, London Road, Croydon – BAFTA award winning series *Peep Show* follows the, generally frustrated, lives of two university friends sharing a flat. Mark (David Mitchell) is financially successful but socially awkward and generally pessimistic. Jeremy (Robert Webb) is far more socially confident and positive but has yet to achieve the recognition and success he believes he deserves.

The characters are mostly seen from their own point of view, or that of others (as opposed to that of the viewer) and the use of voiceover lets us know what they're thinking as well as what they're saying (a feature inspired by Woody Allen's use of subtitles in *Annie Hall*). Scenes are often filmed using cameras strapped to the actors' heads so we also get their visual perspective.

The show attracted a strong cult following when first broadcast by Channel 4 in 2003. By series three (in 2006) the series won the Best TV Comedy award at the British Comedy Awards (which it won again the following year, along with a Best TV Comedy Actor award for Mitchell).

Opera

Yes, believe it or not, there actually is a flatshare-based opera. Not only that, it's a good one!

LA BOHEME

Puccini's *La Bohème* follows the (mis)fortunes of a group of struggling artists living in a garret in Paris in the 1830s. The role of starving poet Rodolfo became one of Pavarotti's signature roles (despite it becoming more difficult over the years to imagine him as a starving anything) and his Act 1 aria *Che Gelida Manina* (generally known in English as *Your Tiny Hand is Frozen*) is one of the most popular and beautiful in all opera.

The opera is often referred to as part of the 'ABC of Opera' referring to *Aida*, *Bohème* and *Carmen*, three operas guaranteed to get bums on seats. When asked by Sir Thomas Beecham what his favourite opera was, King George V supposedly cited *La Bohème*. When asked why this was he replied 'Because it's the shortest'.

La Bohème was the basis for hit Broadway show *Rent*, and Baz Luhrmann's experience directing the opera for Opera Australia in 1990 must surely have had some influence on *Moulin Rouge*, which features a penniless writer, a Parisian garret and a dying heroine.

CHAPTER SIX

Living Together

Okay, so you've found the perfect room in a great flat and your flatmates seem lovely, all's well so far. Unfortunately it's not always as easy as this and, when a group of people live in close proximity to each other, there will be inevitable disputes and differences of opinion. We've all got our own needs when it comes to a place to live, some people prefer a busy, lively house whilst others need peace and quiet. You may be the kind of person who finds it impossible to relax until the washing up is done, whilst your friends don't mind a bit of mess as long as it gets sorted in the end.

According to SpareRoom.co.uk's users the things most likely to provoke an argument between housemates are cleanliness (56%) and noise levels (25%). In addition almost half of those in shared accommodation have argued at some point with their housemates about paying bills. Obviously when you're living with other people you won't always see eye to eye but there are certain problems which will inevitably crop up and steps you can take to avoid them before they do.

So, how do you move in without falling out? Some (if not most) of this may seem obvious but, despite the jokey nature of the advice, these really are some of the simplest things you can do to avoid annoying each other on a daily basis.

Cleanliness

Being next to godliness it's clear that cleanliness is likely to be a major source of conflict (we don't have any statistics on how many flatmates have argued about godliness but I'm guessing it's not the main source of disputes for most people). It stands to reason that any flatshare will only be as tidy as the untidiest person in it so if one of you is extremely houseproud and another is a slob you'll struggle to find the middle ground that's acceptable to both.

There are three main areas of any property that are going to be the obvious battlegrounds, they are:

- kitchen
- bathroom
- living room.

Each presents its own problems and likely trouble spots.

KITCHEN

This is the room with the potential to cause the most trouble, as it's the easiest to turn into a bombsite in minutes. Everyone will need to use the kitchen at some point (even the most committed non-cook will need to get to the kettle) and there's nothing worse than getting in after a day at work and having to wash up before you can cook.

The top trouble spots are:

Microwave

This is a simple one, if you've used the microwave to heat something and it's splattered all over (soup and porridge are best for this if you want a good example to try), clean it up after you've eaten. There's nothing worse than little stalactites of tomato soup hanging down from the roof of a microwave and, before too long, the whole thing will smell awful. There's also nothing quite like the smell of microwaved fish for staying power. A quick wipe down with a wet cloth will get rid of most of the mess, also, the glass plate you put things on is removable for a very good reason – so if you can clean it, do so.

Cooker

Similarly to the microwave an uncleaned cooker is no good to anyone. I'm certainly not suggesting you clean the whole thing every time you use it but wiping any spillages from the hob and cleaning the grill pan are simple basics you should become familiar with.

> **Matt says:**
> 'I can tell you from personal experience that leaving a grill pan you've used to cook sausages never results in it eventually cleaning itself while you're not looking.'

If anyone in the flat is vegetarian you should definitely clean anything you've used to cook meat as a matter of simple human decency.

Generally in any shared house the cooker will need a thorough scrub before you move out but it doesn't need to get so bad in the meantime that it sets off the smoke alarms every time you use the grill.

Fridge

The fridge is the classic image of flatshare neglect. With several people's food in there, and no one keen to throw someone else's stuff away, you can end up with mini civilizations living at the back. It'll be much easier if you buy essentials together so the fridge isn't full of half empty milk bottles, all of which are past their sell by date.

Spillages, drips and anything furry should be dealt with promptly. Milk that doesn't move when you shake the bottle can also be thrown out.

We saw a great invention in the Electrolux design competition last year, which isn't in production yet but certainly should be. It's called a Flatshare Fridge and consists of a stackable, modular set of mini fridges so you get one each and all disputes can be easily avoided. If someone else moves in you just get another module – fantastic! For a look at this simple work of genius just Google 'flatshare fridge' and you'll see what we mean.

Washing up

This is easy, wash up what you've used – it's really that simple. If you're cooking a big meal that requires loads of pots, pans and utensils then wash up as you go along so there are only a few bits left at the end. Everything else should be done soon after you've eaten so other people can use stuff. If you have a dishwasher then this all becomes easier, just pile everything in out of sight and stick a load on once it's full.

Remember, someone has to put the stuff back into cupboards at some point so the next lot of dirty dishes doesn't get added by someone who can't be bothered to see whether what's in there already is clean or not.

Matt says:

'I lived with a friend once who used to cook meals using everything in the kitchen then leave the washing up and go out for the night. As often as not he'd then stay with his girlfriend for a few days so I had to wash up everything before I could eat – no fun.'

Surfaces
Wipe 'em down, easy.

'One guy I lived with used to make coffee in a cafetiere. Somehow he always seemed to leave as much on the surfaces as in the mug and never cleaned up so we got into the habit of writing "clean this please" in the huge brown stains 'til he got the message. This method takes a little patience (or downright stubbornness) at first but works well in the long term.'

Steph

Bins
Empty the bins regularly and make sure you know what day rubbish collection is. Also, sort out your recycling but have a plan of what to do with it too, as there's no point separating it all if you're just going to chuck it in the bin eventually. Lots of supermarkets have recycling bins and more and more councils now collect recycling and provide special bins or boxes to put it in. Contact your local council to see if they provide a recycling collection service if you're not sure.

Bathroom
It shouldn't be that hard to keep a bathroom clean but it never quite manages to work that way. All that should be required is giving the bath a quick rinse after you use it and a more thorough clean every now and then, but there are a few other essentials:

Toilet

Use the toilet brush, that's what it's there for. Any unsightly marks left in the toilet need dealing with, nobody wants to see the consistency of your bowel movements (except Gillian McKeith and I'm guessing you don't live with her). Similarly, if you occasionally suffer from bad aim (I'm talking to you here boys, girls really have to work hard to miss), clean it up. Don't just leave it there and, if questioned, say you must have dripped a bit of water from the sink washing your hands – this is what kids do and we know they're lying so you won't get away with it.

If you've created a new and unusual atmosphere after using the toilet (made it stink basically) it's not okay to just come out and proudly declare 'I wouldn't go in there for a while if I were you'. Open a window, strike a match or (better still) keep a scented candle in there for such occasions. Air freshener is no good, a strong smell of poo is unpleasant, a strong smell of poo with a thick veneer of air freshener is truly horrendous.

Matt says:

'Always (ALWAYS) replace a toilet roll if you finish one and don't squeeze the toothpaste from the top of the tube so it all stays at the end – these are the things which set us above apes. I volunteered at a monkey sanctuary once and never saw a single monkey replace a toilet roll.'

Bath

A quick rinse not only gets rid of soap scum and cleans the bath but also deals with any stray 'intimate' hairs you may have left and which I can guarantee none of your flatmates wants to find floating past their navel when they use the bath after you.

Living room

This is a truly shared space, as you'll spend most of your time as a group here, so keep it tidy. When it comes to your own stuff being left in the living room there's a simple rule to follow; if others will want to use it regularly and you don't mind this then fine, otherwise it lives in your own room.

Examples of stuff you can leave in the living room:

TV/DVD player/stereo/games console

If there isn't one of these in the property already and you have one you're happy to share, then great. Beware of falling into the 'it's my TV so we'll watch whatever I say we will' trap though as this isn't friendly and will cancel out any good will created by leaving your TV in the living room in the first place.

Magazines

If you've read these and think other people may want to then fine; don't just use the living room as a dumping ground though.

Books/DVDs/CDs

Things like this are always good to share but don't just keep all your belongings in the living room because you don't want to clutter up your own room. Also be aware that not everyone has the same attitude to your stuff as you do. If you expect discs to be put back in the correct cases and books to be read without the pages having their corners bent over and the spine broken then maybe you should keep them in your room and lend out at your discretion.

Examples of things you should find somewhere else to put:

Last night's socks

Take them off if you want but don't leave them on the floor for days (or even overnight) as the chance of someone else wanting to use them is fairly slim.

All your shoes

I don't really need to tell you this, do I?

Your bike

Or this, surely?

Your best mate who came for the weekend and is still on the sofa five days later

Friends come and go but, having come, they do need to go at some point.

Washing

If you've done a load of washing and left it on radiators, or in the living room, to dry you should put it away once it is dry. This is partly so your flatmates can use the space to dry their clothes and partly because nobody wants to eat their dinner with a radiator full of someone else's pants watching them.

Noise levels

Noise can prove one of the most intrusive elements of living with other people – even noise from neighbours above, below or sideways can really prove troublesome. In a shared house this is magnified, as you're likely to have more TV, more music, more hairdryers and more conversations going on all at once.

A basic level of noise is inevitable in any shared house but there are a few points worth looking at if you want a happy harmonious household.

PARTIES

It's always a good idea to check with everyone in the house before inviting loads of people over. If you're all happy with this it's probably also worth warning your neighbours in advance (and maybe dropping in a bottle of wine the day after as a thank you for their tolerance). Often people don't mind a bit of noise every now and then, as long as it's not all the time and you have the manners to warn them. You could even invite your neighbours to come along if you get on okay with them.

> **Sharer's tip:**
> 'I live in a shared house in South East London with four other people. We're not a regular party house but do like to have the odd get together now and then and, when we do, they can go on a bit! Our next door neighbours are a lovely couple in their 80s who have lived in the area for 40 years, we always invite them to pop in for a drink if we're having a party and they generally do. On New Year's Eve they came at 11pm and stayed 'til 1.30! Having a good relationship with them means we can make a bit of noise now and then and they don't mind, or feel intimidated by it, as they know us.'
>
> Gemma

MUSIC

With several rooms (and several people wanting to listen to their own music all at the same time) things can get a bit chaotic in a shared house. The first thing to remember is that loud music is not a challenge – it's generally better to get someone to turn their music down, shut the door or buy some headphones than decide you'll drown them out.

If someone repeatedly plays loud music (especially really early or really late) your options generally involve having a word or putting up with it. You should at least do your flatmate the courtesy of talking to them about it instead of second guessing their reaction. If they really won't turn it down then at least they'll know it bothers you and you'll know they're making a conscious choice to be loud. Often people won't realize how obtrusive their music is until you tell them.

Time of day

With any kind of noise (music, TV, hoovering, using your noisy juicer) it's always best not to start too early or go on too late. You run the risk of annoying your flatmates and your neighbours (especially if they have children who go to bed early just on the other side of your bedroom wall).

Remember that things don't have to be that loud to be annoying, the subwoofer of a surround sound speaker set can really rattle the windows a floor up or down without it seeming loud at all to you.

Money and bills

Sort out as much in advance as you can, money has the potential to become a real flashpoint for arguments so the less you leave until there's a problem the better. See Chapter 7, *Finance and Bills*, for advice on this.

Space and privacy

Everyone needs a bit of space of their own, unfortunately not everyone is so good at recognizing this fact in others. Luckily, in these days of mobile phones and wi-fi, it's at least possible to make phone calls and check your emails in peace without having to talk quietly so everyone else in the room can watch *Eastenders*.

PARTNERS

In any shared house space can become an issue, especially if partners become involved. If your flatmates have partners who regularly stay over then it's even harder to use the bathroom in the morning and things can get hectic. This can be fine if you all get on but, if things aren't that harmonious to start with, all out war can soon begin.

It might be an idea to limit the number of nights people can have their partners over to stay, as having an extra person there all the time can get a bit much, especially if they end up practically living with you.

'I moved into a four-bed flat with three of my mates a few years ago; after about a month one of their girlfriends came down for the weekend and didn't leave for six months! It meant we all had an extra flatmate who didn't contribute anything to the bills or rent and spent hours every day in the bathroom. Nobody said anything for the first few weeks and, after that, it became too late to do anything about it.'

Edward

LOCKS AND CLOSING YOUR DOOR

Having locks on your bedroom doors in a shared house can be really useful, especially if you don't know the other housemates when you move in. The problem is, in locking your door to the people you live with, you're basically saying 'I don't trust you completely'. It may stop everyone borrowing your belongings though so what you do with locks is really up to you in the end.

If you have room contents insurance (see Chapter 7) then your policy may require you to have a lock on your bedroom door (and use it while you're out) in which case it's a good idea. It's probably a good idea to lock your room if you'll be away for a few days anyway, though your housemates may well want to use your room for guests while you're away so this in itself may become problematic.

The case of the flatmate and the alleged sister

'I shared a two-bed flat with one of my best friends for a couple of years. One weekend I was due to be away and he asked if it was okay for him to use my room as his sister was coming down for the weekend. He offered her his bed and slept in mine, which seemed best seeing as I didn't even know her. This worked so well that he only ever invited her down while I was away so, in two years of living together, she visited six or seven times and we never met.

I did wonder if she really existed until a few years later when I met her at my friend's wedding!'

Tom

Conflict

Conflict and arguments are bound to feature in any kind of shared accommodation at some stage. There are things you can do to reduce conflict but, every so often, that just won't be possible and you'll have to deal with it. Most people tend to conform to one of the two following types when faced with conflict:

- aggressive
- passive.

Being aggressive looks, at first sight, like you're tackling the problem head on but (more often than not) aggressive behaviour won't sort out a problem and can make things far worse incredibly quickly.

A passive response to conflict will buy you a little time in the short term (and generally won't raise tempers even further straight away). The trouble is it doesn't deal with the problem, it also allows everyone time to go away and go over things on their own and come up with yet more reasons why they're hard done by in this particular instance.

The only real option for dealing with conflict is to talk it through. This can be extremely daunting, especially if you're dealing with someone who becomes aggressive when confronted.

BE BRAVE, BE HONEST

In sitting down to talk through a conflict you've already shown a certain amount of bravery and, even better, a willingness to resolve the problem. Once you're round the table and ready to talk (and hopefully listen) you've got the best chance you'll get to work out your differences. Make sure you're honest about how you feel without straying too much into the territory of blame – if you can say exactly what the problem is, as far as you're concerned, then you're part way there. Try and avoid thinking that the problem is entirely of your housemate's making unless you're 100% certain that's the case.

DON'T JUST TALK – LISTEN

Having the chance to get whatever's bothering you off your chest shouldn't prevent you from letting the other person have their say. If you go into the conversation determined to prove yourself right at all costs you're not giving it a chance to work. You've (hopefully) been honest about how you feel, let the other person (or persons) do the same.

TREAT THE PROCESS (AND THE OTHER PERSON) WITH RESPECT

If you can go into the conversation presuming the other person has the best of intentions and wants to resolve the conflict you'll stand a better chance of dealing with each other with respect. If you both go in looking to be proved right and waiting for the comment you can be justifiably indignant about, then you're missing the point. Surely neither of you really wants tension and arguments?

DO YOUR BEST NOT TO LOSE YOUR TEMPER

However wound up and unfairly treated you feel, try not to lose your temper. If necessary ask for a bit of time to cool off (whether this is ten minutes to make a coffee or walk round the block, or 24 hours). Losing your cool will only allow the other person to respond in kind and feel justified in doing so. The same applies to language.

WATCH YOUR LANGUAGE

Try not to use offensive language (even if the, normally civil, conversations you have with the other person are generally full of swear words and neither of you minds). Using bad language directed at something or someone else (the football on TV, for example) isn't quite the same as having bad language directed at you. If in doubt, leave it out (I'm not sure why all pithy bits of advice have to rhyme but they always seem to – Matt).

COMMUNICATION – LEAVING NOTES

Flat and house shares seem to be the only places in the world where it's considered acceptable (even desirable) to conduct conversations via post-it notes stuck on a fridge. You wouldn't solve a problem at work like this so it's unlikely you'll convince your flatmate of their unreasonable behaviour in this fashion either.

The fridge note works (on one level) for two reasons:

- In most flatshares not everyone will be around at the same time so some form of time delayed communication can be handy.
- Everyone uses the fridge at some point.

It doesn't work for several more:

- Tone of voice is absent so it's hard to judge intent – something may be read as a dig which isn't intended that way.
- Writing something down is a very permanent way of saying something you may have only thought for two seconds.
- The notes are left where everyone can see them so the conversation becomes public.
- Notes end up getting written at times when you're not best able to judge tone and content (such as at midnight when you've finally managed to get your key in the door and have stumbled into the kitchen looking for bread to toast/burn and someone has finished off the last few slices).

Try and resist the impulse to communicate through leaving notes unless all other forms of communication have already broken down.

> ### I got into a note war with my flatmate
> 'We ended up not speaking to each other as we didn't get on, so left notes for each other about house stuff. The notes ended up getting more and more nasty until we had to sort it out (three weeks before we moved out into separate flatshares).'
>
> Sarah

For a hugely entertaining look at fridge communication in flatshares, get a copy of Oonagh O'Hagan's *I Lick My Cheese and Other Notes From the Frontline of Flat-Sharing* (Sphere, 2007).

House rules

While it may seem a bit over the top, it's worth considering a set of house rules so you avoid the majority of arguments before they happen. It's entirely up to you what you include (and you don't have to write them down and pin them up in the kitchen), but a quick discussion about how you all expect things to be in the house when you first move in may well save a serious argument a few months down the line.

Basic things to consider including in the house rules might be:

- what shopping (if any) you're going to buy together
- how you're going to sort out paying the bills
- how often partners can stay over
- who cleans what and when.

Lodgers in your home

Living with others in a flatshare can be fairly straightforward in many ways as everyone has pretty much equal rights to everything. With lodgers though the situation is different, as one of you owns the property, was there first and will be there after the lodger has gone.

As the situation is ultimately in the hands of the live-in landlord they should be prepared and have thought a few things through prior to the lodger moving in, so you can have a few ground rules and both know where you stand.

One of the first things to decide if you're taking in a lodger is how much of the property they can use. Obviously you'll have your own bedrooms but you need to be clear if there are any areas of the house or flat that are off limits. Your lodger will want to use the kitchen and living room and you can't realistically expect them to spend all their time in their own room. If you've got two bathrooms then that will make life easier but if not then that will be shared space too.

A few points to consider before your lodger moves in are:

THE OTHER HALF

Does your lodger have a partner and, if so, will they expect them to be allowed to stay over? If this isn't okay with you make sure they know this in advance of moving in. You might decide it's fine but set a limit on how many nights a week this can happen, which is also okay as long as you're clear from the outset.

KITCHEN

Clear some space in your cupboards and fridge so your lodger has space for their food.

BATHROOM

What time do you both need to get out of the house by? If you can sort out a routine it'll make things easier in the mornings for both of you.

TV

Just because it's your house doesn't mean you get to decide everything. By taking someone's money for your room you should expect to let them live comfortably in your property. Obviously if you don't ever watch the same programmes this may become tricky but have a look at some of the advice on taking in a lodger in Chapter 4, a little time choosing the right person will make everything easier.

What to do if you can't resolve the conflict

This is the tricky bit as, once communication has broken down completely, there may be no way back. There aren't any quick fixes for situations like this and, sometimes, you'll just have to accept that you don't get on and one (or both) of you would be happier living somewhere else. Obviously if you're a landlord living with a lodger then it's clear which of you will end up moving out.

If there's a conflict between sharers then your landlord may be able to help, depending on what the issue is. You can involve the police or your local council but only in serious conflicts (for example if one of the housemates is threatening or violent).

A voice of experience

Melanie Hill took part in the very first series of *Big Brother* in the UK. We asked her if her time in the house had taught her anything about how to live in a large group:

'Nothing can compare to living under the constant gaze of the *Big Brother* cameras with total strangers. It is a little bit like living in an open prison (or so I would imagine). There's nothing real about living in the *Big Brother* house, it's all contrived and artificial. The most valuable lesson I learnt in the house was tolerance and adapting to change. Every day is totally different with different people coming and going and tasks. My advice to people living with others is try to be a relaxed, calm influence – most things we get stressed about don't really matter in the grand scheme of things so why worry?'

Melanie Hill

CHAPTER SEVEN
Finance and Bills

Money can be one of the most likely causes of arguments amongst flatmates – over 50% of those we surveyed had argued with their flatmates about bills at some point. Arguments over who bought or paid for what, and who actually used it, can lead to all kinds of tension and conflict. The more you plan in advance and sort out your financial arrangements, the more of this you can avoid on a daily basis, leaving you plenty of free time to argue about more important things like football, politics, which pub to go to, why (insert band of choice) aren't as good as everyone says they are, why you don't like Bob's new girlfriend – the list is endless.

Even if you're all clear and organized about the financial side of things, it'll help to read through this chapter and make sure there aren't any unexpected bills you hadn't considered.

Rent

By far the biggest chunk of your money will be going on rent so this is the first thing to sort out. The type of flatshare you live in will determine who you have to pay, it's likely to be one of the following:

- a live-out landlord or agent
- a live-in landlord if you're a lodger
- another housemate who you sublet from.

Whoever you pay it's always a good idea to set up a standing order for your rent so you can make sure it's always paid on time and you don't have to think about it every month. This can be especially important if you live with your landlord as it can put a strain on your relationship if they need to keep asking for money. If you get paid at a certain time of the month it's worth asking if you can pay the rent then as it'll leave you with a clearer idea of how much you've got left for everything else. If not then make sure you don't spend all your money before the rent is due.

If you're renting from a landlord or agent and you all pay the same amount direct to the landlord then things are usually pretty straightforward. If you're renting a whole property and dividing the rent between you things can get a little more complicated – make sure you're clear from the outset who's paying what. It can work well to divide the rent according to who has which room – for example, if there's a big master bedroom with an en-suite then one of you may be happy to pay a bit extra to get that room while whoever has the smallest room pays less. This can also be a great way for a group of people with different income levels to share (and paying the same rent for a single room as someone else does for a double can cause resentment long term). If you're happy to pay different amounts then it would be a good idea to work out who can afford what before you look for a property, as your combined budgets might mean you can afford somewhere better than you previously thought.

If there are particularly desirable rooms then you'll need to work out who gets which. You can make this fun.

Matt says:

'I moved into a flat in North London with a good friend back in the 1990s. The first bedroom was a really big double and either of us would have been happy with it in any other property. Then we saw the loft room, which was huge, and we both wanted it. As neither of us could afford to pay extra to get it we had to find a fair way of deciding.

Tossing a coin is a bit boring so we had a couple of pints and went and played air hockey for the room, figuring there's no skill involved (especially after a couple of pints) so neither of us would have an unfair advantage. The point of air hockey seems to be to hit the thing as hard as you possibly can – if you can break all your opponent's fingers in the process then even better. No fingers got broken but I won and got the room, much to the annoyance of my flatmate's girlfriend (sorry Imogen, have you forgiven me yet?).'

You should check your contract if you're renting a whole property, if you have a 'joint and several' agreement (see Chapter 8, *Contracts, Rights and Agreements*) you might find you're all liable if one of you doesn't pay their share. This is fairly standard practice with assured shorthold tenancy agreements as it protects the landlord if one of you fails to pay. It helps to be aware of it from the outset though so you know what you're dealing with if, for example, one of you wants to move out before the agreement is due to end.

Deposits

Under most rental agreements you'll need to pay a deposit before you move in. The standard amount is generally one month's rent (although six weeks is becoming common as well) so you'll have to pay at least two month's rent before you can move in.

The purpose of the deposit is to give the landlord a safeguard against any unpaid rent or damages to the property and furnishings so, provided everything is okay at the end of the tenancy, you should get the full deposit back when you move out. The annoying part is waiting as this usually means, when you next move, you'll need to find another deposit before you get the old one back.

TENANCY DEPOSIT SCHEME

In 2006, the government introduced a new Tenancy Deposit Scheme that requires landlords to hand over your deposit to one of two schemes for safekeeping. This was a result of problems encountered by tenants getting their deposits back – in a recent SpareRoom poll we discovered 65% of people had experienced difficulty getting their deposit back at some point.

For information on deposits and the Tenancy Deposit Scheme, see Chapter 8, *Contracts, Rights and Agreements.*

Bills

Sorting out bills in a shared property can be a nightmare – getting everyone to pay up in full and on time can be a tricky business. Having money conversations with people you're close to can make things awkward, especially if one of you is a little lazy (to put it nicely) when it comes to paying up. However, paying your bills promptly means you won't get faced with a court summons or having your supply cut off, so you might as well get organized.

Some bills, such as council tax, will be easier to deal with, as they're for a fixed amount each month and you can budget accordingly. Others (like gas and electricity) are a little harder as they change each time so become slightly more difficult to budget for.

The bills will all need to be put in someone's name so, unless you live with your landlord and everything's in his or her name, you'll need to sort this out when you move in. It's also vital to check which bills are and aren't included in the rent – water rates and council tax are sometimes paid by the landlord and some rooms are offered all inclusive, so make sure you check what you'll need to pay for on top of your rent before you sign anything.

Remember, having the bills in your name will usually make you liable for any that are unpaid, so don't just put everything in your name to make things easier to sort out.

GAS AND ELECTRICITY

These bills can be the most difficult to deal with as they will be for a different amount each time you pay (especially the bill for whichever heating method you use over the winter months). The fewer of you there are to divide your bills between the quicker (in theory) you should be able to sort them out. Often one person will agree to pay the bill and let everyone else pay them back, which is fine, but this can leave someone seriously out of pocket if the others don't pay up quickly – be warned.

Check with your provider to see if they have any kind of payment plan to help you budget and spread the cost of your bills. At the very least you should contact the supplier with a meter reading when you move in and out and let them know in whose name you want the bill.

'I lived in a shared flat for a year with my girlfriend and a friend of hers. We paid all the bills for gas while we were there (the gas was in my name) but, over a year after we'd moved out, I started getting threatening letters from a debt collection agency saying I owed £850 for gas. Unless we were running a bakery or a hot air balloon business, I can't imagine how they thought three of us could have used this much in a year anyway! I entered into a long correspondence with our gas suppliers (who were extremely unhelpful) but, after almost two years, they eventually stopped pursuing me for the money (especially after I provided a previous tenancy agreement to show I wasn't even living there for part of the period they were trying to make me pay for).'

Steve

KEY METERS

It's common in rental properties, especially shared ones, to have key meters for gas and electricity. These work on a pay-as-you-go basis so you take the key to the nearest top-up point (usually local shops and petrol stations) and put the amount you choose onto it. Once this is getting low you can top-up again. The benefit to the landlord is that the tenants can't run up a huge bill then leave without paying. For tenants it allows them to monitor how much they're spending without getting hit by a huge bill they can't afford. The downside is that most of the gas and electricity suppliers have higher prices for meter customers (and, unless you're really organized, your electricity will run out at a really inconvenient point at least once).

Matt says :

'My first shared flat in London had an electricity key meter and the nearest place you could top it up was a 15-minute walk away. We took it in turns to pay and get top ups but one of us never quite got round to it, so the rest of us ended up paying or having to go out at night to get more put on the key when the power went out. Frustrating is not the word (well, it is but there's a better word which politeness – and my publisher – prevents me from committing to paper).'

PHONE/BROADBAND

The mobile phone is the saviour of flatshares – gone are the days of waiting for three hours to phone out for a takeaway while your flatmate hogged the phone to talk to her boyfriend. Mobiles also mean no boring evenings with a highlighter and the phone bill working out who called which numbers and arguing over the unclaimed ones. You might still need to pay for a landline to get access to broadband but, as long as you don't use it to make calls, that's an easy one to divide between you.

If you, or one of your flatmates, have family overseas who you call on a regular basis you should investigate access numbers. Several companies run these schemes, basically you call them and they put the call through at a much lower cost that most UK phone companies. Just Google 'access number' and the country you need to call.

If you've got broadband it's a great idea to get a wireless router so you can access it from your own computers and rooms. They're not expensive, especially between a few of you, and make it easy for everyone to get online when they need to. Some broadband companies even supply a router when you sign up to their service.

You'll also need to have a conversation at some point about paying for non-essentials like broadband (and cable TV) as some people won't want to pay for services they don't use or want. If some of you want Sky TV, for example, and the others don't then you might find some bills being split between fewer of you. How you deal with this when the people who didn't want it in the first place start watching it is up to you!

COUNCIL TAX

Council tax will be the biggest bill you have to pay and how it gets paid will depend on your situation. Usually one person (known as the 'liable person' for obvious reasons) is liable to pay council tax. This essentially means that the bill is in that person's name, not that it's their responsibility to pay the full amount. Different types of share will mean different ways of paying – here are a few of the most likely scenarios:

Shared house rented by the room

Usually the liable person is whoever lives in the property. If, however, the property is rented by several individuals (or groups) who pay rent separately, the landlord should be the liable person. This will mean the council tax bill is in your landlord's name and he or she will pay. You will possibly still need to pay council tax in this instance but it will most likely be included in your rent.

Shared house rented as a whole

If you rent a whole property, with one contract between you, it's likely you'll have to be responsible for the council tax. This can mean one person has to have the bill in their name, which can lead to problems if one or more people don't pay up. Ask your local authority if it's okay to put the bill in everyone's name as this is fairest and also gives you an extra record of everyone having lived in the property, which can be useful.

You should be able to pay in instalments over the year (or, more commonly, over ten months with a two month break at the end of the financial year), although this might not be possible if you move in the middle of the financial year or fall behind with your payments.

It's essential to inform the council when you move in and out so you don't get stung for a council tax bill for any periods before or after you actually lived in the property.

Lodgers

If you take in a lodger and have previously lived on your own then you'll lose the 25% single occupant discount you've had so far (unless your lodger is a student, in which case you should still be okay). It's reasonable to charge your lodger for his or her half of the council tax (or the increased amount you'll have to pay if you prefer) – this can be included in the rent rather than taking the form of a separate payment. If you're doing this make sure you inform any prospective lodgers that the rent includes council tax.

Students

If some or all of your party are students this will affect your council tax. A flatshare with only students in it is usually exempt from paying council tax. However, if there is a mix of students and professionals then those in employment will still get a council tax bill. As council tax is per household, not per person, the full amount will still be payable (unless there's just one employed person, in which case they can probably apply for a 25% discount). This can mean that some households end up with a couple of people paying a lot of council tax so you should take this into consideration before moving into a mixed house.

An example:

John, Paul, George and Ringo rent a flat for which the council tax bill is £800 a year.

Scenario A

John is at art school full time and Paul is doing a full-time degree in Astrophysics (or something equally rock 'n' roll). George and Ringo both work full time. As John and Paul are both students, and therefore exempt from paying council tax, this leaves the others paying £400 each a year (unless, in the spirit of friendship, they decide to split it four ways anyway).

Scenario B

John and Paul live with other students so their house isn't subject to council tax.

Scenario C

George and Ringo live with two other employed friends (Mick and Keith). Therefore the £800 bill is split four ways and they only pay £200 each.

As you can see, scenario A (where students and those in employment share) results in *someone* paying over the odds – either the students who shouldn't pay at all or the employed sharers who have to take up the shortfall.

Clearly this is a simplified example but you get the picture. We're not saying don't live in a mixed household – just beware of the implications.

WATER

Water bills are another easy one to deal with as suppliers usually bill you for a fixed annual amount and you can spread the payments over at least two terms. However, an increasing number of properties have water meters installed, meaning you pay per usage, so double check first. Some accommodation has the water rates included in the rent so check whether or not this is the case before you move in.

Many people moving out of home for the first time are shocked to get a water bill as they presume water is free – it's not, now you know.

INSURANCE

Your landlord will (or certainly should have) buildings insurance to cover the property but it's a good idea to get your own contents insurance so all your stuff is covered. There are a couple of options for this:

A single contents policy for the flat

Basically you take out insurance to cover the total cost of all your stuff and split the cost between you. This can work out cheaper but you'll need to update the details if one of you moves out and someone else moves in. It can also be tricky working out who needs what coverage (and even if everyone's prepared to pay).

Individual room contents policies

Companies such as Endsleigh offer room contents policies so each of you can insure your own belongings to whatever value you need. This makes it simple for you to protect your own possessions without worrying about everyone else and whether they want to bother with insurance or not. You can then take your policy with you when you move (as long as you let your provider know about your change of address). It's worth checking whether your possessions are covered outside the house as expensive (and easily nickable) stuff like laptops and iPods are going to be taken with you wherever you go. Remember, you're not just insuring against theft, if there was a fire you'd need to replace everything (including your clothes) so take out a policy for a reasonable amount.

Adding your cover to the landlord's insurance

If you live with your landlord they will already have contents insurance and may be happy to add your name to the policy (in return for whatever amount the premium increases by). It may still be easier for you to take out your own room contents policy though, as this will also mean you can take the policy with you when you move and simply update the details with your insurer.

If your landlord says they're going to add you to their policy make sure they actually do as one sharer found out, her's hadn't.

'I lived with my boyfriend and a friend of mine in a two-bed flat for a year or so. We rented the flat from her brother and, when we moved in, he said we could pay him and he'd add us to the existing contents policy (as most of the furniture was his anyway and he had it insured).

We did get burgled while we were there so I was glad we'd paid for insurance but (as it turned out) the brother had taken our money but not actually added our names to the insurance! This made the whole claiming process much trickier as he had to claim for his stuff then give us money towards what we'd lost. Needless to say, we never really got enough to replace everything and we didn't trust our landlord after that!'

Bev

For more information on insurance, including links to companies who offer room contents policies, see: www.SpareRoom.co.uk/essentialguide/insurance.

TV LICENCE

You will need one of these so just cough up and get it over with. It's not so easy to get away without paying these days as the systems used by the licensing people have got more advanced (it's true, I bought a hard disk recorder recently and got a letter from the licensing people saying 'We understand you recently purchased a TV recording device, do you have a licence?' despite the fact that our house already has a licence in my wife's name – Matt).

If it's too much to pay all in one go you can divide the cost over a year. See: www.tvlicensing.co.uk for ways to pay.

Food and shopping

Food is one regular bill that will be difficult to split fairly as everyone eats different amounts and has different tastes. It's worth taking a little time to think about what you buy and use regularly though. Unless you're a really close group of friends and tend to cook and eat together, you probably won't want to buy all your stuff jointly, but it does make sense to have a kitty for some things. After all, there's nothing quite so depressing as five different tubs of butter in the fridge with five different names scrawled on in marker pen – let's face it, everyone will use everyone else's when theirs runs out anyway.

Items like milk, bread, bin bags, butter, toilet roll, cleaning supplies and so on can easily be bought jointly and shared then you can buy other things you want as and when.

A recent poll on SpareRoom showed that around half UK flatshares buy some of their shopping together while the other half just buy for themselves:

- We buy everything together and split the cost – 9%.
- We all buy our own food individually – 52%.
- We buy some stuff together but mostly buy our own – 39%.

Strategy

The first thing to do when you move in is put all the bills in your name and inform the council you're living there so they can sort out your council tax. It's definitely best to put the council tax in everyone's name if you can but bills like electricity you may not want to divvy up, especially if there are several of you in the property.

Next, you need to decide how you're going to pay – it can be easier if one of you pays and everyone settles up with them. If you're going down the 'one person pays the bill' route you should consider each taking responsibility for a bill (i.e. one of you has the electricity in their name and pays that, one does water, one does gas etc.). This will spread the load a bit and make sure no one ends up at their overdraft limit until everyone settles up.

There is the option of everyone just writing a cheque for their share of each bill as it comes in and posting them all together but, as it's generally easier to pay bills online these days, that might be too much hassle. Whoever is responsible for the bills needs to be prompt in paying them, all too often in a flatshare you'll find your supply cut off or get a summons for a bill everyone presumed someone else had paid.

There's a great online resource, which can help you sort out your bills (and general finances) in a shared house, you can find it at: www.ioweyou.co.uk.

Getting behind with your bills

If you do find you get behind with your rent or bills, for whatever reason, there may be something you can do about it, so don't just stick your head in the sand and ignore the problem. What you can do will depend on the nature of the bill and who you're dealing with.

RENT

This is one you'll have real problems with if you fall behind. Don't forget, in most cases, your landlord will need the rent to pay his or her mortgage so if you fall behind it puts them in difficulty too. If you regularly pay late or miss payments you could also be giving your landlord grounds for eviction (see Chapter 8, *Contracts, Rights and Agreements*).

If you think you'll be late paying your rent (whether it's your fault or not) you should give your landlord as much warning as possible. They may not be happy about it but are far more likely to understand if you talk to them than if you just don't pay.

COUNCIL TAX

Getting into arrears with your council tax will eventually lead to a court summons so don't ignore the letters when they start arriving. Also, if you pay monthly and get behind, you may lose the ability to pay in instalments and the council may demand the full amount owing for the rest of the year in one go.

If this does happen it's still worth phoning the council tax office, as they will split the payments if they can – they'd rather you paid than have to take you to court.

UTILITIES

Again with utility bills you will get hounded until you pay up (see Steve's story on page 112) so, if you're struggling, call your supplier and see if they can help work out a payment plan for you. They may also have a scheme to help you spread the cost over a wider period to make things easier.

OTHER BILLS

How other companies treat you when you fail to pay will vary for individual cases. Whoever you're dealing with, a phone call to try and resolve the problem will go down better than no action whatsoever.

Top Tip With all bill disputes or difficulties, it's important to keep a record of any calls you make (with the name of who you spoke to and the date) and copies of all letters or emails you send and receive. This gives you a record of what has been said in case things escalate and you find yourself in trouble down the line.

IF IT COMES TO THE WORST . . .

If you find yourself with mounting debts you can't pay, you should get in touch with one of the non-profit debt counselling services and get some advice. Financial problems never sort themselves out on their own, once the water starts rising it generally doesn't stop. So, get on the phone and spend £1 on the call rather than buying a lottery ticket (your odds of winning the lottery are 14 million-to-1 yet we still go on hoping – if someone told you there was a 1-in-14 million chance of you being hit by a bus you'd presume it would never happen. Aren't we all optimists at heart! – Matt).

Try:

StepChange
Website: http://www.stepchange.org

National Debtline
Tel: 0808 808 4000
Website: http://www.nationaldebtline.org

CHAPTER EIGHT

Contracts, Rights and Agreements

Wherever and however you decide to live, you'll probably find you need to sign an agreement or contract of some kind when you move in. You may think these are in place simply for the benefit of the landlord but, in almost all cases, they protect your rights too so it's useful to know a little about the different types of agreement and what they mean.

The information in this chapter refers mainly to English housing laws; if you live in Wales, Scotland or Northern Ireland, you should check to see if there are any differences in your region. The best source of information of this type is Shelter's website. See the list of useful links at the back of this book, or go to: www.spareroom.co.uk/content/info-flatsharing/guide-to-tenancy-agreements.

Sharers

If you share a property with several people and pay rent to a landlord, you'll probably fall into one of the following groups:

WHOLE PROPERTY

If you rent the whole property you'll most likely have one contract with all your names on it. If you rent direct from the landlord then he or she will deal with all of this but often the landlord uses a letting agent to find tenants – in this case your dealings will be with the agent. You should be aware that, although the landlord pays the agent, you might have extra costs to pay in this situation.

Additional costs you may encounter include:

Administration fee
This is a one-off payment to cover the cost of drawing-up the contracts.

Reference/credit checking fees
These fees are charged to cover the cost of checking with your bank and employer that you can cover the rent, or checking your credit rating.

Re-signing fee
If you decide to extend your lease at the end of a term, you may be asked to pay a re-signing fee, ostensibly to cover the admin costs of renewing the contracts.

Matt says:
'When you sign your contract make sure you've got your landlord or agent's contact details. You may not need them but it's better to double check now than to need something in an emergency (like your boiler breaking down in December) and not be able to get hold of anyone.

Find out who your main point of contact is
This could be your landlord, your agent or whoever manages the property. Ask when you sign the contract who you should call first if there's a problem.

Get a telephone number, preferably a mobile
Make sure you know how to get hold of the person you need. If it's an agent you'll need an out-of-office hours number as well as the regular number.

Ask who you should contact in case of emergency if your landlord or agent isn't available
Get a set of backup contact details in case the first point of contact isn't available. Keep these contact details somewhere you can get at them easily (stuck to the door of the fridge, for example) as you won't want to be emptying out drawers in an emergency.'

From the perspective of the renter it's hard to see why you should be paying all of these, as the agent is already charging the landlord for their services and is working on his behalf, not yours. These types of fees are fairly standard though and there's not much you can do so you'll just have to pay them. One option is to search for lettings that don't use agents or try one of the whole property sites such as: www.findaflat. com. You should always ask beforehand if there will be any additional charges before you sign anything.

Type of contract

You should check to see which type of contract you're signing. By far the most common for rentals in the UK is the assured shorthold tenancy (AST). These are popular as they commit to a fixed term of at least six months and give the landlord more rights and options when it comes to ending a tenancy than an assured tenancy (which gives you the right to remain in a property unless the landlord can convince the court there are good reasons to evict you, such as rent arrears or damage).

The good news about an AST is that it requires the landlord to use a Tenancy Deposit Scheme; at the time of writing, assured shorthold is the only tenancy that requires this. For more on this, see 'Deposits and schemes' later in the chapter.

If you have an AST and the fixed term expires while you continue to live in the property the landlord must get you to sign another fixed term contract or the agreement becomes 'periodic'. Periodic tenancies have different rules and, if you signed for a fixed term, you'll almost always be asked to sign another contract if you remain in the property.

If your contract is joint and several, then this has additional implications, see the boxed text on page 126 for more information on this.

If you have a whole property agreement you should check in advance what the situation is if someone moves out before the agreement expires. The questions you need to ask are:

- If someone moves out, will the rest of us have to pay their rent?
- Can one of us leave before the end of the term if we find a replacement?

- If so, can we change the name on the contract to reflect the new flatmate?
- Will we be charged for this?

Individual contracts

If you rent by the room and each have a separate contract with your landlord then things are a little easier, as each of you is responsible for your own rent and there are no grey areas. You should still check whether you're going to have to pay any additional fees other than a deposit and the first month's rent in advance.

Inter-sharer agreements

One type of agreement which is less common but can prove extremely useful (especially if you rent a whole property) is the inter-sharer agreement. This is a basic contract between flatmates and is separate from any contracts you have with your landlord or agent. The agreement will set out the basic terms under which you share and (crucially) can commit to paper each of your individual obligations regarding rent and bills.

No agreement

If you have moved into an existing flatshare (probably to replace a flatmate who has left) and haven't signed an agreement of any kind then your rights will be limited. In this case your landlord is technically whoever is named in the contract and you're subletting from them. Their contract may well forbid them from subletting in this fashion, which can lead to all sorts of complications. We'd generally advise you to avoid these situations – for more on subletting and other types of tenancy, see Chapter 1.

A note on joint and several contracts

One thing you'll need to check is whether the agreement you have is joint and several – if so, it could mean that the rest of you are liable for any unpaid rent or bills left by any of the other people in the property.

Joint and several is basically a hybrid of joint liability (where all parties are jointly liable for the full amount – in this case rent and bills) and several liability (where parties are liable only for their individual share of the amount).

For an agreement to be joint and several, it must be signed by all parties (council tax is the only exception to this rule). What this type of contract does is allow the claimant (in this case the landlord) to pursue any one party (or tenant) for the full amount owing, it's then up to that tenant to recover what everyone else owes them.

An example

John, Paul, George and Ringo decide to share a flat. They find a great one with four good-sized bedrooms for £500 a month so they sign the agreement and decide between themselves to pay £125 each. After a while the others get fed up with John's new girlfriend, Yoko, hanging round all the time and John leaves to move in with her, naturally he stops paying rent. This leaves Paul, George and Ringo to cover John's share of the rent between them. The landlord won't care that they've agreed between themselves to pay £125 each, he just wants the full rent. He can, if necessary, sue any one of them (not just John) for John's share of the rent if they don't pay up.

If the boys were students it wouldn't be uncommon for their parents to have signed as guarantors for the rent. Under a joint and several agreement, the landlord could have pursued any one of their parents for the whole amount in the event of any unpaid rent.

Lodgers

If you live as a lodger then things are slightly different. The law recognizes that live-in landlords are more vulnerable if the landlord/tenant relationship breaks down as they live with their tenant. As a result, live-in landlords aren't required to give as much notice if they want to evict you.

Not all live-in landlords will ask you to sign a contract or pay a deposit but, as more and more people take in lodgers, it's becoming more standard. Your contract should cover, at the minimum:

- how much rent you will pay
- how long the let is for
- what (both of) you need to do if you want to end the agreement prematurely.

It should also cover your deposit if you've paid one.

If you're taking in a lodger, you should also read Chapter 4.

Deposits and Tenancy Deposit Schemes

DEPOSITS
Most landlords will ask you for a deposit when you move into a property. The standard amount is one month's rent (meaning you will have to pay two months up front before you move in), although six weeks isn't uncommon.

The point of a deposit is to protect the landlord against unpaid rent or damages (other than acceptable wear and tear) caused by you. In theory this should mean that, unless you're behind on rent or have damaged anything, you should get your full deposit back promptly after you move out. It doesn't always work this way in practice and, even if you get your deposit back quickly, you'll probably still need to pay a deposit on your next place before you get it back.

Problems with deposits
We asked SpareRoom users if they'd ever had a problem getting their deposit back from a landlord – 65% said they had. The occasional dodgy landlord will try and get a bit of extra cash out of you by claiming they need some (or all) of your deposit for repairs resulting from damages you've caused. Luckily these landlords are few and far between and the new Tenancy Deposit Scheme (see next page) has made a big difference.

Disputes do occur though when a landlord genuinely feels you've damaged either the property or contents and wants to use your deposit to pay for repairs (as he's fully entitled to do if this is the case – that's what the deposit's for after all). That's where the inventory comes into play, see below for information on inventories.

A NOTE ON CLEANING

Most tenancies will require you to leave the property in a fit state to move into for the next tenants, this means cleaning it. If you're expected to clean before you move out, then the property should have been clean for you to move into. If the place is a mess and needs cleaning before you can even move in, you should tell your landlord or agent – it may be the case that you just want to get on and clean it yourself so you can sort your things out but you should still point out that you had to do this.

Check your contract to see what it says about leaving the property clean when you move out. If you don't, then the landlord may be able to keep some of your deposit towards having the property cleaned. Allow time for this when you're packing up and getting out. If you have a day or two crossover period between moving and needing to be out of your old room, then it'll be much easier to clean once all your stuff has gone.

TENANCY DEPOSIT SCHEMES

Since 6 April 2007, all deposits taken by landlords in England and Wales must be protected by a tenancy deposit scheme. The scheme applies to assured shorthold tenancies, the most common type of tenancy agreement. There are two main reasons for this:

- To ensure that when a tenant has paid a deposit and is entitled to get it back that this actually happens;
- To assist in resolving disputes which arise regarding refund of deposits.

The scheme also hopes to encourage landlords and tenants to make clear from the outset the terms and conditions of the lease to avoid disputes occurring.

There are two types of scheme on offer and it is up to the landlord to choose which they will use.

Custodial
- The tenant pays the deposit direct to the landlord who then pays it into the scheme.
- The landlord must provide information to the tenant about the tenancy and which scheme has been used within 14 days.
- At the end of the tenancy, if both parties agree to the amount of deposit returnable, the scheme is notified and returns the deposit as agreed.
- If there is a dispute as to the amount of deposit to be returned, the scheme will hold on to the deposit until the dispute is resolved.
- Interest on payments held during dispute settlement will be used to pay for the running of the scheme with any left over paid to the tenant (or the landlord if the tenant isn't entitled to it).

Insurance-based
- The tenant pays the deposit direct to the landlord.
- The landlord retains the deposit and pays a premium to the insurer.
- The landlord must provide information to the tenant about the tenancy and which scheme has been used within 14 days.
- At the end of the tenancy, if both parties agree to the amount of deposit returnable, the landlord returns the appropriate amount of the deposit.
- If there is a dispute the landlord must hand over the disputed amount to the scheme for safe-keeping until the dispute is settled.
- If the landlord fails to comply, the insurance arrangements will ensure that the tenant receives their deposit back if they are entitled.

Under both schemes, the deposit must be returned within ten days of agreement or settlement of any dispute. For information on tenancy deposit laws in Scotland see www.spareroom.co.uk/content/info-tenants/tenancy-deposit-scheme-scotland.

Inventories

If you rent a furnished flat, house or room you will almost always be asked to sign an inventory. An inventory is a list of everything your landlord has provided including furniture, curtains, carpets, kitchenware and appliances. It should also contain information on the condition these items are in at the start of the tenancy (especially noting anything that's damaged). The reason for this is that it makes it much easier to settle disputes about damaged or broken items when you move out if you have an agreed upon list to refer to. This should, in theory, make it easier to get your full deposit back when you move out.

If you're given an inventory to check then don't just treat it as another piece of paper, check it thoroughly. If anything is on the list but you can't find it then make a note. Also note down anything that's damaged if it's not mentioned already. This might all seem like a hassle but it won't take long (especially if you break it up by doing a room or two each) and may well end up saving your deposit further down the line. Give a list of any discrepancies to your agent or landlord.

If your landlord doesn't give you an inventory to check, it would be worth having a quick look round anyway and seeing if anything in the property is broken or damaged. If it is, take a photo of the damage (if you use your phone or digital camera to do this it will probably record the date you took the photo which is a bonus) just in case there's a dispute when you move out.

It's also a good idea to keep any receipts for items you've replaced yourself whilst in the property.

HMOs

'HMO' is the new buzzword in landlord circles and can be a confusing topic as there are plenty of rules and regulations regarding HMOs.

HMO stands for House in Multiple Occupation and is basically a term used to describe certain types of rented accommodation shared by more than one household (meaning the rules don't apply to a house shared by a single family).

If your room is in an HMO, you're probably in one of the following:

- bedsits
- a flatshare where everyone has their own tenancy agreement
- student accommodation (unless you're in halls of residence or other university owned property).

If a property is classed as an HMO, then the landlord has a certain set of obligations towards you, including ensuring:

- proper fire safety measures are in place
- the property isn't overcrowded
- cooking and washing facilities are adequate
- communal areas and facilities are in good repair.

To find out whether you live in an HMO, you can contact a local advice centre by using the Shelter tool located at: http://england.shelter.org.uk/get_advice/advice_services_directory.

Your rights

EVICTION

With the best will in the world, some tenancies run into difficulties. In many cases these can be resolved amicably but, sometimes, this just isn't possible. If your landlord decides to evict you (or if you have a lodger and want to evict them) what can you do?

As a sharer

Your rights will depend on the type of agreement you have. There are laws to protect you in this situation and if your landlord fails to comply with the correct procedures it can be a criminal offence.

Your landlord's reason for wanting to evict you may be based on something you've done or could be due to external factors. The most likely reasons your landlord will want to evict you due to something you've done are:

- failure to pay the rent
- anti-social behaviour
- damaging the property.

In any of these cases there may be something you can do to remedy the situation. If you're behind with the rent this will involve paying any arrears (or convincing your landlord that you can do so).

There may be other reasons your landlord wants you out, such as:

- the property is being repossessed
- they want to sell the property.

If the property is being repossessed there's very little you can do, but if the landlord wants you out so he or she can sell the property they'll need to follow the correct procedures, as laid out in your contract. The type of your tenancy will affect how easily you can be evicted. If you're not sure what type of tenancy you have, you can go to: www.SpareRoom. co.uk/essentialguide/eviction where you'll find a link to Shelter's Tenancy Checker.

Tenancy types and eviction

Assured shorthold tenancy (AST) – Fixed term
As this is the most common tenancy in the UK, we'll start here. If you have an AST then your contract will probably be for a fixed period. If this is the case your landlord will need a legal reason to evict you before the end of the contract. Reasons can include:

- being behind with the rent or being constantly late paying
- you have broken the terms set out in your tenancy agreement
- allowing the property or furniture to fall into disrepair
- causing nuisance or annoyance to others
- the property is being repossessed by the landlord's mortgage lender.

Your landlord will need to give you notice which must:

- be in writing
- give the grounds for eviction
- tell you how long the notice period is (usually 14 days or two months, depending on the grounds).

After the notice period has expired you must leave the property, if not the landlord can apply for a court order. If your fixed term has expired and you're on a periodic tenancy, your landlord may not need grounds for eviction.

Assured tenancy

Most tenancies in the UK are ASTs so, unless your landlord informed you before you moved in that you had an assured tenancy, chances are that's what you'll have. Assured tenants can only be evicted if the landlord has suitable grounds (which is why most people don't use assured tenancies any more) so, providing you pay your rent on time and don't break any of the conditions of your tenancy, you can stay as long as you like.

If your landlord has grounds for eviction, they'll still need to give you notice as they would with an AST.

As a lodger or live-in landlord

Most tenants are protected by the law and have rights that are determined by their living arrangements and the terms of their contract. They can only be evicted under certain circumstances and there are procedures which must be followed. If you share accommodation with your landlord, your rights are different and less comprehensive. This is because the law allows for the fact that a live-in landlord is more at risk if the relationship with their tenant breaks down, than a landlord who lives elsewhere.

All a live-in landlord has to do in this instance is give their lodger 'reasonable notice'. There are no set rules regarding how long reasonable notice is. If there's a contract or agreement that includes a notice period then that will be the minimum period deemed reasonable. Otherwise the amount of notice will depend on several factors, including:

- how long the lodger has been living in the property
- how good the landlord/lodger relationship has been
- how quickly the landlord needs to rent the room out again.

Once the notice period has expired, the landlord has the right to change the locks or remove your belongings from the property. It's always advisable for the landlord in these situations to get a possession order from the court, as they will have no option other than to grant an order if the notice period has expired.

Either using or threatening physical violence whilst trying to evict a lodger (or any kind of tenant) can be a criminal offence.

Harassment

Harassment can be defined as your landlord doing something to interfere with your ability to enjoy living in your home in peace or intended to get you to leave the property. Some landlords think that, by making things difficult for you, they can get you to leave without having to follow the correct procedures. Harassment, either by your landlord or someone acting on their behalf is, however, a serious criminal offence. Just because your landlord owns the property you live in doesn't give them the right to harass you.

Harassment can take many forms and behaviour you may see as unacceptable may seem perfectly reasonable to your landlord. Indeed, he or she may not even be aware that certain behaviour is either inappropriate or unpleasant.

FORMS OF HARASSMENT
There are many kinds of behaviour that could be construed as harassment. The list below is far from exhaustive but contains some of the more common forms of behaviour encountered by tenants:

Visiting your home too often or without warning
The fact that he or she owns it doesn't give your landlord the right to just turn up whenever they want to see how you're keeping it. Your landlord should give you at least 24 hours' notice before coming to visit the property, and coming round to check up on you too often can be seen, in some cases, as harassment.

It's natural that your landlord will want to check that everything is okay and that you're not mistreating or damaging the property, but occasional visits with plenty of warning should be the rule.

Entering the property when you're not there or without your permission.
Your landlord has no right to keep a key to the property (unless this is stated in the tenancy agreement) and should never enter the property while you're out unless you've given permission. As stated above, if your landlord needs to access the property you should be given plenty of notice and a time should be agreed that's acceptable to you.

Restricting your access to utilities such as gas, water or electricity
Your landlord isn't allowed to interfere with your ability to access utilities supplied to the property in an attempt to get you to move out. This includes non-payment of bills in order to restrict your access.

Allowing the property to deteriorate to the point where it's dangerous
Your landlord has an obligation to maintain the property to a standard fit for you to live in. Failure to do so can be seen as harassment, particularly if done intentionally with the aim of getting you to move out.

Rupert says:
'The first student house I lived in (with Matt, as it happens) had a leaky kitchen ceiling. We reported it to our landlord but nothing happened and, gradually, the problem got worse. Eventually the whole ceiling came down, narrowly missing my friend's head. We no longer had the problem of a leaky ceiling as we didn't have a ceiling. Eventually it got sorted but it took far longer than it should have.'

Sending builders or workmen round without warning
If your landlord needs to do any work to the property (or any of the appliances or furnishings in it) he should contact you first so you know this is happening and, wherever possible, arrange a convenient time for the work to take place. Obviously your landlord will have to work to the availability of whoever is carrying out the repairs so won't necessarily be able to arrange things to suit you but should certainly see if there's a mutually acceptable time for the work to be done.

Stopping you from having guests

As a tenant you have the right to have guests to stay in the property, unless of course your contract forbids or restricts this.

Threatening you

Threatening behaviour towards you by your landlord (or someone acting on their behalf) can be a criminal offence. You have the right to enjoy the property in peace and any attempt to interfere with this can be reasonably seen as harassment.

WHAT SHOULD I DO?

Talk to your landlord

The first thing you should do is talk to your landlord – in some cases he or she may not even realize their behaviour is upsetting or inconveniencing you. Even if you suspect your landlord is harassing you deliberately, it's worth having the conversation as you may at least find out why it's happening.

Keep records

Once you've done this, unless the situation improves, you should keep a record of all incidents in case you need it for reference later on. You should also put all your communication with your landlord in writing and request that they do the same – if you have a conversation follow it up with a letter confirming what was said so you have it in writing as well. It may be a good idea to have someone else with you if you need to see your landlord.

Seek advice

You have several options if you need to take action. Shelter may be able to help – you should certainly have a look at their website - www.shelter. org.uk. Your local council should also be able to help and you should report any incidents of harassment to them. You should only go to the police to report serious incidents.

Remember, any action you take is likely to have an effect on the relationship you have with your landlord and things may well get unpleasant enough that you want to move out anyway.

Problems getting hold of your landlord

From time to time you'll need to get hold of your landlord. Sometimes it will be with a quick question that can wait a few days, sometimes (for example, if your boiler has packed up and it's the middle of winter) it's more urgent. Your contract should include your landlord's contact details or those of the agent managing the property so double-check that when you sign. Make sure you have an alternative contact person in case you can't get hold of your landlord or agent in an emergency – this is especially important if your landlord lives abroad.

Matt says:

'My current landlord lives in Turkey so my initial point of contact is a friend of his who lives nearby. My boiler broke in the middle of winter last year; without a local contact to sort it all out it would have taken ages to get anything done (and it took long enough as it was).'

If you've tried contacting your landlord and can't get through or get a reply to your messages and your landlord used an agent you can try calling the agent. They may have an alternative number or be prepared to call on your behalf.

Shelter's advice directory can help you find someone to talk to if you need help. Or you can go to www.SpareRoom.co.uk/essentialguide/eviction for links to this and other useful resources.

CHAPTER NINE
Flatshare in London

With a population of 8 million, and a surrounding commuter belt which doubles that figure, London has by far the most thriving flatshare population in the UK (and one of the busiest in the world). High numbers of students, graduates and young professionals (plus a large transitory population) means the demand for both short- and long-term temporary accommodation is high.

Look at any research into the most expensive cities in the world and London will be right up there (along with Moscow, New York and Tokyo). House prices are high and the cost of living is far from cheap, so shared accommodation is the only choice for many Londoners and visitors.

As a result there's always a high demand for rooms over a wide range of budgets and a huge variety of accommodation available. Whether you're looking for a cheap room in a shared house or something in a luxury Chelsea flat with river views there's something out there if you can afford the rent.

A few common questions

ISN'T LONDON HORRENDOUSLY EXPENSIVE?
Compared to most places in the UK (and most places in the world), London is an expensive city to live in. However, rents vary enormously from area to area, so get online and browse a few ads to see what's on offer and get an idea of how much rent you'll need to pay each month.

IS IT SAFE?

The simple answer to this is yes. As with any large city there are certain risks though and there are things you can do to minimize your chances of having anything unpleasant happen to you. See 'Staying safe' on page 149 for more on this.

HOW CAN I FIND ACCOMMODATION?

Online advertising has made it easier than ever to search for a flatshare. If you're coming from outside London, you can do some research into areas, prices and the kind of rooms available long before you get to London. See 'Finding accommodation in London' below for advice on finding somewhere to live.

HOW EASY IS IT TO GET AROUND?

London has a great network of buses, tubes and trains, so wherever you live, it's easy to get to where you want to go. Have a look at 'Getting around' later in the chapter for information on public transport in London.

WHERE SHOULD I LIVE?

There's no easy answer to that I'm afraid – ask half a dozen Londoners and you'll probably get half a dozen answers. Some people swear by North London, some insist South is better and everyone has their favourite places to live. Where you end up will most likely be dictated by your budget and where you need to be for work or study and, once you've been in London for a while, you'll develop your own list of top spots.

'Finding accommodation in London' (below) has some advice to help get you started in your search.

Finding accommodation in London

Finding somewhere to live in London can be a daunting process, especially if you're new to the city. With so many areas to choose from, and so much accommodation on offer, it can be bewildering at first. You'll have a much better chance of narrowing down your search if you answer a couple of basic questions; this will help you discount lots of areas and concentrate your search on the places likely to be best for you.

WHERE DO YOU NEED TO BE?

Whether you're working, studying or just visiting, it makes sense to start looking for accommodation based on where you'll need to be. Living close to where you'll spend most of your time not only cuts down your commute, but will also reduce the amount you spend on travel.

If you already know people in London, you might want to consider living near them. It's certainly worth picking their brains about areas if you can, and going down to stay for a weekend or two before you move, to get a sense of where the different areas are in relation to each other and what they're like.

WHICH AREA?

Popular areas for flatshare in London

London is by far the busiest city in the UK for flatshares. With over 16,000 rooms advertised on SpareRoom in London alone it can be difficult to know where to start.

Here's a list of the most popular areas for flatsharing, to give you a basic starting point:

- Angel
- Brixton
- Balham
- Battersea
- Clapham
- Docklands
- Ealing
- Fulham
- Greenwich
- Hackney
- Hammersmith
- Hoxton

- Islington
- Putney
- Shoreditch
- Wimbledon

Popular commuter areas a little further out include:

- Crawley
- Croydon
- High Wycombe
- Maidenhead
- Slough
- Stevenage
- Windsor

Traditionally, the busiest areas for flatshare in London were South and West of the city, with areas such as Clapham and Ealing topping the lists. Recently though, the Docklands area (and East London in general) has seen a sharp rise in the number of rooms available and people looking to live there. This is mostly due to the relocation of much of London's financial business to Canary Wharf and a huge improvement in transport links to the area. This regeneration of East London was sparked by the Canary Wharf development and continued with the building of the Millennium Dome in Greenwich. The London 2012 Olympic Games brought yet more development to the area, resulting in better transport links and facilities and adding to the growing desirability of (and demand for rooms in) East London.

Docklands is now regularly the busiest area for flatshare in London, and therefore the UK. The map on page 142 shows which London areas have the most rooms to rent, the darker an area, the more rooms there are on offer. Docklands falls into the borough of Tower Hamlets, which as you can see, is one of the busiest areas.

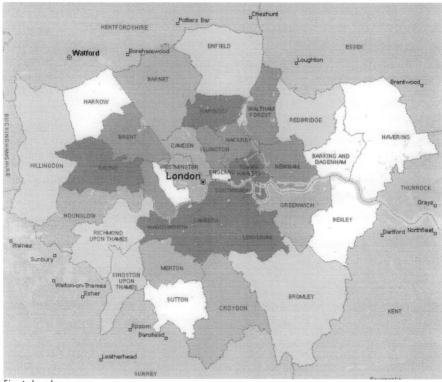

Fig. 1. London rooms

A FEW POINTERS

There isn't space in this book to go into detail about all the areas of London and what they're like, so we've put together a list of a few popular areas by type, just to give you a starting point for your research.

Trendy
- Shoreditch
- Stoke Newington
- Hoxton
- Crouch End

Busy
- Brixton
- Hackney
- Camberwell
- Shepherd's Bush

Cheap
- Walthamstow
- Lewisham
- Tooting

Well-heeled
- Islington
- Crouch End
- Clapham
- Dulwich

Downright posh
- Hampstead
- Chelsea
- Fulham
- South Kensington

Leafy
- Wimbledon
- Finsbury Park
- Epping
- Richmond

Suburban
- Ealing
- Southgate
- Barking

Villagey
- Highgate
- Hampstead
- Dulwich Village
- Blackheath

Central
- Soho
- Covent Garden
- The City

Riverside
- Richmond
- Kew
- Docklands
- Barnes

Alternative
- Camden

WHAT IF I CAN'T AFFORD IT?

The majority of people moving to London for the first time have unrealistic expectations of what they'll be able to afford. Most people can't stretch to a room right in the middle of town so most of London's flatsharing population lives a little further out. Unsurprisingly, the areas with high house prices are similarly expensive to rent in – areas like Clapham, Islington and Fulham are good examples of this. If you can't afford the area you really like, a good tip is to look next door or slightly further out.

Maybe you love Clapham but just can't afford the rents – try Tooting, it's a popular area for flatsharing and is on the same tube line as Clapham, so you'll still be able to go out there. Similarly, if Fulham is where you want to be but the budget just won't stretch, have a look just over the river in Putney (which doesn't have quite the swanky image Fulham does, saving you a few pounds a week on rent). Fancy trendy Stoke Newington? Dalston has less of the cool factor and, accordingly, rents are cheaper (plenty of people who live in Dalston claim their flat is in Stoke Newington anyway! – Matt).

One of the joys of London is that there's always something to do and somewhere new to try – just because you can't afford to live somewhere, doesn't mean you can't go out there. As long as you've got a decent pub, restaurant, bar or cinema near enough for a local night out, the rest is easily available by public transport.

GOING OUT OR STAYING IN?

The temptation in London is to want to live in a busy, vibrant area with lots going on. There's nothing wrong with that, plenty of people live in busy areas, but it's worth thinking about how much you'll be taking advantage of them. You can always go out to somewhere busy but you can't make an area quieter than it is if you want a bit of peace. Why not live somewhere within easy reach of the area you love so you can go there when you want to but take advantage of the quiet life (and probably lower rents) a little further out?

WHAT'S YOUR BUDGET?

Once you've worked out which areas in general will be best, you can start looking at how much you can afford to pay. With rooms in London ranging from £500 per month to over £1,000 (with some even higher – SpareRoom recently had a listing for a room in Chelsea for £1,500 a month), there are bound to be areas you just can't afford. Typically, the closer to the centre of town you are, the more you should expect to pay, but things get interesting once you start looking a little further out.

North London is often more expensive than South as there are far more tube stations North of the river (there are more tube stations with access to more than one line North of the river than there are tube stations in total South of the Thames). However, many South London areas have overground train stations that actually get you into the city quicker as they stop less frequently than tubes. Also, West London is traditionally more expensive than East, although the gap is getting smaller as more of East London is redeveloped.

Have a look at the map below; it shows London boroughs by average room rental – the darker areas are more expensive than the lighter ones. Obviously, there will be different areas within each borough with differently priced rooms but this will give you a general idea which areas are likely to be cheapest.

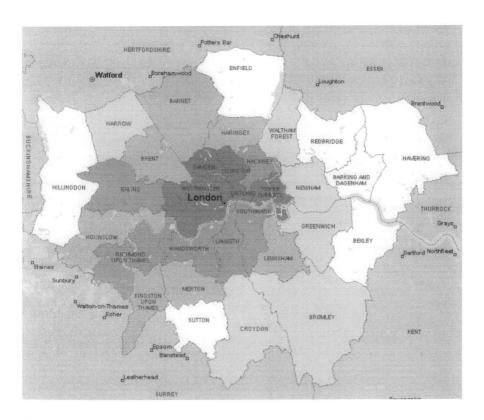

Fig. 2. Map: London rents

How to look

Traditionally, print advertising, in publications such as *Loot*, was the best place to look for accommodation in London. With the advent of online flatshare sites, it's now far easier to use the Internet to find a room. The first London flatshare site (and the first UK site we know of) was: www.IntoLondon.com, founded in 1999. As the site grew and demand rose the site was expanded in 2004 to cover the whole of the UK and SpareRoom was born.

A COUPLE OF HANDY SEARCH TOOLS

SpareRoom's 'advanced search' function gives you the opportunity to search outwards from the centre of London based on the 'zones' system used to organize public transport in the city (for more on this see 'New to London – Getting Around' later in the chapter). This gives you the ability to search for rooms in specific zones, which can help you target the areas you need to look in.

Another great tool is the 'tube line search'. Once you've found the nearest tube station to your work or study, you can search for properties by the line it's on. You can also search by commute time from or to a specific station. Used in conjunction with the other 'advanced search' functions (such as budget) you can really tailor your search to find the best place. All these handy London search tools can be found at london.spareroom.co.uk.

PLACE A 'ROOM WANTED' AD

You can let people know you're looking for a room by placing a 'room wanted' ad. This allows you to tell prospective flatmates where you're looking, what you're looking for and how much you can afford. Room advertisers search the wanted ads and get email updates so you may just find the perfect flatshare comes looking for you. For advice on placing a wanted ad have a look at Chapter 2, *Find a Flatshare*.

SPEED FLATMATING

Another great way of finding accommodation in the capital is to visit one of the regular Speed Flatmating™ events held in Central London.

Speed Flatmating is designed to give those looking for a room in London the chance to meet people with rooms available (both people looking for a lodger and sharers replacing a flatmate who's leaving). The best thing about this way of finding somewhere to live is that it lets you meet the people before you see the room. As we all know, an average property with great people is always better than a fantastic one with flatmates you don't get on with.

Events are held several times a week in bars in London and Manchester. There are events for specific areas (such as Clapham, East London and Angel) and one big central event covering all of zones 1–3 for people looking in several areas. Almost 15,000 people came to Speed Flatmating events in 2015.

Speed Flatmating was the brainchild of SpareRoom's Gemma Allen-Muncey.

Gemma says:

'I first thought of speed flatmating shortly after we launched SpareRoom.co.uk in April 2004. Rupert and I were having a discussion about how we could improve the service we offer our users and whether there was anything else we could offer other than the online advertising. A friend had been to a speed dating event the evening before and as I was telling Rupert about this something clicked and I thought "what about Speed Flatmating events?".

We ran the first event in Clapham Junction in June 2004 and it was a huge success. The really great thing about speed flatmating is that, not only does it enable people to meet with loads of potential flatmates in one evening in a safe environment, it's also really good fun for everyone who attends and we get a lot of people leaving as friends. The events are successful for most who attend and from the very first event we noticed the unexpected outcome of roomseekers buddying up with other roomseekers and forming new houseshares together. We've now modified the event format to take this into account and as a result the events have become even more popular.'

> **Speed flatmating worked for me**
>
> 'I found out about speed flatmating while surfing the Internet in a bid to find a room in London. I was curious to see if it would be an easier way to find a room as I was a bit overwhelmed with all the other sites and trying to find time to organize viewings.
>
> I went along to the event, which was held in a bar – this was great as it was on neutral ground rather than someone's house, which can seem a bit like going to a job interview!
>
> I spent a few minutes with about 10 or 11 people with rooms to let and was able to quickly work out which ones I was interested in going to view by asking questions about price, location, local amenities etc. – it certainly saved me a lot of time.
>
> I organized a meeting with my favourite one and loved it immediately, so I can certainly say for me it was a really effective and enjoyable process with a great end result!'
>
> *Freya*

For more information on speed flatmating, go to: www.speedflatmating. co.uk.

TYPES OF LET IN LONDON

Having the biggest flatshare population in the UK means London also has the widest choice of types of flatshare – if it exists you'll probably find it somewhere in London. Monday to Friday lettings are much more popular in London than most other areas as many people commute long distances to work in the capital and it can be easier to stay during the week and go home for weekends.

> **The lodger's view**
>
> 'I have a family home in Norfolk and commute to London during the week, where I rent a room Monday to Friday. It's really a case of what's best for the family vs what's best for income purposes and the benefits and drawbacks are mostly personal rather than financial. If you can find someone who's prepared to rent to you just for weekdays it can work out really well for them as they can earn a little bit of extra income without losing all their privacy.'
>
> *Dan*

For more information on the different types of let you'll encounter and which will best suit you see Chapter 1, *Types of Let*.

Staying safe

London is a busy 24-hour city and, as in any other city, crime does exist. In general though London is a safe place to live; by using your common sense and observing a few simple precautions (which apply to anywhere, not just London) you can reduce the chances of anything unpleasant happening to you.

DON'T MAKE YOURSELF AN OBVIOUS TARGET

Pickpockets and thieves generally look for easy targets; if you keep a close eye on your belongings and don't draw attention to yourself your chances of having your possessions stolen is much lower.

- Keep an eye on your bag wherever you are and don't leave it open.
- Don't use your mp3 player when walking home alone at night.
- Put your purse or wallet away before you walk away from cash machines.
- Be discrete using your mobile.

DRINK

Booze is a contributing factor in a large percentage of crimes committed. In some respects, however, London feels particularly safe at night. As there are so many reasons for people being out late at night (theatre, restaurants, pubs, cinema, gigs), there's a wide range of people using public transport so getting home can feel less threatening that it does in some smaller towns.

Be careful when you're out on the town not to get so drunk you're not in control. Chances are nothing unpleasant will happen to you but being legless makes you an easy target (especially if you're female), so know your limits.

Keep an eye on your drink when you're in pubs or clubs (or get a friend to), don't leave it unattended and run the risk of having it spiked.

GETTING HOME

If you're out late at night on your own, make sure you know how you're going to get home at the end of an evening and tell someone where you are. Public transport in London is excellent and runs until late so your options for getting home are usually pretty good. If you're going to get a cab home always get a black cab or a mini-cab from a licensed firm or office. Illegal cabs do operate and can be dangerous (for reasons ranging from their being uninsured to attacks on single female passengers). For more information on using public transport, see page 151.

New to London

If you're moving to London for the first time, there are a few things you'll need to know to help you find your way around and get to know the city.

POSTCODES

London is made up of a collection of boroughs but you're more likely to hear people refer to where they live by which tube or train station it's nearest to. Additionally, general areas are often referred to in order to make things easier (e.g. South East, North West, Docklands, and so on). One of the main ways used in flatshare adverts to distinguish areas is the postcode. Now flatshare websites show maps and contain more detailed information on location it's not as essential to know your postcodes as it used to be (in print ads the only indication as to where a property was would be the postcode). It's still handy to understand a little about how postcodes work though.

Most property adverts and estate agents in London (and the rest of the UK) refer at some point to the postcode of the area the property is in, which can be confusing if you're not used to the system. Basically, all London postcodes are made up of two different sections. Take the following as an example:

N11 3RN

The first part refers to the general area the property is in (in this case, New Southgate) and, as a rule, it is this part you will find in property adverts. The second part refers to the street and location of the property on that street. The prefixes of the first part are straightforward (for example SW refers to South West) and give the general part of London, whereas the number gives a more specific location. However, geographically, the numbering appears arbitrary as, for instance, NW1 is central, whereas NW2 is far out and does not border NW1. This is because when the numbered system was first introduced in 1917, the postcodes numbered 1 (E1, NW1, W1, SW1, SE1) were most central and the subsequent numbers assigned alphabetically by the name of the district they represented. The exceptions to this are the central London postcodes of EC and WC (East Central and West Central respectively). *See Appendix – London Postcodes* for a list of London postcodes and areas they cover.

GETTING AROUND

It used to be that the most useful tool for navigating the streets of London was an A-Z. Nowadays you're far more likely to use your phone – most smartphones have great mapping apps that will not only show you where you are but give you directions to where you want to get to. You can also get a huge range of apps to tell you when the next bus is coming, how to get somewhere by Tube or even to call you a cab.

PUBLIC TRANSPORT
Zones explained

The first thing you'll need to get your head around is the concept of zones. Transport for London (TFL), the authority who oversee all aspects of travel in the city, have divided London into six zones which start centrally with Zone 1 (covering the City and Westminster) and spread out in concentric circles to cover the rest of London and some areas of the commuter belt which are actually outside Greater London altogether. You can get a free map from TFL that shows the layout and coverage of Zones 1–6. This map can be obtained at tube and train stations and is handy to keep in your wallet or handbag for quick reference when you're out and about.

Wherever you live in London you'll need to get around and, despite the tendency of Londoners to complain about public transport whenever the opportunity arises, things aren't as bad as you'll be led to believe. With a large network of tubes, buses and trains to choose from, the capital and surrounding areas are pretty well covered, and the more you travel the better you'll get at working out the easiest and quickest way of getting where you need to be.

For more information about planning your journey, visit: http://journeyplanner.tfl.gov.uk.

Travel cards/Oyster cards

The whole ticketing system on London transport changed with the introduction of Oyster cards. Oyster is a pay as you go ticketing system that operates by means of smart cards. The card is read by a sensor in ticket barriers on tube stations so, providing you 'touch in' and 'touch out' at the beginning and end of your journey, it can work out how far you've travelled and deduct an appropriate amount from your card. The card can be topped up at stations or online and buses, and trams also have card readers installed in them. If you travel several times during a day, the fare is capped at a level which is cheaper than buying a one-day travelcard.

Oyster fares are cheaper than buying standard paper singles, in an attempt to get people to switch over from standard tickets. You can now use contactless credit and debit cards to pay for bus, tube and train travel. Just tap your card on the reader as you would with an Oyster card – the payment comes straight out of your account.

TYPES OF TRANSPORT

Tube

Officially called London Underground, but known to most as 'The Tube', the network of subterranean lines criss-crossing London is world famous. Twelve lines cover the capital from East to West and North to South, and the colour-coded map that represents them is a familiar image to most these days. The lines themselves are referred to by name rather than colour (e.g. Central line, Victoria line etc.), so you need to know the name of the line you want to use. The map is available free from tube stations and is easy enough to follow as lines are listed by both name and colour. Once in a station, the direction for platforms for each line is usually indicated by both name and colour as well, so all you'll need to do is make sure you're on the right platform for the direction you want. Most platforms have a large sign on the opposite wall from the platform (i.e. on the other side of the tracks) that shows the line you're on and indicates which direction trains from that platform are travelling in (including the stations you'll travel through after leaving the station you're at). This gives you plenty of opportunities to double check you're getting on the right train (I still occasionally get on the right tube line but going in the wrong direction if I'm not paying attention – Matt).

Unlike many other underground networks, the Paris Metro for example, the tube lines aren't named by terminus but by direction (eastbound, northbound, westbound or southbound) so, having reached the line you need, check your map to see which direction you need to go in. Be aware that some lines (District and Northern for example) split into different branches outside Central London, so check you're getting on the right train. This may all seem a little complicated at first but you'll get used to it quickly and will soon find you don't need the map for many shorter journeys to familiar stations.

The big advantage of tubes is that they are frequent (more so than trains) and it's easy to see when you need to get off (unlike buses) so you can't really go too far wrong. If you do get a bit confused as to where you're going there are maps on most platforms and often members of London Underground staff (usually dressed in blue) you can ask. Failing that you can always ask a fellow passenger as most Londoners pride themselves on knowing how to get about (just ask a group of people the quickest way to get from Richmond to Chalk Farm and watch the debate unfold). Tubes run from early morning to around midnight on most lines but check when your last train is to be on the safe side.

You'll find a downloadable tube map at: www.intolondon.com/tubemap.

Trains

Whilst tubes are often the best bet for navigating the inner parts of the city, trains are great for the outlying zones and beyond. Firstly, you get daylight and fresh air on trains (a definite bonus in the summer), and secondly, the distance between stations is greater so you'll get further more quickly. Trains aren't as frequent as tubes but often serve areas with no tube connections, particularly south of the Thames. Whilst you're within the six zones of the transport system your travelcard covers you for train travel as well as tubes so if it's easiest to get where you're going by train (or if the tubes aren't working!) then it's not a problem. Bear in mind that Oyster pay as you go doesn't cover most of the rail network yet.

When travelling by train it's handy to know exactly when your trains go as missing one by 30 seconds and having to wait 25 minutes is a real pain, especially if you've forgotten your book! You can get train information by calling: 08457 48 49 50 or online at http://www.thetrainline.com.

Buses

There aren't many better ways to see a city than from the top deck of a bus and London is no exception. Buses are usually slower than tubes but, especially since the introduction of congestion charging (see page 157) on London's streets, things are getting better. Despite the fact that London's buses are owned and operated by a number of different companies, they all operate in the same way and recognize the zonal system and accept travelcards, Oyster and bus passes. Some buses now require you to buy a ticket before boarding; signs at bus stops will tell you which buses this applies to.

The bus network is more complicated than the tube and can take a while longer to work out, but bus stops have maps and boards to show you the routes they serve and the numbers of routes serviced by a particular stop are displayed on the bus stop sign itself. Buses display these numbers both on the front and back and, increasingly, on the side by the front doors. The display on the front will also show the final destination of the bus along with major stops along the way. There is also an extensive network of night buses that travel throughout the night, long after tubes and trains have stopped.

Although the iconic Routemaster double decker buses have now been replaced with newer models, they still operate on a couple of heritage routes. These buses have been repainted to look the way they did in the 1960s so a trip on one is a great way to see a bit of London in classic style. The two routes serviced at present are Royal Albert Hall to Aldwych and Trafalgar Square to Tower Hill.

DLR

DLR or Docklands Light Railway was opened in the late 1980s to connect the Docklands area and parts of South-East London to the City. Trains go from Bank and Tower Hill out through Canary Wharf and Greenwich to Lewisham and up to Stratford to link with the Jubilee Line. For some areas the DLR is the easiest option and, now the Jubilee Line covers more of the same areas, is much more integrated with the rest of the transport network. The first time you use it you may feel (especially on some of the elevated sections around Canary Wharf) like you're on a safari park style monorail but that all adds to the fun.

River

As London is on the Thames it's possible to get around by water (as long as the places you need to get from and to are both near the river that is). There are piers all along the river through central London from Putney to Woolwich and regular services run between them. You should be aware though that travelcards aren't valid on river services so you'll have to pay extra to use them. This makes them less than ideal for commuting which is a pity as a journey to work along the river would be a great start to the day (in most weather conditions anyway).

Whether you use the river to get around or not you should definitely take a sightseeing trip along the Thames at some point as it's a great way to see some of the highlights of London's heritage (such as the Houses of Parliament, Tower Bridge, St. Paul's and The Tower of London). For a great way to see the best of London by both road and river (and this has nothing to do with flatshare or London transport so please forgive me), have a look at www.londonducktours.co.uk.

For more info on getting around on the river see: www.tfl.gov.uk/gettingaround/9442.aspx.

Bike

As with many large cities, a bicycle can be a great way to get around. With the congestion charge reducing traffic in the city centre (and increasing the cost of driving) many people have opted to switch to bike. There is an extensive network of cycle routes around London that make it easier to avoid the traffic.

If you're not sure you want to commit to buying a bike just yet – or you don't need to cycle regularly – then the Santander Cycles scheme (or 'Boris Bikes' as they're more widely known) might be the answer. The scheme has thousands of bikes available for hire from special docking stations across London. You need to register for the scheme but, once that's done, you can hire a bike for as long as you need one.

How it works

You pay an access fee – from £2 for 24 hours up to £90 for a year. Hire charges start at £2 for up to an hour (with the first 30 minutes being free).

For more on Boris Bikes, and cycling in London in general, visit https://tfl.gov.uk/modes/cycling/santander-cycles

Taxis and cabs

Anyone who's spent time in London will be familiar with the sight of a black cab. Along with the red double decker Routemaster buses they are one of the most iconic images of the London streets. For short journeys in the centre of town and getting home late at night, taxis can be invaluable, just flag one down on the street and away you go.

Minicabs can often be cheaper than taxis, especially on longer journeys, so look out for licensed minicab offices too. Be careful though as there are a large number of unlicensed minicabs operating in London and, apart from being uninsured, these can be highly dangerous. These generally operate by hanging around busy areas and touting for business. Licensed cabs should all have their licence on display so check before you get in. There are numerous apps available to help you book a black cab (Hailo or Gett) or licenced minicab from your phone.

You can also text 'home' to 60835 to receive a text message listing local hire firms.

DRIVING

Driving in London has a certain stigma attached to it, especially for those who have never tried. London is one of the busiest cities in the world and, naturally, traffic can be horrendous but don't let that put you off. As long as you're well prepared and able to stay relatively calm you'll be fine. The first and most important thing to know is where you're going and how to get there – if you've done a bit of homework you'll find yourself less likely to be going round in circles for the afternoon. You can also get detailed routes with instructions to print out from the AA and RAC at: www.theaa.com and www.rac.co.uk.

Other than knowing where you're going, it's also worth knowing a couple of other things, firstly about congestion charging.

Congestion charging

By far the biggest change to driving habits in the capital in recent times has been the introduction of congestion charging. Congestion charging came into effect on 17 February 2003 and was intended not only to decrease traffic on the city's roads but also to encourage people onto (and increase funding for) public transport. The scheme works by charging vehicles to enter Central London. The designated zone inside which the charge applies stretches from Marylebone and Euston Road in the north, and Kensington in the west, to Lambeth and Newington in the south, and Tower Bridge Road and Commercial Street in the east.

The charge applies from 7am to 6pm Monday to Friday (excluding public holidays) and the cost for one day is £11.50 if you pay before midnight on the day of travel. You can also pay the following day at an increased cost of £14 (this effectively means next charging day so, if you travel on a Friday you have until midnight on the Monday to pay the next day fee). Methods of payment include shops and garages, telephone and online payment and even payment by SMS text message.

There are plenty of warning signs on the roads around the zone plus several on motorways and A roads coming into London, so (in theory) you should be well aware of where the boundaries are. In practice it helps to be aware before you travel if you may need to enter the zone. Several pocket maps are available showing the exact boundaries of the zone (both A–Z and the AA publish maps such as these and they are readily available in petrol stations and bookshops around London) and most A–Zs have it clearly marked. If you're heading into London but won't be entering the congestion charging zone it's also important to bear in mind roads such as the North and South Circular Roads (A406 and A205) are often busier as a result of traffic avoiding Central London.

If you drive a motorbike or scooter, you should be exempt from the charge. Also, anyone driving an electrically powered car is exempt.

For more information on the congestion charge and how to pay, log on to the official website: https://tfl.gov.uk/modes/driving/congestion charge.

Parking
After the congestion charge, the second most hotly-debated issue concerning driving in London is parking. Parking in and around London can be difficult and expensive and restrictions apply in the centre of the city from 8.30am to 6.30pm Monday to Friday and 8.30am to 1.30pm on Saturdays. Meters and car parks are expensive and it's not even guaranteed you'll find anywhere to park at all. Further out in the more

residential areas, parking conditions vary wildly – in some areas you may even need to buy a permit to park outside your own house.

Useful contacts for parking in central London:

NCP (National Car Parks)
Website: www.ncp.co.uk

For more information on all aspects of travel in London, go to:
https://www.tfl.gov.uk

CHAPTER TEN

Staying Safe

The Internet has changed our lives in so many ways. We can shop, chat, play games, find information – the benefits are endless. The downside is that the Internet provides the possibility of concealing your identity, making it possible to conduct scams and fraud in new ways.

The aim of this chapter is not to scare you into thinking the Internet is unsafe, but to give you a little information with which to approach any transaction confidently. Roads are dangerous to cross, so rather than tell our children never to cross roads, we give them the knowledge they need to reduce the risks and navigate them safely. Rather than say 'Never cross the road, it's dangerous', we tell them 'Don't cross without an adult' or 'Always use the pedestrian crossings and remember to look both ways'.

Just as you wouldn't cross the road without performing a few simple checks, you shouldn't conduct any form of business online without a similar amount of caution. The following information should give you the guidance you need to 'look both ways' before parting with any money as well as some basic advice to follow, whether you found your room online or not.

Online safety

In any online transaction involving a relatively large amount of money, there will always be risks but, by learning a little about how the scams operate (and using a safe website), you can drastically reduce the chance of anything untoward happening to your or your money.

USE A REPUTABLE SITE

The first thing to do is decide which website(s) you want to use. By picking a reputable site you've taken the first step to avoid scams, as the site should be filtering listings before they even hit your screen. Sites that require users to register before they can respond to listings have the added benefit of another level of safety in place so, although it may seem like a pain to have to register your details, it has its benefits in terms of security.

HOW SITES PROTECT YOU

By providing a space for you to advertise sites should feel an obligation to do their utmost to ensure any fraudulent listings or scam attempts are dealt with. There's plenty a site can do to keep its users safe. As an example here are some of the tactics we employ at SpareRoom to make sure your experience with us is positive.

Keeping you safe

SpareRoom has a team of dedicated staff who spend their time checking the listings submitted before they go live. With over 5 million registered users, it's not possible to check every single ad so that's where the machines come in. We have an extensive (and ever growing) set of filters we run all our listings through which are set to look for any inconsistencies or typical scam language. They also check ads by location and flag anything originating from a country we know to be the source of attempted scam listings (Nigeria is the most common – it has been estimated that the Nigerian scam industry is second only to its oil industry in terms of revenue created). The filters then quarantine any dubious ads and we sort through them manually to check they're okay (which by far the majority are) before letting them onto the site.

We also check all the photos and videos uploaded and weed out any which are either unsuitable (we had one particularly 'intimate' video submitted a couple of years ago – I'll leave the rest up to your imagination – Rupert) or contain direct contact information. Which leads us on to . . .

Keeping your email address safe

Many classified listings sites publish your contact details directly onscreen for anyone to see. SpareRoom don't do this for a couple of reasons.

Firstly, displaying your address directly on the advert allows automated software to scan the page, copy your email address and add it to a mailing list, resulting in you getting loads of spam emails. This process, known as 'email harvesting' or 'trawling', goes on undetected all the time and is one of the major ways spammers get your contact details so they can offer you Viagra and breast implants.

Secondly, only allowing registered users to contact you through the site makes everyone subject to our anti-scam checks. This doesn't mean we check up on everyone using the site (with over 5 million users we'd never manage it anyway), just that we check any messages flagged by our filters as suspicious. It also means that if a scam advert does make it onto the site (it does happen occasionally) we can see who has received messages from the fraudulent user and warn them.

Rupert says:

'In ten years of running flatshare sites, we've come across most of the ways people use to try and con unsuspecting members of the public. Some of them seem so ludicrously obvious to us now that we wonder why anyone falls for them (although someone, somewhere must, or the scammers wouldn't persist), others can be subtle and far more difficult to spot. That's why we employ several methods of quarantining suspect ads (both manual and automated) so we can check them before they get as far as our users. We can't vouch that everyone who advertises with us will make a great flatmate but we can ensure that, as far as is humanly possible, we protect you from anyone intent on defrauding our users.'

General security tips

The first golden rule in dealing with anything involving large amounts of money is IF IT SEEMS TOO GOOD A DEAL TO BE TRUE, IT PROBABLY IS.

Most successful scams play on our desire to either get something for nothing or get a great deal on a transaction. When it comes to renting rooms, if something looks amazing and is much cheaper than other rooms in the area then exercise caution. By all means contact the advertiser but maintain a healthy level of scepticism.

Rupert says:

'Don't forget, all ads on SpareRoom have a "report this ad" link. If you think something looks dodgy then let us know and we'll have a look at it for you. We spend hours each week looking at fake or suspect ads so we'll be better at spotting them than you. It's all part of the service so don't think you can't get in touch if in doubt.'

In addition, there are a few general rules you can follow to make sure your room or flatmate hunting experience is a safe one.

DON'T PART WITH ANY CASH UNTIL YOU'VE SEEN THE ROOM

If you're looking for a room, you should never hand over any money or sign a contract until you've seen the property. However plausible the reasons you can't see it today may seem, hold off – if the landlord is genuine they won't mind and will understand your caution.

Similarly, if you're renting out a room, don't let someone take it unless they've been to see it (or, at the very least, met you in person). Remember, if you're renting out a room or taking in a lodger and need a little more peace of mind, you can always perform a few standard security checks before you sign the contracts.

SpareRoom offers a tenant referencing service, which you can access via www.SpareRoom.co.uk/content/info-landlords/tenant-referencing.

EMAIL ADDRESSES ARE NOT PROOF OF IDENTITY

If your prospective flatmate, tenant or lodger conducts all their correspondence by email, you shouldn't take their email address as sole proof of identity. Most free email addresses (Yahoo, Hotmail and the like) don't require any form of ID to sign up for so are easy to set up and use. Obviously if the person you're dealing with has a (functioning) work email address with a recognized company or organization, then you have a bit more security in terms of knowing where they work. You should always get a telephone number as well as an email address though.

BE WARY OF 070 NUMBERS

Phone numbers beginning 070 may look like UK mobile numbers but can, in fact, be routed to almost any number in the world. There are legitimate uses for these numbers (the user may not want their personal number appearing in an advert for example) so don't assume they're suspect, just make sure that anyone you intend to move in with gives you a landline or UK mobile number too. If they're genuine and the 070 number was just for their own security then they'll be fine with this.

DON'T PRESUME, IF YOU'RE NOT SURE THEN ASK

If you are unsure at any point in your dealings with someone, then ask for clarification. Any genuine landlord, flatmate or agent will be happy to answer questions. The golden rule is always 'if it seems too good a deal to be true, it usually is'.

DON'T LEAVE SENSITIVE DOCUMENTS LYING AROUND

If you're conducting viewings for a new lodger or flatmate, then make sure you don't leave any bank statements, cheque books, passports or other sensitive documents lying around in full view. This may seem like being over cautious (and in most instances that will be true), but why take the risk?

FEEL SAFE

If you're worried about heading off to viewings in areas you don't know (particularly late at night), you can always take a friend with you. Failing that at least let someone know where you're going and tell them you'll give them a quick call to let them know when you're done and on your way back (if you do this make sure you do call).

DON'T USE WESTERN UNION TO SEND MONEY

If a landlord asks you to send your rent and deposit via Western Union be extremely cautious, especially if the landlord lives overseas. Western Union payments are untraceable so there's not much you can do if someone takes your money and does a runner. Western Union is fine for sending money to friends and family (which is what most people use it for) but it's not suited for other transactions like paying rent so avoid it wherever you can.

ALWAYS GET A RECEIPT

If you're paying money to a landlord, agent or flatmate for rent or a deposit, make sure you get a receipt. If you pay by bank transfer or cheque then you've got a record of the transaction but otherwise get it in writing. Your landlord shouldn't mind doing this (and agents should expect it) – if you're paying money for a tenancy, you have a right to a receipt of your payments.

BEWARE ANYONE OFFERING TO OVERPAY YOU FOR ANYTHING

By far the most common form of online scam is the one known as the 'overpayment scam'. You don't need to know all the details – simply put, if anyone offers to pay you over the odds (usually by cheque) and asks you refund the balance, then walk away. The scam uses fake or stolen cheques and works on the perception that cheques clear in a few days when, in fact, they don't finally clear until the issuing bank has got the cheque back. By paying any money back you're giving your own cash away as the original cheque will be cancelled.

ALWAYS EXPECT A CONTRACT

If you see a room you like and the landlord or agent lets you take it without a contract of any kind, stop and think before handing over any money. If there's no contract, you have no legal right to be there and very little in the way of other rights. A contract will protect you as well as your landlord, so don't presume that no contract is good news.

If you pay your rent by standing order or cheque then you'll have a record you've paid money to the landlord, which suggests some form of verbal agreement at the very least. This should be enough, in the event of any dispute, to prove that you are a tenant but a clear contract will make things much easier if anything does go wrong.

KEY POINTS TO REMEMBER

- Never send money to anyone using Western Union unless you know them and trust them absolutely.

- If something appears to good to be true, then it probably is.
- Never agree to take a room until you've seen it.
- Don't let anyone take your room who hasn't been to see it or met you in person first.
- Get a receipt for any money you hand over.
- If you're showing someone around your flat don't leave sensitive documents out.
- Take someone with you or let them know where you're going (particularly late at night).

Useful Resources and Links

We've put any useful resources and links into the relevant chapters but, as a quick reference guide, they're listed here as well so you can find what you need in a hurry, without having to remember which chapter you saw it in. We've also put any relevant content you may want to print out and use (such as checklists and sets of questions) in a special micro-site for this book, which you can find at: www.SpareRoom.co.uk/ essentialguide.

Flatshare and related sites

www.SpareRoom.co.uk
www.speedflatmating.co.uk

Information and advice

www.gov.uk/browse/housing-local-services
www.stepchange.org
www.adviceguide.org.uk
http://england.shelter.org.uk
http://scotland.shelter.org.uk/home
www.tvlicensing.co.uk

Useful tools

Budget calculator:
http:/www.moneyadviceservice.org.uk/en/tools/budget-planner

Find a Gas Safe Register accredited installer:
www.gassaferegister.co.uk

Tenant referencing:
www.SpareRoom.co.uk/content/info-landlords/tenant-referencing

London links

https://tfl.gov.uk

Appendix: London Postcodes

Here's a quick reference guide to the postcodes you'll find in London flatshare ads. These cover London itself; as you venture further out you'll find some of the outlying areas have their own postcodes (such as Croydon – CR). For information on UK postcodes in general, and a list of what the prefixes stand for, go to: www.listmasters.co.uk/postcodes. php

EC

EC1	Aldersgate, Finsbury, Holborn
EC2	Bishopsgate, Cheapside
EC3	Aldgate
EC4	St. Paul's

E

E1	Whitechapel, Shoreditch
E2	Bethnal Green
E3	Bow
E4	Chingford
E5	Clapton, Homerton
E6	East Ham
E7	Forest Gate
E8	Dalston
E9	Homerton
E10	Leyton
E11	Leytonstone
E12	Manor Park
E13	Plaistow
E14	Poplar (Isle of Dogs)
E15	Stratford, West Ham

E16	Victoria Docks, North Woolwich
E17	Walthamstow
E18	South Woodford
E20	Walford (just kidding – this is the fictional postcode where the soap opera *Eastenders* is set)

NW

NW1	Regent's Park, St. Pancras
NW2	Cricklewood, Dollis Hill
NW3	Hampstead
NW4	Hendon
NW5	Kentish Town
NW6	Maida Vale, Kilburn
NW7	Mill Hill
NW8	St. John's Wood
NW9	Colindale
NW10	Willesden
NW11	Golders Green

SE

SE1	Borough, Waterloo
SE2	Abbey Wood
SE3	Blackheath
SE4	Brockley
SE5	Camberwell
SE6	Catford
SE7	Charlton
SE8	Deptford
SE9	Eltham
SE10	Greenwich
SE11	Kennington
SE12	Lee
SE13	Lewisham
SE14	New Cross
SE15	Peckham
SE16	Bermondsey, Rotherhithe
SE17	Walworth
SE18	Plumstead

SE19	Crystal Palace
SE20	Penge
SE21, SE22	Dulwich
SE23	Forest Hill
SE24	Herne Hill
SE25	Norwood
SE26	Sydenham
SE27	West Norwood
SE28	Thamesmead

WC

WC1	Bloomsbury, High Holborn
WC2	Strand, Holborn

W

W1	West End
W2	Bayswater, Paddington
W3	Acton
W4	Chiswick
W5	Ealing
W6	Hammersmith
W7	Hanwell
W8	Holland Park
W9	Maida Vale, Paddington
W10	North Kensington
W11	Notting Hill
W12	Shepherd's Bush
W13	West Ealing
W14	West Kensington

N

N1	Angel
N2	East Finchley
N3	Finchley
N4	Finsbury Park
N5	Highbury
N6	Highgate

N7	Holloway
N8	Hornsey, Crouch End
N9	Lower Edmonton
N10	Muswell Hill
N11	New Southgate
N12	North Finchley
N13	Palmers Green
N14	Southgate
N15	Stamford Hill, South Tottenham
N16	Stoke Newington
N17	Tottenham
N18	Upper Edmonton
N19	Upper Holloway
N20	Whetstone, Totteridge, Oakleigh Park
N21	Winchmore Hill, Bush Hill, Grange Park
N22	Wood Green, Bounds Green, Bowes Park

SW

SW1	Westminster, Victoria
SW2	Brixton
SW3	Chelsea
SW4	Clapham
SW5	Earl's Court, West Brompton
SW6	Fulham
SW7	South Kensington, Knightsbridge
SW8	South Lambeth
SW9	Stockwell
SW10	West Brompton, Chelsea
SW11	Battersea
SW12	Balham
SW13	Barnes
SW14	Mortlake
SW15	Putney
SW16	Streatham
SW17	Tooting
SW18	West Wandsworth
SW19	Wimbledon
SW20	Raynes Park, Lower Morden, Merton Park, Wimbledon Chase

Index

Kissing Frogs
IN CYBERSPACE

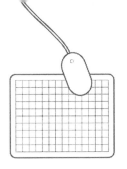

Kissing Frogs
IN CYBERSPACE

DIANNE SWEENEY

Kissing Frogs in Cyberspace
Copyright © 2009 by Dianne Sweeney

ISBN: 978-0-578-04179-7
Library of Congress Control Number: 1-257700361

Dedication

*To all of the men and women who put their hearts
on the line online—you are not alone.*

Dianne's Acknowledgement

I would like to thank Chris Haskett, Ellen Welt, and Josh Hancock for their timely insights and suggestions during the writing of this memoir. I would also like to thank Alison LaBouff for her optimism and suggestions during this process. You have my most sincere gratitude.

In order to capture the essence of my experiences, correspondence (emails, IM's, or questions and answers) have not been edited.

Training Wheels

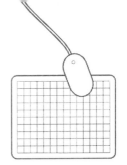

I have a question. How does a single, 35-year-old woman who has been in and out of meaningful and meaningless relationships since she was sixteen find that one true love? I've been a high school English teacher for over thirteen years, so my weekends are filled mostly with grading papers on Earnest Gaines and Shakespeare. That doesn't leave a girl much time to date even though I live in the Bay Area, one of the top five places in the United States to meet men. I never thought it would be this difficult to find a man with whom I wanted to spend the rest of my life.

Ever since I was little, I have always watched movies or read fairy tales in which the man and woman eventually end up together despite the odds stacked against them. Cinderella finds her Prince Charming at a ball. Sleeping Beauty falls asleep, and she still ends up with a Prince. Even Fiona, an ugly ogre, finds true love. Harry meets Sally, and twelve years later they fall in love and get married. Even in times of tragedy people fall in love. In the midst of chaos, death inevitably around them, the ship sinking steadfast into the depths of the sea, Jack and Rose profess their undying love to each other. But one question remains: what happens to all of these couples when the cameras stop rolling?

It doesn't matter how crazy the movie plots are, we all love to escape reality once in a while. We root for these couples to get together. The world of make believe is a wonderful place. But, eventually, the theater lights come up, and we are forced to face reality again.

Can't your average, thirty-something, working woman—sometimes too sarcastic, sometimes too honest for my own good—of today catch a break? Professionally, I'm set. Friends—I have plenty. But love…well, isn't that what we're all looking for? I feel like I'm on a merry-go-round that is spinning out of control. I'm exhausted. Part of me is ready to just give up. Forget about the fairy tale. If one more person tells me, "There are plenty of fish in the sea," or "When you stop looking for love, it will happen," or my personal favorite, "When you fall off your bike, you just have to get back up and start again," I think I will let out a scream that will be literally heard around the world.

Is going on a date after months or years away from the scene really as easy as getting back on a bike? I walk into my garage and glance at my neglected bike sitting in the corner covered in dust and cobwebs, and I think about the first time I learned to ride a two-wheeler.

My first bike was royal blue and gleamed in the sunlight. I refused to ride around the neighborhood with a pink bike. I have two older brothers, so I wanted a blue bike. I wanted to be one of the guys! But of course I had to have a basket on it; where else would I put Barbie?

I was fearless. My training wheels and I would careen around corners, the wind whipping through my pigtails. Every week, there was a contest amongst the neighborhood kids to see who could make the longest black streak on the concrete right next to Mrs. Moore's house. Mine were never that long, but I made my mark—just like one of the boys.

I still remember the day my father called me over to the garage. I peddled over and looked up at him. In his hand he held a screwdriver. He looked down at me and said, "It's time to take off your training wheels."

He must have seen the horror in my face because he said, "Don't worry; I'll be right behind you."

Within a few moments, my training wheels were gone.

My father came up behind me and held onto the seat and asked, "You ready?"

With his help, I was able to straighten out my wheels, and I began to peddle. Once I was more confident, I started peddling faster. However, I didn't want my father to let go of the back of my seat. I kept looking behind me to make sure he was still holding on.

There I was, peddling faster and faster, screaming back at him, "Don't let go!"

I could feel him jogging beside me the whole time, but then I began to hear him panting as he tried to keep up with me. Fathers are invincible, right? I assumed I could go warp speed, and he would be able to keep up. I slowed a little bit for fear that he might let go, and there he was right beside me. As my confidence soared, I quickly forgot about my father and started peddling harder and harder. I then yelled one more time, "Hang on. Don't let go, yet."

Then from a distance my father yelled, "Too late. I already did."

Frantic, I turned around and lost my balance. Screeech! Bam! Crash! Thud! I braked so hard that my bike skidded across the street, and I toppled over the handlebars. I lay on the ground, stunned. This was long before bike helmets mind you, so I was extremely lucky I didn't crack my head open. Immediately, I burst into tears.

My father calmly walked over to me and said, "Are you hurt?"

"Yes, I think I scraped my elbow," I said, teary-eyed. I looked down at my elbow and noticed a red burn mark and a few specks of blood along the newly scratched skin. Slowly, I started to sit up and noticed that that was the extent of my injuries.

"Well, it's too far from your heart to kill you, so get up so we can do this again."

I looked at him incredulously. I was angry. Why wasn't he hugging me and telling me that everything would be okay? He was joking, right?

He wasn't. He quietly picked up my bicycle, rescued Barbie from the scorching asphalt, and patted the seat of the bike.

He looked at me and said, "The only thing you have to fear is fear itself."

Being five years old, I didn't understand what he meant. Thirty years later, I now understand his words exactly. I'm sometimes controlled by my fears. I sometimes don't know how to act when I can't control a situation. Dating is not really something that too many of us can control. There are so many pitfalls to think about. Are there training wheels for people who are just starting to date again?

As I turn to leave the garage, I can't help but wonder—does art imitate life, or does life imitate art? I can't live my life through movies, fairy tales, or old adages, so what is a woman to do? Pick myself up, dust myself off, and start again (another old adage).

I'm about to take control of my love life and embark on a six-month quest for the man of my dreams. I don't know what will happen in two weeks or two months, but here-we-go…

Wrap it Up

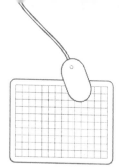

I'm not doing this," I say to Christy as she hovers outside of my dressing room. Christy has been one of my closest friends since the day we first met in college. She has an infectious laugh, a sarcastic wit, and an opinion on just about everything. Even more impressive, she's been happily married for eight years and has two beautiful children.

"Come on, it's my present to you," she goads from behind the door.

"This is what you chose to get me? Are you holding some sort of grudge against me?"

"Get out here!" she says, laughing.

My attendant opens the door, and I walk out.

Actually, walk is not the right word. *Waddle* is more like it.

Christy has decided that she and I deserve a day of pampering. She's treating me to a day at It's a Wrap, a spa that will wrap away unwanted inches, reduce cellulite, and eliminate stretch marks. Hmmm, now that I think about it, what is she trying to tell me?

"I look ridiculous," I mumble. My face is completely smooshed. Only my eyes, nose and mouth are visible.

Have you heard of this new form of torture that women subject themselves to? For a mere $139.00, a cute, petite, twenty-something-year-old will wrap your body from head to toe in mineral-soaked bandages. The objective? To lose ten to thirty inches in one hour. So, here I am in my bra and underwear, being wrapped in wet Ace bandages. I feel like a sausage about to burst.

Once I'm mummified, my attendant places a huge, black raincoat over my head. The raincoat is used to keep the heat in, I think, or it could be that I don't look silly enough already standing there in nude colored bandages with mineral water dripping off of me. Nonetheless, I step out into an open area where women (or other sausages) are jumping up and down on mini-trampolines. Every inch of the room is being used. Mummified women are jumping and twisting those inches away. In front of us, a large flat screen television plays *My Big Fat Greek Wedding*. It wouldn't really matter what movie is playing because underneath the television is every chick flick known to womankind with the same synopsis—girl meets boy; girl changes image for boy; boy falls in love; they live happily ever after.

"You look like everyone else. Besides, don't you want to look good for your date tonight?" Christy says as if reading my thoughts, a trait she seems to be annoyingly good at much of the time.

"Just imagine how good we will feel. God, I hope I lose twenty inches," Christy says and begins to bounce enthusiastically.

Well, here I am. Mummified, thirty-five, and within in an hour there will hopefully be ten to thirty inches less of me. But what is the rest of me to do? I haven't been on a first date in ages. I honestly don't know what happened. After I broke up with my last boyfriend, I just retreated into my own world. The days became weeks, the weeks became months, and I looked up one day and realized I hadn't been on a date in a long time. Yet, some things never seem to change—bikini and eyebrow waxes, electrolysis, bleach cream, tanning, shopping, haircuts, diets, shrink wraps—it never ends no matter how much older we get. I wonder if men appreciate or even realize all the things we do to impress them. I glance around at the other women and then my eyes find their way back to the movie, and I begin to cheer on the starlet's quest to find the perfect man.

After twenty minutes, my attendant calls me down to squirt more minerals on my body. I also have plastic baggies on my hands and feet which are now full of water. The attendant takes them off my feet and drains each bag, then does the same with my hands.

"Wow, this water is really cloudy," she says as she pours it into a bucket. I'm not sure if that is a good or bad thing, so I don't say anything. After she finishes draining my bags, I waddle back over to the trampoline and continue to bounce those inches away.

Twenty minutes later, I hear, "Dianne. Come on down. You're done. Let's go take those bandages off and get you measured," from my perky attendant (who, by the way, would disappear if someone were to try and wrap her because she is already a size zero).

I shoot Christy a death glare. This has been one of the most uncomfortable experiences I have ever had. I mouth, "I hate you." I cannot wait to get out of these bandages. I feel like I have been in a straitjacket for the last hour. In the meantime, tick…tick…tick…I have to start getting ready for my blind date tonight.

As I arrive home, I realize I only have an hour to prepare for my date. Wait, I know what you're thinking—who cares about the date? How many inches did you lose? Fourteen point seven inches, to be exact. That was the total after they re-measured my arms and my legs and my thighs and my chest and my chin. I didn't walk out of there a pin-head. However, I did lose two inches around my thighs. Could you imagine if I spent all that time being wrapped up, and I only lost a couple inches around my ears? Trust me, with the luck I have, it's possible.

Now, I don't know about you, but I have been through some very painful procedures in the name of beauty. I remember one time I spent $500.00 on a device that was supposed to make my legs look and feel silky and smooth. In the end, I damaged a nerve, and my legs were red, black, and blue for weeks. You'd think that would teach me something.

However, when I saw that I had lost all those inches, I couldn't resist more torture. I quickly bought a whole series of the mummification-trampoline-torture treatments. You knew that was coming, right?

Blind Date

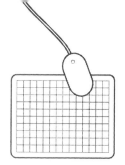

As I'm just about to put on my outfit, I hear my cell phone ring. It's Doug, my blind date. My house is a little bit hard to find, so I assume he is calling for directions.

"Hey there," I answer.

"Dianne, this is Doug."

"Hi, are you lost?"

"Ummm, no. I'm afraid I have to cancel. My back really hurts."

"Your back hurts?" I say a little surprised.

"Yeah, sometimes it hurts and I need to sit perfectly still for a few hours. I'm really sorry. Can we make plans for another time?"

"Yeah, sure. Do you need help? Is there anything I can do for you?" I ask.

"No, my mom is coming over to help me. I always call her when I don't feel well."

After a long pause I mutter, "Okay. Well. Feel better. Bye."

"Bye. I hope you didn't spend a lot of time getting ready."

As I hang up, I mutter to myself, "You have no idea."

I call Christy. The phone rings a couple of times, and she picks up.

"What's up?" she says with a mouth full of food.

"He called and cancelled. His back is hurting." I say with obvious disappointment.

Christy is quiet for a moment. "Okay. That's weird."

"Thank you. I thought so, too. He said his mom is coming over to help him."

"Ha, now that is even weirder. Well, what are you going to do now?" she asks.

"I don't know. Nothing, I guess. See what's on TV." I say as I begin removing my earrings.

"Come on, Dianne. Just shrug it off. Don't get down about this."

"Uh, he cancelled on me, remember. I think I have the right to be a little upset."

"I know, but I *know* you. You are going to put on your sweats and turn on the TV and use this as an excuse to not make any more effort to find a man."

I sigh loudly into the phone and glance longingly at my sweats crumpled up in the corner of my room.

"You need to get back out there and start dating on a regular basis. Listen, I was watching Oprah the other day, and there was this dating expert on. She said that women shouldn't deliberately look for men, that when you stop looking for men, that's when they appear. But, there is one thing you have to do."

"Walk down the street naked after a few more body wraps?" I ask dryly.

"No, you have to be visible. You have to go where men hang out."

"I see a lot of men at the bookstore. I could try that," I say, exasperated and only half-serious.

"Yeah, the bookstore would be a good start. But remember, you are not looking. You are just…"

"Browsing?" I say, and we both start to laugh.

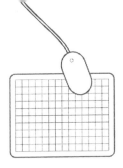

A Clean, Well-lighted Place for Men

As I walk into the bookstore, my eyes are immediately drawn to the "Must Read Books" table; I start toward it and stop myself. *You are here to find men, not a book.*

I walk toward the middle of the store and see a tall, sleek man standing there. I take a step forward and then stop. I look at the section heading: Diseases.

Okay, maybe he's doing research. Maybe he's a doctor looking up information, or maybe…my mind races ahead in time. I don't even know this man's name, but I'm imagining us at a party surrounded by our mutual friends, when a woman turns to us and says, "How did the two of you meet?"

I cough nervously, "Well, he was in the Diseases section of Barnes and Noble, reading *How to Stop the Spread of the Human Papillomavirus*…and…well…it was love at first sight." No, I can't. I just can't get that image out of my head.

I take a step backward and move on to the Sports section. I imagine I'm going to find a big burly man with muscles protruding through his jersey, reading a book about football or baseball. As I turn down that aisle, there is a man standing there, and what do you know, he has very nice forearms. I can tell he definitely works out. He is engrossed in a book, but I cannot tell what it is. He is so engrossed, in fact, that he doesn't even notice I'm there. Casually, I peer over his shoulder. To my surprise, it's an Asian Biker Chick Calendar. Is that drool coming out of his mouth? I glance at the pictures; I look at their perfectly sculpted bodies. Dubiously, I glance down at my own and move on to another section.

I decide to check out the True Crime section as that is a not-so-secret interest of mine. Now, this could go one of two ways, but I figure, let's just see if there is anyone there.

I turn down the aisle; it's empty. I stop and glance at the titles: *The Real JonBenet Ramsey Story, Jack the Ripper,* and *Cabin 28: The Keddie Murders.* My eyes are quickly scanning the titles when I come across one that sends my imagination racing: *Women Who Kill.* Can you imagine if I were to purchase this book and have it out on my coffee table when my date comes to pick me up? Better yet, what if I left it in the guest bathroom for a little light reading? I could even highlight some passages and take notes on the sides. The notes could say, "This doesn't work. You need a ten-inch blade, not a six-inch."

Placing the book back on the shelf, I turn around and leave the bookstore. I leave my Mr. Right standing there gazing at the science fiction novels, dreaming of a woman who looks like Princess Leia in her gold bikini.

Okay, Now What?

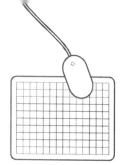

"Well, you only went there one time. You have to make this a weekly adventure," Christy says.

Downing a gummy worm, I say, "Easier said than done."

"Well, you know there's one place that has tons and tons of men looking for women."

"Don't say it. Please don't say it. I'm begging you... not the..."

"Internet," she says without missing a beat.

Pleading with her, I say, "No, please don't make me go into cyberspace. It's too traumatizing."

"Come on, what do you have to lose?"

"My dignity. My sense of self-worth!"

"Well, what else are you going to do?"

After I get off the phone with Christy, I start thinking about what she said. Why is this so difficult? All I'm looking for is that one person who will make my stomach do flip-flops. Is that too much to ask? But how would I even begin my search in cyberspace?

Do I google Prince Charming? Desperate?

Help!

New User

I'm sitting at home with my glasses on, my hair piled on top of my head, an old blanket wrapped around me, and my 2-liter of Diet Pepsi. I have on a baggy pair of sweats, and my legs haven't seen a razor in days. Yet, I'm still able to shop for a boyfriend in today's modern world. In the background Fergie fills the room with her hit song, *Big Girls Don't Cry*. I swear she wrote that song just for me.

I stare at my laptop. The computer goads me, eggs me on. *Open me*, it whispers.

I turn off my cell phone, so I can't be disturbed. Then I lock the front and back doors. Casually, I walk over to my computer and run my fingers over the top of it. It's warm to my touch. Click! In an instant, I'm alone in cyberspace.

At the click of a mouse, we can get any information we desire. The word google has now become a verb. We can "google" restaurants, vacation spots, cars, companies, and dating websites. Googling dating websites will get 30,700,000 hits. Over thirty million websites are devoted to dating, matchmaking, matchmaking advice, and relationship therapy, for those brave (or stupid) enough to take a stranger's dating advice.

Again, I'm reminded of all the movies I've watched in which the man and woman eventually end up together despite the odds stacked against them. Aren't the odds in my favor with all of these websites? They've gotta be.

As I'm scrolling through the thirty million hits, each website entices me with guarantees and promotions—and all of them promising me I will find my Prince Charming. "Find your true love in six months; we guarantee it." Wait! They're actually going to guarantee that I'm going to find the love of my life in six months? This is too good to be true. I'm definitely checking this out!

The next website is a buy one get one free offer. Buy what? Buy one man and get another man free? Half of the time, I don't even know what to do with one man; what am I going to do with two? I always get into trouble when I go to the grocery store with a buy one get one free coupon. Currently, I have two boxes of oatmeal, two cans of Spam, and four boxes of chocolate chip cookies. I hate oatmeal and Spam is disgusting, but how could I resist a BOGO offer? Upon closer inspection, I realize that they mean buy one month, get the second month free. Okay, that makes more sense. Hmmmm, this site is a maybe.

On another site, they claim that they are a lot better than a grocery store. It took me a minute to understand the reference, but then I got it. While I'm at the grocery store, I often muse about how relationship experts claim that this is a great place to meet men. Come on, how many of us really dress up to go to the grocery store? If I could get away with it, I would probably shuffle through the aisles in my robe and slippers.

However, it has dawned on me as I get older, what if the relationship experts are right? Have I been doing everything wrong this whole time? Maybe I should take a minute or two to look in the mirror before running out the door. Maybe I should walk right up to that man squeezing an avocado and say, "Hey, how about squeezing this?" Maybe I will just ram my cart into his and apologize profusely as his wife walks up looking annoyed. I wonder how many "relationship experts" met their significant other by following their own advice. Then I wonder how many have been kicked out of their local grocery store for harassing other customers. I think I will pass.

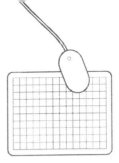

http//:www.needaman.com

*A*lthough many people joke about Al Gore crediting himself with having invented the Internet, many of us have no idea why or how it was created. It actually was created to transfer data to military sites. How ironic that this quirky technology is now the vehicle for love for so many. A cold tool of math, science, numbers, data, cash, porn, Christmas shopping, and viruses is how people now try to call up to balconies looking for love at first click.

Is dating on the Internet still considered taboo? What will it be like to put myself out there whole-heartedly to hundreds of men and say, *Your prayers have been answered. Here I am!* If everybody is "doing it," why am I embarrassed when I tell someone I'm "online"? For me, it's a feeling of personal failure that I can't find love in the "real world." Is virtual reality the last resort when "real" reality fails? Right now, it seems like the best option. But what if I don't find love in cyberspace either? What then? I have a fulfilling life. I travel, I have good friends, but I do want to be in a healthy relationship. However, I'm not willing to be in one for the sake of being in one. As of yet, the real world hasn't worked out for me, the Internet is a gamble, and if that fails, I'm not sure what to do. They have yet to find life on other planets.

And Here-We-Go

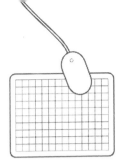

Okay, if I'm going to do this, I'm going to go all out. No guts, no glory, right? I think I'm going to try a few different websites. I don't have the time or money to try all thirty million. Unless this book becomes a bestseller; then I could have a trilogy, or even a "millogy." Can you imagine hobbling into the bookstore in fifty years and seeing, *Kissing Frogs in Cyberspace: Part 569*? I can just picture the back of the cover. *Follow Dianne as she turns 90 and is still looking for love. We are taking odds that this will be her year to either find love...or kick the bucket.* Classy, I know.

I have narrowed the dating websites down to three. I don't think I will need any more than that because one site has guaranteed me that I will find my match in six months. Can you believe it? I'm just a few clicks away from true love—they boast. Okay, well, if they guarantee I will be in love in six months, they must know something I don't because I have been looking for twenty years. I decide right then and there that I'm going to take them up on their offer. What do I have to lose—except six months?

On each of the websites I'm required to write an autobiography and post a picture of me. Oh brother. Now, I know that we are our own worst critics, but I'm seriously not photogenic. On each of the dating websites, you can post as many as twenty pictures. Who has twenty pictures of themselves? Who do they think I am, Tyra Banks?

Trust me, the picture on my website is airbrushed. At one point, I think I even heard the word "body double" as the photographer was taking my picture. If pictures say a thousand words, can I just post my picture and say, "Come and get me!" I don't even know if it matters what I write for my profile. I think I could write that I had an alien encounter; I love to pick lint out of my belly button; and I can eat with my toes, as long as my picture makes me look alluring. You can see my cynicism creeping in. Nonetheless, I strive to write that one profile that will send endless men into a frenzy, clamoring to write me. It has to be funny, but not too funny. I have to sound smart, but not too smart. I have to be alluring, but not too alluring. I'm starting to feel like Goldilocks. After many rewrites and changes, here is what I come up with:

Dear Santa,

July is here and not that I'm complaining or anything, but you did not send me Mr. Right like I asked for when I saw you at the mall. I'm writing to you early this year, so you can get to work right away. Remember, he should be funny and tall—very important! I hope you don't think I'm being selfish; I really did appreciate the luggage you left under my tree since you know my goal is to visit every Hard Rock Cafe in the world. I will work on slowing down in my car and stop singing horribly at the top of my lungs to 80's music. Gosh, do you see everything? Just in case you forgot me: I'm the funny, sarcastic one who told you I hopped a plane a few years ago to see Billy Joel because he wasn't playing in the Bay Area. Does that ring a bell? Also, I told you I wanted a man to complement my life, not complicate it. He also must enjoy traveling and have his own life but be willing to blend his life with mine. I'm just as content being single, but I would like to be in a great relationship.

If you, the one reading this, (Not Santa) do not want to be in a caring, passionate, loving relationship, then we would not be a good match. Couch potatoes are okay, but not every night. I love movies, going to new places, and basically want to see the world. Got a passport? There are so many things I could write about, but I think the first thing we need to do is communicate and see where it goes. I don't want to take away your hobbies and passions, nor would I want you to take away mine. I think that is how people lose themselves in relationships and become miserable and bitter.

Thank you, Santa, for working on Mr. Right for me. Do I need to get a bigger stocking?

With a little trepidation, I let the dating website search its database for my matches. Within five and a half seconds, fifty pages of men come dancing across my screen. Are all of these men potentially my future Mr. Right? Are some of them going to be Mr. Right Now? Or worse yet, are some of them going to be Mr. Right Now, You Need To Leave? I've hit the mother lode. Like a kid in a candy store, I decide to write to my number one match.

He refers to himself as a, "…romantic, good natured, caring guy with a good sense of humor." I like that in a man. Later, he writes, "I'm confident, funny, sometimes elusive and a challenge. Are you up for it?"

I'm up for it. His entire profile intrigues me. Anxiously, I move on to his pictures. In his primary portrait, his features are indistinct because he is sitting far away and wearing sunglasses, so I begin to browse his other photos. Slowly, my face drains of all color. I know this person. I mean, *I know* him.

Return of an Old Flame

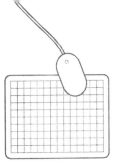

*M*any of us have that one person we never really get over. It may be love, it may be infatuation, it may be just a fantasy, but there is something that makes this person linger in our minds.

When I was twenty-two, we shared a fleeting moment together, and it changed my life. Working my way through college, I was a supervisor at a fast food restaurant. The hurried atmosphere, the long lines of impatient customers, and the anger in their eyes when their $2.99 hamburger didn't taste like a gourmet steak did not make this my ideal job. In fact, I hated it. Occasionally, I would strike up a conversation with our regulars. One in particular caught my eye from the beginning. I like blonde-haired, blue-eyed men, and this man was exactly my type. Whenever he came into the restaurant, I would give the cashier on duty a break so I could take his order. Sneaky, I know. I never really expected it to go anywhere. Until one day, my boss said to me, "There was a guy asking about you today."

"Oh yeah?" I said casually, acting as if I couldn't care less, though I was hoping it was Nick.

"Yeah, you know, the one with the goatee who always orders the same thing?"

"Oh yeah, I know him." Was that nonchalant or what?

After a while, I began working a different shift, as my schedule of classes had changed. Working until midnight every night, I doubted I would ever see my favorite customer again. He only came in for lunch.

One night, I was cleaning up after the dinner rush, not really paying attention to the front line. Suddenly, I heard, "Hey, can't a guy get some service around here?"

I looked up, and there he was. His eyes twinkling. His smile intoxicating. I was smitten.

"I guess," I said and smiled back at him. While he was eating, I talked to him for about an hour, oblivious to the fact that the cook was setting the fryers on fire, there was a long line out the door, and the restaurant looked like a war zone. At the end of our conversation, we ended up making plans to go see *Batman*.

Before the movie, we decided to grab a bite to eat. We headed for Pedro's and ordered margaritas and appetizers. We were talking and laughing so much that we ended up missing most of the movie. Disappointed that our date was about to end, I said, "Well, now what are we going to do?"

Confidently, he said, "We can rent a movie and order a pizza."

My heart skipped a beat, "Yeah, we could do that." I was trying to play it cool, but my hands were sweating, and I knew that he could see the beads of sweat on my forehead.

With Nick, there was a chemistry that sent my mind reeling. I don't know why we bothered to rent a movie—we didn't even watch it. After a while, we began to slowly move closer together. He pulled me into his arms, and we began to kiss. It was one of the most passionate kisses I have ever had. All of these emotions began running through my mind and body. I had dated a few boys in high school, but there were never any fireworks. With Nick, it was like the 4th of July.

We continued to see each other, and each date was better than the last. I never knew that so much passion could exist between two people.

However, after a few dates, I panicked and lost track of myself. I became this immature brat who ignored him when he came into the restaurant. I was playing hard to get. Isn't that how they do it in the movies? I was struggling with emotions that were new to me, and I didn't know how to deal with them. It was as if I was right back in high school.

Not into the drama, Nick walked away and didn't look back. He moved on to a different restaurant for lunch, and I graduated from college and began my career as a teacher. Any feelings we shared disappeared quickly, like a bowl of candy on Halloween night.

However, Nick made a lasting impression on me. To this day, I don't think he knows that. For him, it could have been a couple of nights with someone he thought he was attracted to until she turned into a psycho.

Now that I know that this kind of passion exists, I'm committed to finding it again, and it's not just going to last for a few brief moments. This time it will last a lifetime. God willing, when I find it again, I will be a lot wiser and won't plot or scheme along the way.

Nick always lingered on my mind. I used to wonder what he was doing, or if he was happy. Three years after we parted ways, I was pumping iron at the gym, (okay pumping ten pound dumbbells at the gym), when I looked up and saw Nick. I slowly moved away from the workout area, so he wouldn't see me. I looked a mess. I couldn't let the man with whom I had spent a few of the most romantic nights of my life see me this way. No way! Quickly, I exited.

Later that night, I couldn't stop thinking about Nick. I decided to email him.

He was actually glad to hear from me and asked me to call. Could this be the time when we could actually connect and be free from playing games and just get to know each other? Just for the record, I wasn't holding out for him for three years; I was curious, not pathetic (that comes much later).

As if no time had passed, we talked on the phone for two hours. After a few more phone calls, he asked me out to dinner. The chemistry was still there between us. We laughed and talked about everything. Later on, we went back to my place and the passion was still there, until Nick bolted up and said, "I have to get going. I haven't got any of my things here."

"Oh, okay," I said. "Sure." All I could do was just stare at him with this dumbfounded expression on my face. Was I the only one in the room that night? Didn't he feel what I was feeling?

During the next few months, it was a Charlie-Brown Christmas-Tree Disaster. I barely heard from him. It was frustrating. He told me that he liked me and cared about me, but he needed to focus on his own wants and needs. I was constantly annoyed, and then his emails and phone calls eventually stopped, and I refused to email or call him.

Fast forward all these years later, here he is on this dating website; here he is as my number one match. I haven't thought about him in ages, and now all of these feelings come flooding back when I see his profile.

What is a woman to do? Are the gods playing tricks on me? Is this some cosmic force telling me now is the right time to go out on a date to see if there is any real chemistry between us? Both of us are more mature and settled in our lives. No games, no preconceived notions; no thoughts about the future, no living in the past—just two people meeting for coffee or a movie. Will there be a second date, or will he float slowly back into cyberspace after we meet? There is a part of me that says, let it go. Let it go. Of course, I turn a deaf ear to that voice.

Thinking about it for awhile, I finally write to him:

```
To:  Nick@Nick.com
From: Dianne@dontdoitatall.com
Subject:  Hey Nick
Dear Nick-
     I recently placed an ad on this dating
website, and guess what?  You turned out
to be my number one match.  Isn't that
funny?  You don't have to write me back or
```

anything. I just thought I would at least
say hello and hope you are doing well.
Take Care-

    Dianne

I hold my breath. That same afternoon, an email
arrives from him. His email is casual. It's as if no time has
passed between us. He asks me how I'm doing. He even
tells me that he "completed [his] first triathlon in Maui a
few weeks ago." Then he asks me, "What have you been up
to?" There it is—the invitation to write back. So I do.

To: Nick@Nick.com
From: Dianne@dontdoitatall.com
Subject: Hey Nick
Nick:

    Hawaii must have been amazing! I
think that is awesome that you did that.
Where the hell does the time go? I
can't believe that you will almost be 40.
Notice I go to your age first, LOL, and
skip the fact that I'm 35. Holy cow!

    At first, when I saw your profile, I
was like, cool we do match on everything,
and I started to write you about liking
your profile and what not, and then I went
back to look at the pictures and stopped
and was like, are you kidding me?

    Things have been great with me. I
don't want to drone on and on, however,

> I would like to get to know a little bit
> more about you (Isn't that the typical
> verbiage for online dating? LOL). Hope to
> hear from you.
>   Dianne

I think my email is witty, casual, and breezy. I anticipate a response. One week passes, then two weeks, and I never hear from him. With nothing to do but move forward, I have no choice but to close the door; however, I have to admit, I don't exactly lock it.

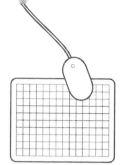

Dontdoitall@aol.com

*W*riting about Nick has been the most difficult part of this experience because it's the closest to my heart. Nick's vignette has been written over and over again. It was first written in resentment, then frustration, and in the end forthrightness. A term I struggled with before moving forward into rightness. If this were a Hollywood movie, we all know what would happen. He and I would realize that this is fate bringing us back together time after time. Next, we would ride off into the sunset together. However, this is reality. He is not Harry, and I am not Sally, and yet it's hard to let him go.

Some people have asked me if I regret writing to Nick. No, I don't. He and I had a history together. I needed to make sure that he wasn't the love that I'd been searching for. He wasn't, and I'm glad that I finally realized it.

However, there comes a time when we must close the door to the past completely. Let's make me the sacrificial lamb. All I did when I wrote Nick or called him was give him the opportunity to reject me over and over again. Do not make this same mistake. Put down the phone! Do not send that email you have spent hours writing and re-writing! If you have to send it, send it to me—Dontdoitatall@aol. com. Use me as a sounding board. Because, in the end, we really just want to send our thoughts and emotions out to the "universe" so someone will listen. And hey—you're listening to me; I'll listen to you.

Romeo? Um, Wherefore Art Thou, Exactly?

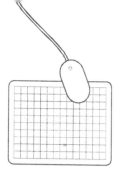

With Nick behind me, I decide to respond to two men who pique my curiosity. One never responds, and the other, Tony, replies right away. It's short and to the point. I like that.

During our first string of emails, Tony tells me that his friends have given him the nickname, "The Joker." I don't ask him why. I'm not sure if I really want to know at this point. He asks when he can call me, so I give him a couple of different times when he can reach me. I'm excited. He seems like a really nice guy.

We have a great conversation. It's always hard to pinpoint exactly what we should reveal and not reveal about ourselves when we first talk to someone. I don't think it would be a good idea to tell him I spent last Saturday night eating a pint of Ben and Jerry's and journaling about my experiences with Internet dating. It seems to be a good call on my part, because our conversation goes well, and we decide to meet in person.

I'm about to say something that many people might disagree with. I think seeing a movie together makes an awesome first date. I mean, let's be honest. This is not a date (I know, I just said it was). It's a meeting to see if the person we have spent the last couple of days communicating with looks like his or her online picture. Naturally, if there is a spark, or the chemistry is there, dinner or drinks could follow the movie. If the date is a total bomb, and you just want to be back in your bed devouring Chunky Monkey and reading *US Weekly*, you've only wasted two hours. No big whoop. Besides, it gets you out of the house, doesn't it?

Trust me, this method is so much better than sitting through an hour or so of excruciating conversation when both of you know that this will be the one and only time you will ever see each other.

Waiting for The Joker to appear, I sit in a chair and take strange pleasure in the butterflies in my stomach. I feel good. I just had my second mummy wrap, so I fit nicely into my new pair of jeans. What could go wrong? A few minutes later, I see a man walking toward me. He looks exactly like his picture–clear blue eyes and a steely jaw. He is dressed casually, in jeans and boots. His grip is smooth and gentle when he takes my hand to introduce himself. This is my kind of man. We converse for a few moments, then head into the theater.

Now, like everyone, I have flaws. Believe me. I will be chatting about my imperfections throughout our journey. However, no matter how badly we want the date to go well, there are warning signs that should not be ignored when meeting someone for the first time. Let's call them red flags.

Lately, Public Service Announcements are becoming more and more common at the movies. It's bad enough that they charge $29.50 for a tub of artery-clogging popcorn; however, since they have a captive audience, we are at their mercy. Some of the PSA's are quite creative. I love the one that seems like it's an upcoming attraction. The hunter is about to kill his quest when all of a sudden a cell phone goes off and the hunter turns around, annoyed. It cracks me up!

Red Flag #1

The Joker and I are munching on popcorn and chatting about ourselves during that PSA when the on-screen cell phone rings. In an instant, The Joker is on his feet and yelling out, "Put your cell phone away, now! Damn it."

As I'm watching this unfold, my mouth gapes wide open in utter disbelief.

Seriously, did that just happen? I'm mortified. Everybody around us is snickering and pointing at us. One man is shaking his head and looking at me as if to say, "You picked him, now deal with it." I sink as low as I can in my seat. I lean toward him, whispering, "That is part of the commercial. They fooled ya, huh?"

He looks at me sheepishly and says, "I haven't been to the movies in three years. Can't you tell?"

Wait, what?

Now, I know not everyone goes to the movies as much as I do, but three years? That's a little too long. Why is that? Is he a homebody? Does he not have any friends that he can go with to the movies? Would we find ourselves incompatible since I love going to the movies and he doesn't?

Red Flag #2

Upon leaving the movie theater, he pulls me a little closer and asks me if I want to go to dinner. Thinking that it can't get any worse than what happened in the movie theater, I agree to go. Not missing a beat he says, "We have to take your car, though. I drive a shit box, and it stalled two times on the way over here."

The hits just keep on coming. Even if his car is a junker, I think he could have saved that information for later. Doesn't he want to impress me? I mean we could argue that he is just being a gentleman and telling me all of this because he doesn't want his car to stall in the middle of an intersection on the way to dinner. But I don't think that's it.

Red Flag #3

During our dinner, we make polite conversation with one another. After awhile, he wipes his mouth with his napkin, places it back in his lap, and looks at me with those piercing blue eyes. I'm just about to forgive his previous faux pas when he says, "I want you to know I'm a very sexual person. For Christmas, I gave my mother and sister a dildo."

Whoa! Alert! Alert! First, I process the idea that he gave his mother and sister rubber penises in celebration of the birth of Christ. Then I process his use of the word "a." Wait, did he just say "a dildo?"—just one dildo? As in they have to share? There are two possibilities here: either he's serious, in which case, ewww!, or he's joking, in which case, ewww! I don't really want to find out which it is, and besides, who wants a man who jokes about giving his mom sex toys?

All I can do is stare at him. I don't know what to say to that, so I respond with, "Oh really?"

Perhaps he would have rather heard me say, "Oh yeah, big boy, tell me more?" or, "Oh yeah? Was it the Rabbit 460 or the Rabbit 555?"

Discouraged, I leave the restaurant that night knowing that The Joker is not the man for me. I go home to start the dating process all over again.

And Now?

"I don't know if I have the stomach for this."

"Rabbit 555, ha!" Christy laughs.

"I'm so glad you find so much joy in my misery," I say, beginning to chuckle myself.

"Just keep going. You'll be fine."

"Thanks, you know you are going on this journey with me, right?"

"I will be there for you—frog after frog," Christy says.

After I hang up the phone with Christy, I realize that she is right. The only thing I can do is keep moving forward. Eventually, one frog will turn into a prince, right? *Right?*

I have come to realize that in order to be successful at this, I can't compartmentalize any of the men I meet, like I have in the past. Otherwise, I will always see them as frogs, and they won't have a chance to become my prince. They aren't all going to be like Tony or Nick.

I now have no more images of how my soul mate should look and act. So what if he doesn't have blue eyes or a certain type of look? So what if he's not a typical white-collar worker? I need to toss all of those "requirements" out the window.

Time is ticking. The promotional offers will not be around forever! Also, I have over $350.00 charged to my credit card for various dating websites. Surely this must be a small price to pay for finding everlasting happiness? We will see. Although money can't buy you love, you still need it to find love in this modern-day society.

Secret Decoder

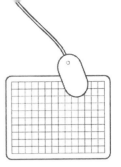

*U*ndoubtedly, I will have to get used to both being the rejected and the rejecter. In order for me to get through this, I just have to remember—you have nothing to fear but fear itself. Rejection is hard, but it's a part of the process.

My aunt, God bless her, sends me four to five emails a day. They are jokes, chain letters, or surveys about how I can register to win a million dollars. Most of the time, I delete them (Sorry, Auntie!). However, she did send me one that made me laugh out loud. Enjoy!

To: Dianne@dontdoitatall.com
From: AuntyEm4444@AuntyEm.com
Subject: I Thought This Would Help You with Dating

Rejection

Top 10 Rejection Lines Given By Women (and what they actually mean...)

10. I think of you as a brother.
(You remind me of that inbred banjo-playing geek in *Deliverance*.)

9. There's a slight difference in our ages.
   (You are one Jurassic geezer.)
8. I'm not attracted to you in 'that' way.
   (You are the ugliest dork I've ever laid
   eyes upon.)
7. My life is too complicated right now.
   (I don't want you spending the whole
   night or else you may hear phone calls
   from all the other guys I'm seeing.)
6. I've got a boyfriend.
   (Who's really my male cat and a half
   gallon of Ben and Jerry's).
5. I don't date men where I work.
   (I wouldn't even date you if you were
   in the same 'solar system', much less
   the same building.)
4. It's not you, it's me.
   (It's not me, it's you.)
3. I'm concentrating on my career.
   (Even something as boring and
   unfulfilling as my job is better than
   dating you.)
2. I'm celibate.
   (I've sworn off only the men like you.)
   ...and the number 1 rejection line given
   by women
   (and what it actually means)
1. Let's be friends.
   (I want you to stay around so I can
   tell you in excruciating detail about
   all the other men I meet and have sex
   with. It's that male perspective thing)
   In response to the first joke, here is

the male perspective on the same issue
...

Top 10 Rejection Lines Given By Men
(and what they actually mean...)

10.   I think of you as a sister. (You're ugly.)

9. There's a slight difference in our ages. (You're ugly.)

8. I'm not attracted to you in 'that' way. (You're ugly.)

7. My life is too complicated right now. (You're ugly.)

6. I've got a girlfriend. (You're ugly.)

5. I don't date women where I work. (You're ugly.)

4. It's not you, it's me. (You're ugly.)

3. I'm concentrating on my career. (You're ugly.)

2. I'm celibate. (You're ugly.)

...and the number 1 rejection line given by men (and what it actually means)

1. Let's be friends. (You're sinfully ugly.)

Wow, I don't know whether to laugh or cry. Rejection is hard, and I have to realize that it's going to happen. It's just interesting how fast paced our lives have become. Everything happens at warp speed these days—including rejection. It used to be that you could go to a bar, and at worst you'd be rejected by three or four people. With the wonders of technology, you can sit back and be rejected by dozens of people in half the time. Most of us aren't prepared to deal with the sheer magnitude of it; however, it's the price we pay for having a better chance of meeting "the one."

Bachelor #2

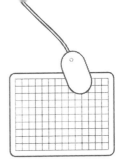

$\mathcal{T}$oday, I open up my email, and I have a wink. A wink is a flirtatious gesture on a man's part to let me know he likes my profile. I think for many of us it's less risky than sending an email. Upon receiving this wink, I can either wink back or send an email. However, if I wink at him, and he winks at me again, we could end up going through this endless series of winking at each other. That wouldn't be a good thing. After reading his profile, I decide to write to him.

```
To:  ILuVPoPcoRn@ILuVPopcoRn.com
From: Dianne@dontdoitatall.com
Subject:  Hello There
Dear ILuVPoPcoRn-
     Thanks for the wink.  I liked your
profile.  You take great pictures.  How
was your weekend? Do you have a busy week
coming up?  I look forward to hearing from
you.
Dianne
```

Within two hours, he responds. Eagerly, I open his email. First, he compliments me on my pictures. Next, he tells me how much he "lovd writing motocyces." Okay, time out. I'm willing to bet that he doesn't actually write on motorcycles. I think he means that he likes riding on them. Silencing my inner English teacher, I forgive all of his typos.

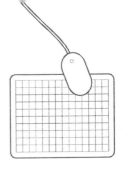

ILuVPopcoRn...or Do I?

*A*s I sit outside Starbucks, I watch the people rushing in and out of the café. Some people look frazzled; some people look annoyed as they see the long line that awaits them inside; some people are smiling and talking on their cell phones. I wonder where all of these people are hurrying off to, and how many of them have casually met someone for coffee in the hope that it will lead to something more.

I'm anxiously waiting for ILuVPoPcoRn (do you know how hard that is to type?) because I always arrive early. It just makes me more comfortable sitting there when my "date" approaches. Although I would rather have gone to a movie, James did not have a lot of time to meet. Thus, we decide to meet for a quick cup of coffee on his lunch hour. I wonder if that is Internet speak for, if you don't look like your profile, or if you used Photoshop on it, I'm outta here.

"Hi, Dianne," a voice says to the side of me.

I turn, "Hi James, have a seat." Before he sits, he asks, "Do you want something to drink?"

"Sure, a bottle of water would be great," I say with a smile.

"Alright, I'll be right back." He says as he disappears into the coffee shop and stands in line behind all of the non-fat, tall, non-whip coffee drinkers. Before the door closes behind him, I quickly call out, "Do you want some money?"

"No, I got it."

Okay, while he is inside the café getting coffee and a bottled water, I can give you the 411. I'm a little bit more on guard this time, after meeting The Joker. James is 6'2", rents an apartment in Milpitas, and works with his brother. Together, they started a company. I'm really impressed by his work ethic. He has sandy brown hair and blue eyes. He is not traditionally handsome. He is your average male who blends into the sea of faces at a crowded Starbucks.

He comes outside. "Nice day, isn't it?" he asks as he sits down.

"Yea, it really is. Thanks for the water."

"No problem." He smiles. I smile shyly at him, too. I remove my sunglasses, so we can look at each other.

The conversation is smooth, and it naturally flows from one topic to another. He is very nice.

Trying to be casual, I ask, "So, what exactly do you and your brother do?" I don't want him to think that my next question is going to be, "And how rich are you?"

"Well, it just so happens I have it right here." He reaches into his pocket and pulls out a long plastic tube.

"This looks really cool; what is it?"

"The tube is used to test dirt in people's backyards. You fill up the tube, and mark it, and you can have it tested to make sure the dirt isn't contaminated."

"Oh, that's neat," I say, desperately trying to hide the lack of enthusiasm in my voice. "How did you come up with that idea?"

"It was really my dad's idea. My brother and I just run the company."

"Do you have a factory around here, or is it based overseas?" At this point, I'm being serious. You never know how some of these crazy inventions turn out. I could be sitting right beside the next Donald Trump.

"No, we just make them in my dad's garage. We turned it into an office and warehouse."

"Well, that must keep you extremely busy. I hope your company does well," I say, my water bottle poised at my mouth. I take a long sip, clear my throat, and switch to a different topic. There is only so much room for plastic tube talk.

"Have you been anywhere exciting?" I ask.

"Oh no, where I live I don't have to go anywhere. In fact, I rarely use my car."

That feeling of doubt is beginning to stir inside me. The red flag is waving in the distance, but I ignore it. I forge on, not ready to face defeat.

"What do you mean?" I say, clearing my throat.

"I have a Taco Bell, a Subway, and a McDonald's all within walking distance. I'm all set. Oh, and my dad lives two blocks away."

I sigh loudly. "Ummm, no. I meant traveled anywhere?" I press on. Our conversation is becoming stale and rough.

"Yeah, I know what you meant; I don't have any desire to leave this area." He says without any expression on his face. He reaches for his caramel macchiato and sips it slowly.

"Oh, hmmm, you didn't see the part in my profile that said I wanted to travel? Remember, my goal is to visit every Hard Rock Café in the world?" I say, becoming frustrated.

"Oh yeah, I read that, but everyone says they want to travel. If everyone was always traveling, why are there still so many people around here?"

Admittedly, he has me on that one. I'm unable to come up with a counter argument. Nor do I want to.

I look at him, drink my last sip of water, smile, and talk to him for a few more minutes. I look down at my watch and tell him I can't believe how quickly times goes by. It has already been a half-hour. Okay, it has only been twenty-two minutes, but who's counting?

"It was great meeting you," I say.

"You too," he says. He leans in to give me a hug.

"Where are you eating tonight?" I ask.

"Last night it was Taco Bell, tonight is Subway. My dad and I have a lot of work to do."

I nod and walk away. When I get into my car, I have a sudden craving for McDonald's.

This has been one eye-opening experience after another. Hopefully, the next few months will be more exhilarating.

The Plumber

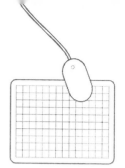

Someone's been checking out my profile. I love when I get email like this. I anxiously click on the link to see who has been darkening my page. First, I look at his headline and my eyes scan his introduction. I casually peruse through his pictures. Wow! He's hot! I continue to read his profile, and there, three lines down, I see the answer to the question I dread most: Do you have children? Yes, 3.

I'm disappointed that The Plumber has three children. I have had two relationships with men who have children. Both of those relationships ended in complete disasters, partly because of the kids or more accurately, because of the guys' inability or unwillingness to include me in their families.

I don't want to relive those experiences. Ever again!

Memories of Love

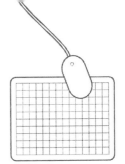

When I first met John, three years ago, he became my first true love. He doted on me, he desired me, and he was so much fun. With him, I found that passion I was looking for. I had never met anyone like John before. He was emotionally available and extremely attentive.

The beginning of a relationship is always exciting. Everything our partner does is precious. We are careful not to reveal too many of our secret single behaviors, but we reveal just enough to keep each other guessing. Everything is so fresh and new. The playful touch, the all night make-out sessions, the foreplay. We are smitten. We love when the man opens a door for us or pulls out our chair at the restaurant. Then, the days turn into weeks, the weeks into months, and suddenly the door remains closed when we approach the car; the chair remains pushed in to the table. The cute little thing he or she did at the beginning of the relationship begins to become annoying, even grating.

"Why do you always have to do that?" John asked me, glancing sideways.

"It's just a habit I have," I said placing the lid back on my soda. It drives me crazy when soda is not filled to the top of the cup at a fast food restaurant.

"Hmmmm…." John said more to himself than me.

"Is something the matter?" I asked, a little irked that he had called me on my quirks.

"No, I just have been thinking about us lately. Sometimes I think you should date someone who doesn't have a son," he said, staring straight ahead.

I glanced at him. I turned toward him more so he could see me. "All this because I checked to see if my soda was full?"

"I don't know, Dianne. I just don't see you and David connecting the way he needs to connect to a woman."

"Well, he should be connecting with his mother. I'm a part of your life, which makes him a part of our life. How can I connect with him? I don't want to get close to him if you and I have no future. What is it you want me to do? I have never dated anyone with a kid before. I need your help."

"I don't think there is anything you can do," he replied stiffly.

Reliving this moment in my mind, I realize that he was trying to give me an out, so that he wouldn't have to break up with me. However, at the time I didn't get it. I became "super-girlfriend." Only without the red cape. I tried so hard to get close to David, but to no avail.

"You aren't helping me, John. Where does this leave us, you know, the two of us?"

No reply.

Even though we had our problems, we continued to date, and we had an amazing time when it was just the two of us.

However, when David was with us, I have to admit, I didn't know how to act around him. Should I correct his behavior when he did or said something wrong? Was it okay to show John public displays of affection? John gave me no guidance, and because of this, I began to resent him, and I didn't really know how to deal with that. I thought I was being nice to David, but we weren't connecting. Whenever he was sick, or he was having a bad day, or he didn't know how to do his math homework, John would cast me aside and forgot about me rather than include me in his family.

At times, I felt like John was torn between the two of us. It was just too much for our relationship to bear. John and I had talked about marriage, and were planning our future together, but then his son started having trouble in school, getting into fights, fighting with his mother, and in the end, John told me that right now he had to be a father first. I told him I wasn't willing to wait around and be a girlfriend on the days his son was feeling fine; he needed to include me in his entire life. John said, "Well, I'm a father first above all else."

The final blow to our relationship occurred when John told me he and his son were going to Mexico for the weekend. They needed some time alone together to bond.

"We all need time together to bond, John," I told him.

"I know, but I promised him I would teach him how to SCUBA dive, and you don't like to do that."

"So, what are you saying? I would just be in the way?"

"Well, no, but the three of us just want to dive."

My head reared up, "The three of you?"

"You know I dive with Jill. She's coming with us."

"You're not serious?" I asked him. "You're taking another woman with you?"

His silence was deafening. Literally, feeling the arrow shoot through my heart, I placed John's keys on his table and said, "You're a coward. Thank God, you have your son to hide behind when the going gets tough."

"Don't use my son as an excuse for our problems."

"No, John, I don't have to. You and I are the root of our problems. Your son just brought them to the surface a lot faster. I can't believe this is happening to us. I'm in love with you."

"Sometimes love just isn't enough. I love you, but…"

Not wanting to hear any more, I turned and left.

I entered post break-up hell. Every love song that had ever been written reminded me of him. I didn't want to see any of my friends or talk about it. I became numb.

More Memories

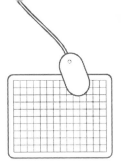

The next man I dated also had a son. This time, I made sure at the beginning that he could juggle a relationship and fatherhood at the same time. I should have realized that when you compare a relationship to any part of a circus act, disaster eventually will follow.

I was not going to get my heart broken again. Getting over John was the hardest thing I ever had to do. I had wanted to spend my life with him.

Justin, the new man in my life, assured me that he could do both. Our relationship started with a bang and then fizzled. I wasn't prepared to open myself up the way I had with John.

I'm not saying that there are not wonderful, caring and loving men out there who have children, but when I find the right man, he'll be a central character in the story of my life, and I want to be the same to him, not just a footnote.

Later that night, I email the Plumber and confess that I have been hurt in the past by men trying to balance love and fatherhood, and I just don't think I can do it again. I wish him all the best.

Letting go of the past is difficult for me. For most of my life, I have either lived in the past or lived in the future. That can be destructive. Many of us carry grudges, torches, and memories that just clutter our lives. I'm slowly beginning to realize that sometimes the old has to fall away to make room for the new.

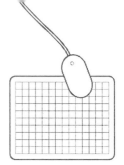

August

*W*ith July behind me, I think about the different men I have talked to and met during the last thirty days. My dates haven't gone exactly as planned. I also think about all the different websites that exist. Am I on the right ones? I did browse quite a few sites before I settled on the three that I chose. However, there are a few that I have to pass on for various reasons.

One site is an exclusive dating club for a select group of very hot singles. Anyone can apply, but you have to be voted in by a panel of judges. Are you kidding me? No, thank you. Who did they hire, Simon Cowell? I can imagine him writing me and saying, "Can I be honest with you? You look like the back end of a horse, and you have no business being in the dating world."

Moving on, I find "the best website for meeting women from the former Soviet Union." Thousands upon thousands of women are on this site. All of them have one goal—to marry an American man. Well, I wasn't born in Russia, so I pass on this site as well.

Fortunately, I have saved the best for last. "Would you like to communicate with a female inmate?" Seriously, this is a website where a man (or a woman, I suppose) can pay $3.00 for each person they want to write to. I have sinned, but I have never committed any crimes. I pass on this site, too.

Does everything cost money? Aren't there sites where I can post my ad for free? I want to try as many websites as possible. Wouldn't that increase my chances of success? Not exactly.

Rule of thumb, if men don't want to pay for their ad to be up, run, don't walk, in the other direction. I find this out the hard way. I come across one website where you can post anything you want. You can sell your car, your pets, your house, and even your soul.

One man is looking for someone cool to hang out with. Intrigued, I read on. He begins by saying that he is "fun and free." Wait, did he just come from confinement? Further down he states, "I dig the beach and sporting events." He doesn't sound half bad. My finger is poised ready to hit the reply button when my eyes scan the last line of his profile, "Ya, I enjoy an occasional joint, it's cool. Go green, baby!" Delete. On to the next ad.

The next man is a "semi-retired bad boy who likes to ride motorcycles." What is it with men and motorcycles? He is also, "wild at heart." He is open to "all types of women." Interesting. This one could have some possibilities. However, I already made a rookie mistake with the last man's ad. I scan through the rest of his profile and there at the end is the following line, "Your picture gets mine. If you are fat, please do not email me. Yeah, I know you are a person, but I can't do a fatty." Strike two.

There must be a few good men on this website. Wait isn't that a movie? Anyway, I scroll through hundreds of ads until I find one profile that is quite charming. He is funny and smart. He has no grammatical errors, and best of all he doesn't end his profile with a derogatory remark or some inane dribble. This is a man whom I'm going to write to. He writes me back right away. He tells me that he is a people pleaser, and he would love to get to know me more. He suggests we have dinner as soon as possible. I think that is a little odd, but then again, look where I am. I'm just about to write him when I read his final sentence. "I look forward to meeting you; however, I must be discreet because my wife doesn't know that I frequent this site." Strike three. I'm outta here.

Okay, so maybe being able to post your ad for free isn't the way to go. I guess when you are not paying a monthly fee to find the love of your life, you can forego any signs of intelligence or ethics. However, there are people who do pay for matchmaking services and are still in dire need of coaching.

You've Got Mail

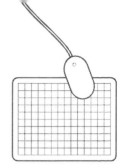

*I*n order to fulfill the "contract" with some of these dating websites, I have to write to men at least three to five times a month. Hell, I can do that in my sleep. However, I'm having a hard time finding someone with whom I want to correspond with this month. Then I come across a man's profile that really leaves me baffled. I don't know if he is trying to be funny, or if he has become numb to the world of online dating. Even though I have to write to one more guy this month, I just can't bring myself to do it.

Mr. HereIamForU

*M*ost people write about what they like to do for fun. Instead Mr. U writes, "If you get to the point where you're feeling really good about yourself, merely scroll through all the people who viewed your profile but didn't deem you to be wink-worthy." Wow, he does have a point. However, is that what he does for fun? Angry, he scrolls through life scowling at people who do not want to be in his presence? That doesn't sound like fun to me. Come on Mr. U, don't let the Internet get you down. Why don't you tell me about your job?

Mr. U refuses to write about his job. Instead, he takes the opportunity to tell me about an Internet dating fun fact, "Would you believe there are only 89 women in the entire US who make $150K or more and list chest as their best feature? Who knew?" Mr. U, what are you trying to tell me? That I better have big boobs and be willing to support you?

Okay, let's forget about your job. Why don't you tell me about your religion? For this he writes, "I can respect the fact that people out there have strong religious beliefs, however, if you have a Jesus fish on your car, I will punch you." Mama Mia! What Sunday school did he go to? Okay, so he won't tell me about his religion, he won't tell me about his job, and he won't tell me what he likes to do for fun, maybe he will tell me about some of his favorite things. For his favorite things he writes, "I'm not sure if this qualifies as one of my favorite things just yet, but I've become quite fond of making fun of people who still don't know the difference between you're, your, their, they're and there. Ummm… wasn't that 3rd grade?" Well. I'm not quite sure how I should respond to this. He seems so angry.

Who is this man? In the end he writes that he genuinely likes nice people and is very positive. Huh? But a few lines later he writes, "If you tell me that you're looking for a guy who is as comfortable in a pair of jeans as he is in a tux, I'll be forced to gag myself with a spork. Also, I will not respond to anyone who uses the phrase, 'I work hard and play hard;' unless you are really hot, but just know that I really think you are an idiot." Shaking my head, all I can do is wish Mr. U the best of luck. He is probably sitting at home wondering why no one deems him wink-worthy.

Thinking I need to turn my attention to a different website for awhile, I devote a few days to my third choice, and the men on that site.

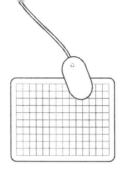

Don't Worry, We Will Take Care of Everything

I don't know if I like this particular website or not. I'm supposed to give up total control to them, and let them find my match based on their scientific approach. Dating in the 21st century sure has its advantages... or does it?

Over the last couple of months, I have adjusted my "must have" list when looking for my perfect match. However, I do not want the man of my dreams to be shorter than me. This presents a problem, because I'm 5'11". Now, there are many wonderful men out there who are not 5'11", but I would just feel uncomfortable dating them.

When you sign up for this particular site, you are at its mercy. I distinctly put in my preferences: I want a man who is 5'11" or taller. After my initial profile, I wait for the men to come pouring in. I receive fourteen matches in one day. I'm impressed. Eagerly, I go online to see what my matches look like, and what they have to say.

Profile 1

Age 38 Height 5'7"

Profile 2

Age 34 Height 5'6"

Profile 3

Age 41 Height 5'5"

Profile 4

Age 56 Height 5'0"

Exasperated, I decide to write to this dating website:

```
To: DatingExperts@DatingExperts.com
From: Dianne@dontdoitatall.com
Subject:  Question for you?
Dear Sir or Madam-
    Could you please make sure my matches
are 5'11" or taller?  I automatically
won't think the chemistry is there if I'm
uncomfortable dating men who are not as
tall as me.
Thank You,
Dianne Sweeney
```

Within 48 hours, I get a reply. I know I'm in trouble when they start my letter with "Dear ..." They can't even be bothered to type in my name or at least Dear Customer. When you get a standard form letter you know that all hope is lost. I notice they don't even address my concerns, but they do take the opportunity to tell me that their success is based on mathematical computations, based on each person's response to critical relationship questions. They continue to write, "We are pleased to announce that, on average, 3% of our members are getting married every day."

I think what she really means to say is:

```
To:  Dianne@dontdoitatall.com
From: DatingExperts@DatingExperts.com
Subject:  What's Your Problem?
Dear (I can't be bothered to enter your
name),
    Have 3% of the people you met asked
you to marry them?  I didn't think so.  We
know what we are doing.  You are going
to quit your bitching and date whomever
our mathematical matching process tells
you to date.  This has nothing to do with
fulfilling your desires, damn it.
Sincerely,
Masters of Picking Who You Belong With
```

I'm starting to worry that this is going nowhere fast. It's already late August, and the winks, the emails, even the mini-me matches are only coming in sporadically.

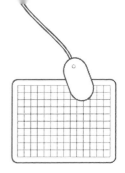

New and Improved or Tired of the Same Ol' Thing

I have noticed that many men have a much wider age range than most women. For the men, the average 35-year-old has no problem putting his age preference for his potential mate to be between 18 and 52. If it weren't illegal in 50 states, they would probably put 16. My age range for men is between 33 and 43. This is because I'm afraid that if I put anything older, it will invite the 50 or 60-year-olds to write me and tell me how they may be in their 50s or 60s, but they feel like they are 40. Take this man for example. Here is a good looking man who is 41. He put that his ideal match would be between 19 and 36. That is a huge age gap, but to each his own. However, let's take a look at the last portion of his profile:

"Are you honest, have a very positive outlook on life and can you share your feelings with relative ease? Ok, I'm 56 yrs old not 41. Why do I have 41 and not 56 in my profile? I want to have children and I get too much interest from 50 year-old women who can't have children. Also, most women in their 30's - 40's assume that I do not want to have children. Ok, so shoot me for trying to "game" the personals search engine. And, all pictures are current. 1-2 yrs old at most. I'm honest and you will not have to prod and poke at me for honesty."

So, why not just say this at the beginning? Why make me read the entire profile before springing this on me? If his pictures are only two years old, why is he standing in front of a calendar that says 2002 when it's 2006? Why would I want to start any relationship off with a lie?

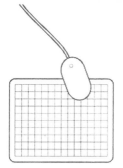

$\mathcal{S}$ kinman 2005

When I first start talking to Skinman2005, he tells me he's 6'3", forty years old and "ready for action." He has no children and lives on a farm. We email each other a couple of times, and we have some great conversations; however, there is something noticeably strange about his pictures. He looks different in all of them. In some of them he is really far away, while in others, he is right up in the camera's face. It's as if he has one for every decade he has been alive.

Not having any luck on certain dating websites, I decide to explore a couple of new ones. My friend shows me some ads from one particular website. It's a pretty good site, and I like their set-up. As I'm looking at their personal ads, I come across Skinman2005 once again. This doesn't strike me as odd. Many of us, me included, are on multiple sites.

Username: *Skinman2005*

Height: *6'3"*

Age: *51*

Children: *2*

Wait, what just happened here? How did he age eleven years? Where did these two children come from? I want to ask him about his new profile, so I send him an email.

```
To:   Chris@Chrisforyourightnow.com
From: Dianne@dontdoitatall.com
Subject:  Hey Chris
Hey Chris:
    My friend was showing me a picture of
her boyfriend whom she met on a dating
site and to my surprise; I came across
your profile. Which profile should I
believe?  The one that says you are 40
or the one that says you are 51 and have
children?

    Dianne
```

Skinman2005 doesn't reply. I, of course, am ignored. One of the things that really bothers me about these websites and the people on them is that it's easy to disregard people's feelings. We wink at people and get no response; we take a risk and email a person and tell him or her how much we enjoyed reading his or her profile, and many times we do not get any reply in return. It only takes a minute to write to a person and say, "Thanks for emailing me; however, I don't feel like there is a connection. Good luck to you." Okay, I was wrong. That took me fifteen seconds to write.

We often forget about the human connection when we use online dating. It's easier and safer to hide behind the computer and email or ignore someone than it is to speak to him or her on the phone. Because we are looking at a screen, we forget that there is a human being on the other end waiting for us to reply.

September

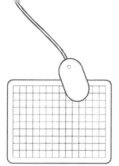

*I*t's time to say good-bye to August as September slowly creeps in. There are four months left of this journey.

Lately, I have been getting emails from men who are twice my age and half my height (Ok, they're not literally three feet-tall septuagenarians, but you know what I mean). I gotta tell ya, this really worries me. I'm starting to get a complex. Maybe I'm not as good-looking as the other women on these sites. Maybe they have more to offer than I do. Maybe I shouldn't be worrying about all of this, but I do. Is it my weight? Is there something in my profile that is turning men off? Are there other women out there who are going through the same thing as me? What makes these women more appealing? It's time to meet my competition.

The Other Woman

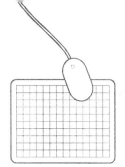

While scanning the profiles of all the women who, like me, are looking for the man of their dreams, I come across the same line over and over again:

"I'm easy to get along with and lots of fun."

"What am I really like? One word: Fun."

"I would be perfect for someone who likes to have fun, and I'm sexy."

One woman writes, "Fun and sexy are my middle name."

Fun? Sexy? I wonder how many men would respond to an ad that read, "I'm a nymphomaniac who has the ability to turn into a pizza and a 6-pack of beer at midnight." I'm willing to bet hundreds, maybe even thousands.

The other line that really amuses me is, "I love wearing a baseball cap, but I also like to dress-up. However, I don't wear a baseball cap with a dress." I'm so glad that she clears that up for us. Another amusing line, "I'm *diversable* from wearing a baseball cap and dressing up in an evening gown."

And the list goes on and on. What is happening to us? Obviously, we all want someone who is fun and wants to have a good time. Who in their right mind is going to put, "please be boring and pessimistic?"

Dressing up? Of course many of us love to dress up. However, I know I don't have an evening gown in my closet. I threw my prom dress away years ago. I love to shop, so if I have to "dress up" for a night on the town, you can bet that I will rummage through my closet, look at the tons of skirts, pants, and tops I have, and utter these five words: "I have nothing to wear." Off to the mall I go…

What would happen if we all had to write about who we really are quirks and all? Would that yield more matches or be a total turn off? I think there is only one way to find out. It's time to write a new profile and spice things up. Perhaps my candor will attract more (and saner) men. Fingers crossed.

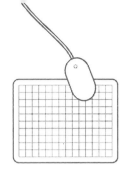

Want the Truth, but Can You Handle the Truth?

Username: *WhoAmI*

Tell Us About Yourself: *"All right men, let's be honest with each other. What would happen if we had to tell who we really are, not who we want you to believe we are? I honestly don't think it matters what I write as long as I have a cute picture up. Am I right or wrong about that?*

It amazes me that everyone is looking for someone who is fun. Of course we are. What are we supposed to write? Please be boring, uneducated, and cheap? If we were to approach each other in the grocery store, would I say, "Hi, my name is WhoAmI. I'm fun, educated, and cute—your turn!"

That doesn't happen in the real world, but since this is cyberspace, all bets are off.

One of my secret single behaviors is that I love watching Ghost Hunters and Girls Next Door.

Rarely do I chew gum, but when I do, I always have to have two pieces. One of my biggest pet peeves is when I go to a drive-thru window and the drink I order is not filled up to the top. I never complain, but now every time I order a drink, I have to look underneath the cap to see if it's filled up enough or not. I can't help it.

You can bet that if I need to dress up for a night on the town with you, I will always use that as an excuse to go shopping. I tend to put a small wall up when I first meet people, but I'm working hard at knocking that wall down. I have realized that some people settle because they are afraid to be alone, some people are settling down, and some people, like me, refuse to settle for anything less than that butterfly feeling in the pit of my stomach when I know I'm going to see you.

I hate cooking for one, and no one can explain to me why it's not cheaper to eat out than to stay in when you are a bachelor/bachelorette. Oh, and I hate mayo—it's the most disgusting thing ever invented.

I will freak out if a guy is glued to my hip 24/7. I never understand when some of my married friends say, "I don't know if I can go, I have to get permission from my _husband/wife." We're going to lunch, not the local strip club!_

I hate working out, but I do it. Often times my trainer wants to shove a weight into my mouth because of all the smart remarks I make during our sessions.

One of my flaws is that I say what everyone else is thinking, and that always gets me into trouble. Sometimes, my motto is, if you don't have anything nice to say, come sit by me.

I'm forever looking for my keys. I have lost work keys, house keys, and I will always ask you if you have seen my keys.

So if you want to find out if I'm fun, cute, witty, look good in an evening gown or a baseball cap, nice, sweet, sexy, educated, and out-going, and whatever else it is you are looking for, you are going to have to email me to find out. That's the fun part."

My prospects are starting to look good. I'm not getting thousands of hits per day, but they are steady. When Jake first emails me, I'm not sure if we would be a good match. A few things in his profile make me a bit wary. "I lead a simple life," Jake explains. What does that mean? Is there anyone out there who enjoys leading a complicated life? When I think of the simple life, I think of Paris Hilton and Nicole Ritchie! "Please be low maintenance; I want a Toyota not a Lexus," Jake writes near the end of his profile. I guess no one has ever told Jake that using automotive terms to describe romance is not the way to a woman's heart.

But when Jake and I talk on the phone for the first time, he seems nice. Polite. Respectful. We have a few lapses in our conversation, but we decide to meet anyway. "Would you like to meet at San Jose State?" Jake asks eagerly. He works in the downtown area, and it will be easier for him to take a lunch break near his work.

As usual, I arrive early and find a place to sit down as I wait for Jake to arrive. Out of the corner of my eye, I see a man who is about 5'9" approaching me instead of the 5'11 ½" I'm supposed to be meeting. Oh boy.

"Dianne?"

"Jake?"

"Yeah, how are you?"

"Great, and you?"

"Fine, fine."

Okay, this is awkward. What do you do when there is absolutely no chemistry? As we sit there in silence, I can't help but think about why people lie in their profiles. Why put a picture up that is ten years old? Why say we are active when we love sitting on the couch watching soap operas? I wonder if there has ever been a time when the two people look at each other, shake hands, and say, "Thanks for coming out, but let's stop right here." Probably not. I clear my throat to break the silence.

Jake looks at me, "So, do you want to walk around for a little bit?"

No, and you don't either. Why are we torturing ourselves?

"Yeah, sounds good," I say.

Now, I'm not opposed to walking. I actually love to walk. Although this time, I hesitate because my cute sandals, which I wore to impress him, are rather tight. Maybe I am high maintenance. However, I suck it up and walk around with him anyway.

The walk isn't too bad. However, there are these long pauses before either one of us begins to talk again. So what do two people who have nothing in common and have no chemistry with each other do next? They go for coffee, of course.

"Would you like to get some coffee?" he asks politely.

"Sure," I say. I need to sit down because the back of my sandal is beginning to rub my heel raw.

Jake opens the door, and we get in line at Starbucks behind two or three other people. After a minute or two, the cashier says, "Next in line."

Jake gives me a gentle nudge and says, "Go ahead."

Thinking Jake is right behind me, I walk up to the cashier and order a bottle of water. However, Jake is still waiting in line. The other cashier calls out, "May I help you?"

Jake walks up to that register.

Now, let me say this right here and now. I have picked up the check quite a few times when dating a man, but I'm always surprised when the man doesn't at least offer to pay when we first meet. I always ask if they would like some money for the bill. However, when they tell me no, I'll admit it, I'm pleased. I just think the whole notion of going Dutch is strange, and it makes me feel uncomfortable. I think one person or the other should treat; in the end, it all evens out.

As if he is reading my mind, Jake turns to me and says, "I always go Dutch throughout my relationships. That way we won't owe each other anything in the end."

"Hmmmm, interesting," I say. How else am I supposed to respond to that? I wonder if his approach is a good one. Isn't that self-destructive, though? Imagine if we went into every relationship wondering how this one was going to end. Aren't we just setting ourselves up for failure? If we are always looking to the end, how are we going to enjoy the beginning?

I reach over and hand his cashier a five dollar bill. "His money is all counterfeit."

She laughs and takes the money.

I look at Jake and smile, "You don't have to worry; I won't expect a thing."

He smiles, too, but I can tell that he isn't sure what to make of what just happened. I hope he doesn't go through life thinking that everyone has a motive. I've lived that life. It isn't healthy.

After that, we sit outside the café in agony, both of us rapidly drinking our beverages. After a few more moments I lean over and say, "This has been great, but I really do need to get going." I can't really thank him for anything because he didn't pay for my drink, so I thank him for taking the time to meet me.

I don't know if I'm a Toyota or a Lexus, but maybe Jake should just take the bus for awhile while he figures things out.

Tomorrow is a new day, and I have another date. Hopefully, Pat will be the ray of sunshine I have been craving.

Wifeless4565576

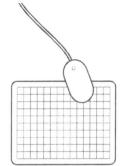

*E*xcitement is in the air. I have been emailing a man who is witty, charming, and handsome. Could this be the man who makes me cancel my membership? Who knows? I'm having fun chatting with him. After a few playful banters through email, he asks for my phone number. Eagerly, I give it to him. I can't wait to hear his voice. A phone conversation can make or break a potential relationship. Admittedly, there have been a few men who turned me off after I talked with them on the phone. However, that is not the case with Pat, AKA, Wifeless4565576. He is a great conversationalist. Not even realizing that time has slipped away, I look up at the clock— we are already an hour and a half into our conversation. That is a dating no-no! The first conversation should only be about 10-15 minutes. Otherwise, it takes away some of the mystery. Not wanting to appear too eager, I tell him that it's time to say good-night. He says, "This must be the part where I ask you out then?"

I think he hears my smile through the phone. I'm grinning from ear to ear. "Are you asking me out?" I ask coyly.

"Yes, I am."

We agree to meet at Starbucks before going to the movies. Not only do I want to make a good impression, I want to lift Pat's spirits a little, since he too has had limited luck with online dating. He is about to cancel his membership.

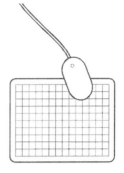

$Pat's$ $Dating$ $Nightmares$

*L*ike me, Pat is less than thrilled with Internet dating; the last two girls he's met online have been beyond strange.

He has been online for a little over five months, and he is losing his patience. Amy was the last person Pat met. They agreed to meet at a restaurant; however, she did not want to talk on the phone with him beforehand (Red Flag, alert). When he met Amy, she was about thirty pounds heavier than her photo, and she asked him if she could tape-record their date (Red Flag, Red Flag). Halfway through their lunch, she dipped her finger into his bowl of soup and seductively put it into her mouth. Astonished, Pat quickly signaled for the check and walked her to her car. Then he bolted to his, got in, and drove far, far away.

Pat's next encounter might have been with a woman, or it might have been with a man pretending to be a woman—only on the Internet can true deception like this occur.

Here's the point. Cunning men and women are lurking in the shadows of the Internet, preying on all the lonely hearts out there, and taking no prisoners in the process. Women will often email men and begin a seductive, misleading game of cat and mouse. Once they've sunk their claws into their unsuspecting victims through half-nude photos, they strike. Let me show you what I mean.

A woman will email a man whom she just met online and write:

```
To:   Pat56565@Pat56565.com
From: Sandy@Iamallyoueverneed.com
Subject:  Hello There

Pat-
   Hey babe.  It was great talking to
you.  I had some photos taken of me, and
I want your opinion on them.  Because they
were for my modeling career, they were
really expensive.  I want you to look at
them, but my agent charges a small fee.
However, I got him to release the first
one so you can look at it.  Tell me what
you think.  I can't wait to see you.
Love,
Sandy
```

Curious men click on the link and see the most beautiful, busty woman imaginable. She is ever so alluring, on the verge of unbuttoning her shirt. The men, foaming at the mouth, click on the next picture and an ad pops up. *Don't let her slip away, for less than $5.00 dollars a week, you can have "Sandy" with you throughout the day.* Men, even though you're shaking your head, I know some of you have actually paid this fee. These websites rake in about $15,000 a month—which reveals just how deceitful the Internet can be.

Of course, men never get to meet "Sandy" even though she portrays herself as an online dating member. Once they fork over the money, she disappears into the shadows and moves on to her next victim.

Because of Pat's experiences, I decide to arrive early to buy the movie tickets. I purchase the tickets and wait.

When Pat walks up, he immediately embraces me. He is so warm. He is 6'3", has dark brown hair, and the sweetest smile. As if we have known each other all our lives, we settle into a conversation before the movie starts. He is pleased that I already have the tickets, and I think I may have even scored a few points with that move.

After the movies, he asks me to dinner. I say, "Yes."

"Great," he says, as he takes my hand and we walk to the nearest restaurant. Throughout dinner, we flirt with each other. I put my hand down in the middle of the table, and he places his hand on mine. After we finish our dinner, he walks me to my car.

At this point, I don't want to just give him a hug. I want to give him a kiss good-bye, but I let him take the lead. When we arrive at my car, we just stand there awkwardly for a few moments, our eyes glued to the pavement. Finally, he says, "I have to go to Colorado for a few days. Can I call you when I get back?"

"Sure, of course," and as I'm finishing my sentence, he leans in and kisses me softly. I kiss him back. It lasts for a few tender moments. As I pull back, he smiles and says, "I will talk to you later."

At this point I could write something like, "and with that kiss, my feet float off the ground." But let's face it... that's not reality. I get in my car, and I drive home.

Cyberstalker

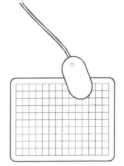

While Pat is in Colorado, I think about the way that people interact with each other. We receive an email from an old flame, and our instinct may be to delete it, but curiosity gives way, and we have to read it. We fly off the handle and write a scathing email to someone we are angry with, and immediately regret it. It always seems like humans are testing each other. Reluctantly, I have to admit that I don't trust people when I first start a relationship. That goes for potential female friends as well. I also have this bad habit of testing their friendship or the relationship. This is a problem that has cost me quite a few friends and potential relationships.

When I first meet a man, I tend to lose confidence in myself. I begin doubting the situation, and I look for things that are wrong. I look high and low, leaving no rock unturned. Knowing that this is one of my flaws, I'm trying to work through it. I don't want to sacrifice any of my needs and desires because I have to test the relationship.

Having said this, I do what ninety percent of women do when they meet a potential mate. Slyly, we check, day after day, to see if the man we have just met has logged back onto the dating website. Men don't seem to do this as much, but I do it all the time.

Over the next few days, I log on to the website to see if Pat has been active (not active in three days!). Isn't that a crazy notion? He just met me, and he is supposed to swear off all women? I'm shaking my head as I write this because I realize how stupid this sounds. My goal from now on is not to look. It will be hard, but I'm going to try and stop doing it.

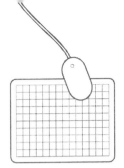

He's Back

$\mathcal{F}$our days later, Pat calls. My heart skips a beat when I hear his voice. The conversation is light-hearted. He enjoyed Colorado, and I enjoy listening to him talk about it. After an hour of conversation, he asks me out to dinner. Strangely, however, he asks if we can meet at the restaurant because he doesn't think he is ready to come to my house and pick me up.

Odd, I think, but I respect his decision.

We decide to meet at a trendy restaurant in the downtown area.

I meet him there at 6:00 sharp. He walks in and immediately gives me a hug. We walk further into the restaurant to find a long line of cell phone addicts, crying babies, and couples in various stages of the dating process. At this restaurant, you have to place your order first, and then find a table. When we approach the cashier, I realize that it's Kelly, a former student of mine. Of course, her teenage curiosity gives way; she has to know who Pat is. I introduce him to her, and then she says, "Ms. Sweeney was one of the best teachers I ever had. You are so lucky."

That gives my ego a boost! I smile at Kelly and the three of us make small talk while we wait for our number to be called.

Number 68. Number 68.

Pat excuses himself to pick-up our trays. I smile at Kelly and give her a hug good-bye.

We find a table in the corner of the dining room and continue to make small talk. However, the sparks between us are beginning to fade. Trying to ignite them again, I nonchalantly put my hand down on the table; he does not put his hand over mine. After a few more tries, my curiosity gives way, "I get the feeling there is something wrong with you tonight," I say demurely.

He looks down at his plate, plays with an imaginary piece of food, and after what seems like an hour says, "Well, I have to be honest with you. I do have a couple of concerns, red flags if you will, and I don't know what to do with those."

Red flags? Isn't that my line? I *have* red flags? Well, of course I do, but what have I done to give him a red flag? Oh no, did he notice I had been stalking his personal ad the last couple of days?

I clear my throat, "Uh, do you wanna talk about it?"

Okay, couldn't we do this over the phone? I'm not used to straightforwardness. I didn't want to burst into tears like Reese Witherspoon in *Legally Blonde*.

"My mom was a teacher," he begins, slowly. "It used to really bother me when we would go to a store or a restaurant and her students would always stop her and say hello. It pissed me off when they told me how lucky I was to have her for a mother. When your student said that about you…well…it just made me think I was with my mother."

Is he serious? I thought I was the neurotic one. I don't know what to say.

I want to reach over and rip that napkin right out of his hands. Trying to get past this, trying to smooth over the situation and reclaim that spark that is now completely extinguished, I look up at him, and smile. Mustering up all my wit and charm and giving him a mischievous grin, I say, "Well, actually I have a confession to make. I'm really a hooker."

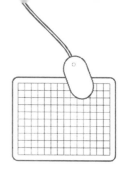

What am I Doing Out Here?

*T*he days are fading into one another and October is not too far off. I didn't have a lot of dates in September; however, each date I encounter or each time I venture out into cyberspace gives me a chance to reflect on who I am and how I have ended up here to begin with. The people that come in and out of our lives can make lasting impressions, whether through a chance encounter, a rival, or a colleague. Slowly, I'm beginning to get rid of the clutter that I have surrounded myself with so that I can make room for someone who dares to venture into my space.

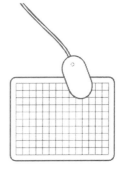

http://www.ionlywanttheretobeone-datingwebsite.com

*M*any of us pay a lot of money to be on these various websites. Wouldn't it be great if there was just one website that combined all of the major dating websites together? A few of the men whom I have encountered could save a ton of money if such a site existed. I chatted with one man who told me that he was on 15 different sites. I asked him why he was on so many. He said that dating was a numbers game. What does it matter if he was on 1 or 100? I thought that was interesting, but I also wondered if it gave him too many choices.

I'm on three different websites, but I've pretty much cut and pasted my introduction from one site to the other. I guess I could create a persona for each one like my friend, Rogerthat.

Rogerthat writes, "I can get along with almost everyone, down to earth, love to laugh, hard-working, but most of all I like to have fun" (again, aren't we all like this?). He goes on to say, "I've reached a point in my life where I'm ready to settle down." I like what he has to say, so I email him. He emails me back, but says he isn't feeling very well and needs to chill for a few days. So much for his fun-loving free spirit!

Later on that day, I'm searching through the thousands of personal ads on another site, and I come across AREUREADY?

Looking at his screen name, I say aloud, "Yes, I'm ready. Are you ready for me?" After I finish reading his profile, I look at all of his pictures. He looks oddly familiar to me. Wait a minute. This is Rogerthat, my sick friend. His pictures are different, but it's him.

> Rogerthat: I'm looking to settle down and live my life with that one special person.
>
> AREUREADY: I'm full of life, but I'm not looking for a LTR (Long Term Relationship). If I could I would just write I'm interested in one night stands only.

Oh, my God. What happened to all of his attributes? Is he hoping to find someone to have sex with while he is getting to know his perfect wife? Is he the type who, after he finds his perfect wife, "forgets" that he still has an open account on one of the dating websites? What if a beautiful woman contacted him after he was already married? Will the real Rogerthat please stand up?

Click, Click, Click

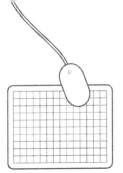

With two bad dates in a row, I retreat back into my own world for a breather. This has been a degrading experience. Do you notice that all of these dating websites claim that because of them, there are millions of people who are now married? It's great that all of these people found each other because of Al Gore's invention, but how many couples are torn apart *because* of a click of the mouse, because we rekindle an old flame, or meet someone who pays attention to us in a chat room?

We google an old boyfriend to see if we get any hits. We wonder about the man we dated a few times a year ago, or we go back to our school days and see what is happening with our high school sweetheart, for many of us, our first love. For some, it's a chance meeting in a chat room, a game room, or a posting on a message board; meeting people is safer and easier through the Internet than in the real world. Online, you can be the person you want to be. Maybe better looking, richer, happier, and it's safe to be that person. Bruce, who was a mechanic in the Navy ten years ago in real life, becomes Bruce, the former "Navy Seal," online. Melanie, whose distant cousin became a model in the real world, "does some modeling." You can type things on the Internet that you would never say in the real world. In short, cyberspace gives people a place to fill their lagging self-esteem or to compensate for the shortcomings of their real life.

I have a secret single behavior that causes me to sit for hours in front of the computer. It's not searching for personal ads. It's playing online games. You can sit and play any game you want and chat with people from all over the world. There is one game in particular that I can't stop playing. It's called Stomp.

While playing Stomp in the "Destruction Room," I begin chatting with the other players. There we all are, typing away. I have even met people who fell in love while playing these online games and are now married. It's harmless fun, as long as you don't become too obsessed, as I tend to do.

It's while playing this game that I meet a man who happens to be on a business trip in San Jose. He lives in Portland. I start to ask him about Oregon and if he enjoys living there. Soon we were chit-chatting about all sorts of different topics. He often travels for business, and he travels to San Jose quite frequently.

After a few more nights of conversation and a little harmless flirting, our dialogue veers in another direction—a more personal one. It goes something like this:

> Sillyguy: Hey, you wanna go get dinner with me tomorrow night? This is the only thing I hate about business trips, eating alone.

> Me: Oh I'm bummed. I have to work.
>
> Sillyguy: Oh, sure. No biggy.

I do want to meet him. He's charming and says some really funny things. We have never exchanged pictures. So I have no idea what he looks like. How funny would it be if I met my future husband while playing games online? Yet, it's not to be, because he is about to lower the boom. Why does this always happen at the last second? I think I'm going to start reading my emails and instant messages from the bottom up.

> Me: That is the only night I have to work.
>
> Sillyguy: I think I'm free the other nights I'm there. But I think you need to know one thing. I don't know if I mentioned this or not, but I'm married.

Sometimes I wonder...am I the only sane person in cyberspace?

> Me: Does your wife mind that you are online so much?

All of a sudden a small screen pops-up. *Sillyguy has asked you to chat with him privately.* I press okay, and there we are...alone in a room in cyberspace.

> Sillyguy: My wife and I have an understanding. I didn't want to say that because everyone is in the chat room, and I don't want them to see this.

Me: What do you mean by understanding? You can sleep with whomever you want?

Sillyguy: Well, she asked if we could have this understanding because I'm away so much.

Me: So your wife is the one who initiated this?

Sillyguy: Yeah, I mean we get along great and everything, but we are staying together for the kids.

Me: Well, be careful out there; STD's are pretty common these days.

Sillyguy: Oh, we are. We promised each other not to let anything get too serious. So do you want to have dinner still?

Is he kidding me? Sadly, no, he isn't. At this point, I wondered how many people he "has dinner with" when he is away on business trips.

Me: I think it's great that you and your wife have an understanding, if that is how you want to live your lives. However, I don't need any more drama in my life. I'm looking for more than just dinner, and I'm looking for someone who is single. Let's go back and play the game.

Sillyguy: Sure, I totally get it. But we would only have dinner. I think we could have a really good time.

> Me: Thanks for the offer, but I don't think it would
> be a good idea.

I log out of that room and quickly go to another room. I'm not going to give up my games because of him.

Do not underestimate this format for people meeting and growing closer on the Internet. I have met many people in chat rooms who use these forums to vent their frustrations about their loved ones, work, or just life in general. I have also witnessed many men and women who happen to be in the same room strike up conversations that begin innocently, but then grow into a flirtation and sometimes a lot more. Internet affairs happen daily, in every town and chat room across the country and around the world.

It's sad because studies have shown that thirty percent of cyber affairs escalate from personal emails or instant messaging to personal contact regardless if one or the other is married. There is even an online social network for men and women seeking extra-marital affairs. Wow! Nothing is sacred anymore.

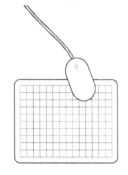

You've Got No Mail (or Male for That Matter)

$\mathcal{I}$ have not received any emails, winks, or "clicks" from anyone lately. I know that people are looking at me because the websites have a feature which allows me to see who's viewed me. I hate this feature. Why do I care who has viewed me? I only care about the ones who write me. I don't want to see that over seventy-eight men have viewed me and have decided that I'm not the one for them based on a couple of pictures and some words.

I write to one dating website because I want to see why this function would appeal to its members.

To: DatingExperts@DatingExperts.com
From: Dianne@dontdoitatall.com
Subject: Hello There

Dear Dating Website:
    I was curious as to the purpose of

the "See Who Has Viewed Me" function
on your website. To me, it's a little
disappointing to see that many men have
viewed me, but do not find me appealing.
I would rather not know than know. Thanks
for any clarification that you can give
me.
Dianne Sweeney

Within two days, I get a response. I'm thanked for my inquiry. As I scroll through the form letter, the following sentence catches my eye. "We find this function vital. Many people are too shy to make the first connection. Don't wait for them, now is the time to take action. Send them an email and say hello."

Now is the time to take action? Hmmm. Okay, Mr. Customer Service Representative, I'm going to take your advice, even though I don't think what you say is really true. People just click, click, click. I think I'm going to test his theory. I'm going to send an email to every man who has viewed me. All seventy-eight of them. Let's just see how many are "too shy." I'm going to become a 'googolo.'

In the end, Mr. Customer Service Representative is wrong. Out of the seventy-eight, I hear back from twelve. In many cases, I just casually mention to them that I had noticed they had viewed my profile but didn't say "hi" and wanted to give them a nudge. One man writes back and says, "to be honest, I click on everyone. It doesn't matter to me if they are my type or not, I'm just looking for ones that I think will be easy or sound desperate enough to talk into a friends with benefits relationship. Since you did write to me, you interested?"

I guess I should be relieved that he didn't think I sounded desperate or easy. However, he is the epitome of a googolo—a gigolo in cyberspace.

How Do They Survive?

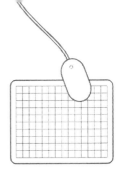

I wonder if men have the same fears as women. Do men worry because they don't receive any winks? Do men stress out about old age, about wrinkles and gray hair? Or worse yet, losing their hair? I know that men think about sex every day, every hour…for some men I know, it's every second! But when they are free to focus on other thoughts, however briefly, do they worry about the same problems as women? Is it easier for a man to date online than it is for a woman? These are the questions I have always wanted to have answered. Are there any men out there willing to give me some honest answers? I'm going to find out.

    I consider all the men I have dated in the past, but decide they will just think I want to go out with them again. I don't know if I can rely on complete strangers, or if they will even talk to me, but it's worth a shot. I need a forum where I can get a variety of opinions. Hesitantly, I go back to one of those free websites and post this ad:

Looking for the Male Perspective

If you could take a few minutes to answer my questions I would greatly appreciate it. I'm doing research for a book I'm writing, and I need your honest answers. Thank you and take care.

1. What is your viewpoint on Internet Dating?

2. Are you seriously looking for someone or just looking?

3. How many dating websites are you on?

4. Have you had any bad experiences?

5. Do you really think, in the end, you will find your soul mate in cyberspace?

Within an hour, I have 189 emails in my box. Oh, my God! No wonder there are no single men in the real world anymore. They are all hanging out in cyberspace. The first email that I receive says that, "women need to just be themselves." His next piece of advice is, "don't be vague. If you can't handle a NSA (No Strings Attached) don't intrigue us." I'm not really sure what he means by all of this, so let's not take his advice.

However, another piece of advice that I do like is "don't sleep with him if you like him. If it went well, he will be back." I start to really warm up to this man. I am about to write him back when I get to the last line of his email, "Some guys are here for sex; some guys are hanging [their] heart on a string, so fish them up. I'm one of the ones who prefer sex.

Want to go out for coffee sometime? Here is my picture."
Man, those last few words are always a killer.

Well, you can't win them all. We do need to give
him props for being honest. I thank him for his words of
wisdom and wish him well on his quest—which is kind of
strange when you think about it.

As I scroll through their emails, I can feel their pain.
Some of them aren't having any more luck than I am. One
man writes that he went out with a woman who brought a
suitcase along with her on their date. She asked him if he
could store it at his place for awhile because she was in the
process of moving. Here's a hint: leave the baggage, both
literal and metaphorical, at home.

The next man is so frustrated with Internet dating,
he can't even spell correctly. He writes, "ads dose not sem
to wok. I don't hav strgest dats becuae women wont rit me
back."

I think women would write him back if they could
decipher what he is saying to them. I'm willing to bet his job
requires no use of a pen or a piece of paper. Spell correctly!
As I'm writing this, I have to laugh, because my editor always
yells at me to spell correctly.

I read every one of those emails.   I can sum up the
results in a few lines. I am:

- Propositioned: 79 times
- Asked on a date: 98 times
- Asked what I would give in return for their answers:
  43 times
- Afraid for my life: 3 times

And Mr. Personality writes, "Why don't we get together and I will screw your brains out, and then I will tell you all you want to know." Okay all, I must apologize. I want to know what every man is thinking just as much as you do, but I didn't take him up on his offer. We are never going to know his pearls of wisdom.

One of the last emails I receive is the most disheartening of all.

> To: Dianne@dontdoitatall.com
> From: phunontheside6969@phunontheside6969.com
> Subject: YOU
>   I'm a married man with completely dishonorable intentions. Would you consider such a liaison? I'm 5'10'', athletic, very easy going, very highly educated, playful, and always a gentleman. I have very recent clean STD results also available, in case that is of importance to you. I'm also on Yahoo Messenger during work hours. If you are interested, you know what to do.
> Would love to LOVE you,
> JS

This email really bothers me for a number of reasons. I think about him; I think about his wife. Then I think about myself. Here I am looking for someone to spend my life with, and here we have two people who found each other and one or both are still not satisfied. Is his wife happy? Are they miserable? Do they have an "understanding"? Are they one of those couples I see having dinner in a restaurant, not talking, not even really looking at each other? Did their relationship start out full of love and laughter, and now they are complete strangers? Or the thing that I'm most terrified about: Did they just stop trying and fall out of love? Occasionally, I hear people say, "When so and so first met they were so in love. Now, they can't even stand to be in the same room together." Depressing! Where did I put my bag of gummy worms?

Okay, we need to laugh. I have saved the best email for last:

To: Dianne@dontdoitatall.com
From: Fartmaster4545@Fartmaster4545.com
Subject: I'm a Decent Guy
    I'm a decent looking guy. Don't have a problem attracting the opposite sex. My problem is flatulence. Every time I start a relationship there is doom and gloom. Why? Because you women are difficult to please. I can only keep my farting problem a secret for so long. They are loud, very long and usually very smelly. What can I do? Whenever I start ripping em in front of my significant other, she always gets turned-off and eventually wants to leave. It's normal to fart. Don't tell me that you haven't farted in the last 24 hours. So, why am I the bad one? Am I normal or are you women just too damn picky?
F

I think I gagged at least four times typing this.

As in life, we will always come across a variety of people. It just goes to show you there are the good, the bad, and the smelly everywhere—even if they are only a click away.

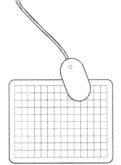

Violations

$\mathcal{T}$he most shocking email I receive is from the web host. My ad is being flagged for violating one of their rules. Seriously? They have the most disgusting ads posted on their site, and my ad is removed? I read through their terms of use and still can't figure it out. I'm not unlawfully selling body parts. I'm curious–can one really sell a body part lawfully? I'm neither stalking nor harassing other users, nor am I engaging in the illegal selling of unlawful substances. Oh well, just another day in cyberspace.

A couple of days later, I receive an email from a man who saw my post but couldn't reply right away. He says he is honest and sincere. He tells me that he wants to show me something really cool. I hold my breath. What can he possibly want to show me? A few minutes later, he sends me an email with an attachment. The subject line is "It's Me." I open the first picture, and there stands a handsome man. He is holding a little puppy in his arms and smiling at the camera. The next picture, however, blows me away. There he is dressed as a leprechaun from the waist up. He has on the green hat, the white shirt, and the suspenders…but no pants or underwear. He has his hands on his hips and is wearing elf-like shoes. He tells me that many women find this photo very sexy, and he wanted to share it with me. He also tells me that many women have asked him to take them to bed wearing this outfit. How exhilarating that must be. Ugh. I thank him for sharing his uh…uh…email with me, and he drifts back into cyberspace.

I have to admit there is a small part of me that might have considered him if he came with a pot of gold, but alas, he didn't. I mean, the guy can't even afford pants.

The Male Perspective

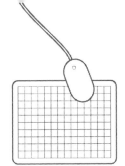

*C*hristy is rolling on the ground as she pours through all of the emails. Tears rolling down her cheeks, she says, "You have to email the farter. Look how open and honest he is. That is rare in most men."

"You're such a jerk," I scoff.

"Well, what are you going to do now?" she says, wiping the tears from her eyes.

I laugh, "I don't know. I emailed a few men on the other dating websites, but I only got one line answers."

"You need to find one man—one man who would be willing to sit down and talk to you openly and honestly, without farting on you, of course."

"I know. But who? He would have to be someone who is good-looking, funny, and considered a good catch. Not necessarily a good catch for me, but a good catch."

We both look at each other. As if reading my thoughts, she pushes the laptop toward me.

I reach back into my past and rely on the one man who has always been truthful with me when it came to dating. I reach for that unlocked door and open it slightly. I email Nick.

I'm not sure if I will get a response, but it's worth a try. Many people might say, Dianne, who are you kidding? You just wrote to him so you could attempt to make one last connection. And you know what? Absolutely! On the one hand, I needed to connect with him one more time. On the other hand, I knew that he would tell me the truth no matter what–a trait that I both admire and hate.

```
To:  Nick@Nick.com
From:  Dianne@dontdoitatall.com
Subject:  Seeking the Truth
Dear Nick:
     I need a huge favor from you. I was
hoping that you and I would converse back
and forth through email before I asked you
this, however, that didn't happen. Which
is okay. I completely understand.
     I was wondering if you would answer
some questions for me. I tried asking
other people, but they would only answer
my questions if I took off all of my
clothes for them. I even tried posting an
ad. That was a disaster. Anyway, if you
could answer these questions for me, I
would greatly appreciate it.
     Just imagine that the world wants to
know about Internet dating from the male
perspective.
Sincerely,
Dianne
```

He responds to my email right away, and I eagerly read his reply. He is more than happy to answer my questions, and he is extremely insightful. In order to capture the essence of Nick's thoughts, I didn't want to edit his words.

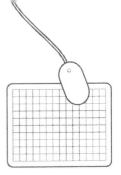

Mr. Perspective

Age and Occupation?   *39- Account Manager*

Q. How long have you been Internet dating?

A. 38.5 yrs. I used to etch-a-sketch a little hottie in the crib next to me. No, off and on for about 8 years, I guess.

Q. Why do use online personals?

A. Hmmm...lots of reasons...efficiency...can screen for basic compatibility and availability from home 24/7 without having to deal with bars or? Live interactions are better in many ways, but you never know if someone is single, straight, lives nearby, has some of the same values/beliefs until you've invested lots of time/energy.

Q. How many women have you met?

A. Fumbles to get calculator...uh, about 30?

Q. What is the biggest deception that you notice that the women claim to be or are or look like on their profile and how they are in real life?

A. Weight!   Pictures are old or glamour shots, or face pictures only.

Q. What was the worst date you have ever been on? How so?

A. Hmm...I've been lucky, I haven't had any horror stories.   Some have gone better than others, but none that were that bad.   LOL...no wait...just thought of a couple.   Cooked dinner for a girl I met on your favorite site, and she had to leave in the middle of dinner to do a drug deal. And she wanted to come back later. NOT! Then there was the stalker...too painful to go into detail (mostly kidding, it wasn't that bad, but she brought up the idea of marriage on the first date then emailed/called way too much).

Q. When you look at the profile, do you just look at the picture, and does it really matter what they say as long as they are good-looking?

A. LOL...yes, it matters a lot. Looks only go so far...they are important in some ways, to create chemistry, but I'm not interested in dating anyone that is brainless, mean, bitchy, sour, jaded, rude, conceited, lazy, visionless...a guy's gotta have standards you know!

Q. How many dating sites are you on? I don't need to know which ones.

A. One, right now. I have sampled as many as five or six.

Q. What would be the number one advice you would give men and women about online dating? Be as detailed as possible.

A. Be honest without being too serious. I think most people want someone fun. For example, even though I'm open to something very serious, if a woman mentions that she is ONLY interested in a serious relationship/marriage, it's a deal breaker for me. Not because I don't want a relationship/marriage, but because there is already built-in pressure before we even meet. It sets me up to be the bad guy before even getting to the starting line, if things don't work out.

Q. (Little personal) How many of your dates have turned into one night stands on the first meeting?

A. Two

Q. How many of your first dates went really well, and then the person or you just disappeared? Ever have a personal experience about that?

A. About six. Some of them were more one-sided, I think. I thought they went well, but maybe she felt more like friends than romantic...and vice versa. There were several dates that were really fun/interesting, but no chemistry.

Q. If you are just not into the person, do you ever email her and tell her thanks but no thanks, or do

you disappear into the night? Give me an average range here. I always email, sometimes email, never email.

A. Almost always email, unless I felt deceived or if the date was an obvious dud. It seems pointless, if the feeling is mutual. The other exceptions were when I get busy and don't reply for a while, then feel weird about emailing weeks later.

Q. What is your biggest disappointment about online dating?

A. I've realized that body language, looks, vocal tonality, the sound of a person's laugh, her smile, smell, play such a complex role in attraction. You really get none of that until you meet. So, while it's great to be able to screen for certain things, you really miss out on the chemistry piece of attraction until you meet live.

Q. Do you use any other venues for dating outside of cyber dating?

A. The occasional referral from friends, or just meeting people through activities (band/volleyball/triathlon training).

Q. What advice would you give women about trying to meet a man in a different venue? Besides a bar, where do you think the best place to meet a man is?

A. Activities, bookstores, restaurants, grocery stores, public restrooms (scratch that one). It doesn't take much to interest a guy... if a woman makes a little eye contact and/or smiles, it could be on. I think women don't realize how much a guy fears rejection, even a guy that is confident in many areas of life in his thirties, forties, fifties, can be paralyzed by the thought of approaching a woman. It wouldn't hurt to make it a little easier on us. Many women make it very difficult (some guys call it a "bitch shield"), which only reinforces the fear.

Q. On average how many women do you email in a week? How many women respond?

A. *One or two, I'm pretty selective. Most respond, I think because I put thought and humor into the message.*

Q. On a scale of one to ten how truthful are the personal ads that you read?

A. Seven

Q. How many of the personal ads you read pretty much say the same thing? On a scale of one to ten.

A. Seven

Q. What is the one thing you look for when reading a personal ad? What advice would you give women about writing a personal ad?

A. 1. I check basic info to see if she is a match for me....age range, single (you'd be surprised), etc.

2. Pictures, pictures, pictures. If there is no potential for chemistry, I don't waste my/their time.

3. See if I'm an overall match for her, race, height, age, etc.

4. Scan text for basic compatibility, look for humor, likes/dislikes, does she exercise regularly, values/beliefs, religion....yada, yada.

Advice would be to include at least two and as many as five plus pictures. The unfortunate truth is that ninety-nine percent of guys are visual, and chemistry is triggered primarily by looks. Because this is not as true for women, they don't always put as much focus on it, or they try to deceive, which really wastes everyone's time. I think that because women's attraction is triggered differently (more by lifestyle, confidence, attitude, strength, intelligence, ability to provide), they think that it's OK to put old/outdated photos because looks are not that important to them. It's the equivalent of a guy saying that he has an exciting/rewarding job, tons of friends, plays sports regularly, travels, etc., when he really is an-out-of work janitor, that plays Xbox in his house alone all day/night. OK, I feel better now that I got that out of my system. Boiled down it would be: Relax, have/be fun. It's OK to want to get married, but talking about it too early will scare the fish away. If you do mention it, it would be wise to temper it with verbiage like, "if things work out over time, or if we find that we are compatible down the road, eventually I would like to get married, but want to take the time to find the right guy."

Hope that helps. Good luck with everything. I want to read your manuscript.

Nick

Over the next few days, the questions that Mr. Perspective responded to begin to weigh on my mind. The two words that keep replaying in my head are "bitch shield." I think I have one of those. In fact, I think my bitch shield is plated with heavy-duty armor. Not because I'm a mean, snotty person, but because, like all of us, I fear rejection.

Usually when a man looks at me, I quickly look away. I wear my sunglasses, so men don't realize I'm looking at them. I remember one time when my friend and I were at a routine traffic stop, and the police officer looked into our car with his flashlight and said, "Good evening, ladies, have you had anything to drink tonight?"

"Not a drop," I said. "Unless you count a super-sized Diet Pepsi."

The cop smiled. "Okay, you are set to go. But before you do, I have to tell you, you have beautiful eyes."

Embarrassed, I said, "Oh, thank you."

At that point I should have jotted down my phone number and given it to him. So why didn't I? Looking back on it now, I know why. I was afraid of being rejected or laughed at when I drove away. However, he was taking a risk by flirting with me. I could have at least returned the favor.

Isn't it funny that I'm confident in every aspect of my life, but I can't look at a man and smile? I have decided that, for the last remaining days of my quest, I'm going to remove my "bitch shield." I'm going to make it a point to smile more at the men I encounter and to make eye contact with them. This will be difficult, but I refuse to hide behind a shield, a wall, or anything else that stops me from finding a man I want to seriously date.

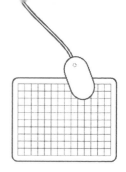

May the Force Be With Me!

With my shield tucked safely out of sight, I decide to go to the gym. My goal is to talk to at least two men. When I arrive, the gym is full. Wall-to-wall bouncing bodies and sweat. However, there are two lonely treadmills pushed into a corner. This is going to be harder than I think. In order to make eye contact with a man, I will have to exercise backwards.

But since the treadmills are the only machines available, I climb on to one of them and begin a long walk uphill with my back to everyone else. Then I see a huge black and red spider. He is trying to crawl back up to the web he has created in the corner of the window. A few minutes later, a man gets on the treadmill next to me

Here goes nothing, I think.

I turn to him and say, "I'm laying odds that the spider will fall to his death."

He turns to me with a look of confusion. "What's that?"

As I turn toward him, I can tell that he is a much older man, probably in his mid-to-late sixties. Okay, so he is old enough to be my dad; however, this isn't about dating him. It's about making eye contact with a man and striking up a conversation. He looks at the spider. "Oh, I see. You're right. That is a big one."

"Yeah, it is."

Okay, now what? I glance over at him, he glances at me. I glance at him again and turn to watch the lonely spider struggle to crawl back up to the home he has created in the outside corner of the gym—tucked away from the hustle and bustle of the rest of the world. How does he find a date, I wonder? I shake the thoughts out of my head; I don't have time to delve into the relationship sagas of a spider that may or may not have commitment phobias.

I clear my throat; okay, say something to this man. *But what?*

Do you come here often?

My, you have a big…cane…

What was it like in WWII?

I can't think of anything to say, so I turn to see if there are any machines that have not been claimed yet.

I glance around the gym, and my eyes rest on Mr. Universe. His body is muscular, and from where I'm standing, there is not one ounce of fat on him. The sweat is dripping down his face as he listens to music drumming from his iPod. Watching him run, I hear the *Rocky* theme song when Rocky is running to the top of the steps of the

Philadelphia Museum of Arts. *Dun na na…dun na na…dun na na…dun na na …* Right next to him, there is a treadmill that is not in use. I hop off my machine, hurry over, and leave Grandpa to deal with the spider's relationship issues. I almost knock another person out of the way, as I dive for the machine. I make it.

Now, by nature, I'm not a runner. I trip more than I walk. However, I need to muster all my strength to make it appear that I can run, or at least jog.

As I hop onto the machine, I glance at Mr. Universe, *dun na na…dun na na…*he is too busy keeping up with the tempo of the music. I begin walking at a decent pace; I sneak a look at Mr. Universe, and he begins running faster on the treadmill. Oh yeah, watch this. I increase my speed and break into a jog, rejoicing in the fact that I'm jogging, a concept foreign to my body. Nonetheless, I'm trudging along. But then my body begins to tire a little. I cannot keep this facade up much longer. I lean forward to slow the machine down, and I rip the ear piece to my iPod out of my ear. Struggling to get it back in, and not paying attention to my feet, I hurtle backwards, until gravity takes its course, and I land with a thud on the ground. Dazed, I look up and the treadmill is still going 'round and 'round and 'round.

Mr. Universe turns to see what all the commotion is about and sees me sprawled out on the ground. "Holy shit," he utters. "Are you okay?"

No, I'm not okay! I'm lying in the middle of the gym floor. People are gawking at me. If I was a cartoon character, I would have a lump emerging from my head with birds circling around it—tweet, tweet, tweet.

"Oh, of course. I'm fine."

"Here, my girlfriend picked up your iPod for you." He hands it to me.

Girlfriend, Girlfriend, Girlfriend begins echoing through my head. Humiliated, I slowly pick myself up and take my iPod from his hands. Too embarrassed to look at her, I slowly begin to limp away. Out of the corner of my eye, I can see them standing there in utter disbelief.

"Honey, did you see how that girl biffed it?" are the last words I hear, as Mr. Universe turns to his girlfriend, and I walk away.

So, if this had happened four or five years ago, I would have grabbed my heavy-plated "bitch shield" and put it on so securely that it would have become my second skin; however, I have learned a lot since then, and this quest I'm now on makes me stronger every day.

Arriving home that night, I toss my "bitch shield" into the trash can. I do, however, go into my dresser drawer and dig out my elbow pads, just in case I need a little protection out there now and again.

Laughter is the best medicine, but the aspirin I take far outweighs the laughter in this situation. Can laughter be used to remove the huge bruise I have on my ass?

Mr. Perspective and I are becoming fast friends. I no longer perceive him as the man I thought he was, or the man I created in my mind. He is just Mr. Perspective now. Is that the reason why Nick keeps returning over and over again? Each time he comes back into my life, I discover new things about men. What is he supposed to teach me this time? I crave his words of wisdom, and he, in turn, takes on the role of Yoda. Learn, I say.

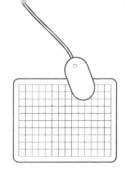

What Have I Actually Learned?

I have learned a lot over the last few months. One of the things that I have learned is that having the right screen name is extremely important. I can't tell you how many men I have been turned off by when I find out their real screen name. One man I corresponded with felt comfortable enough to give me his—gottajohnson4u. By now, you should know I'm not kidding. He was forty-three. Another man told me his was GreatGuyButBitter. Hello, Mr. Wonderful. I can't wait to spend my life with you.

Also, it's important to have the right catch phrase. I worry when I see, "You will never be alone again." or this one, "You think you can hang with me?" What are we monkeys?

I get that this is the World Wide Web, but why on earth do men email me who live in Tulsa, Oklahoma? There have got to be women there, I'm sure of it. Once, I received an email from a man who lived in Atlanta, Georgia. He wrote, "I would get on a plane and fly to you." Then, he had no picture. That got me thinking. Does he have his own jet? Is that why he was so readily available? There are thousands of men in my area; do I really have to go cross-country to find my true love?

The inner English teacher can no longer be silenced. I have to say this again—spelling counts. Holy Cow! Whit wuld u do if the hole book ws writn lke this? Do you know how many emails I have received from men who do not take the time to spell correctly? I even had a man write me and call me "Den." Who is that?

One of the other things that I have learned is to listen. People of all races, backgrounds and faiths have stories to tell about online dating. I also learned that I'm not the only one out there who is going through this.

While I scroll through the various dating websites, I always read articles from the "dating experts." Many of the dating experts say to keep the conversation short and sweet. "Leave them wanting more." So I'm trying that. More what though? More short conversations? More me? It's driving me crazy, this whole notion of "leave them wanting more." I have received the following advice from three different "dating experts." "Don't reveal too much about yourself." Also, "Don't appear too smart." and my favorite, "Don't dress too classy. He might think that he can't keep you in the luxuries that you desire." So based on that, I'm supposed to be a dumb, mute hobo. Is this ever going to be easy? I have been trying to keep my conversations short, and trust me, for some, they are not short enough.

The phone rings one night, and I pick it up to hear a friendly, "Hi."

"Hi. You must be Craig." I'm not psychic; I know it's Craig because I gave him my number a few hours ago, and I told him I would be home around 7:00 p.m. It's 7:08.

"I am indeed."

Lull in the conversation.

"So, how was your day?" I ask.

"Great. So you are a teacher, eh?"

"Yes, I am."

"Do you ever have students make passes at you?"

I jiggle my phone because I don't think I've heard him correctly. "Ummm, excuse me?"

"You know, I had this huge crush on my 3rd and 5th grade teacher. Come to think about it, I was in love with my 7th grade teacher, too, so I was just wondering."

"Uh-no. That actually makes my stomach turn." Who is this person?

"Oh, sorry. Do you live with roommates?"

"Yes, actually I live with two."

"They aren't men are they? That would be a deal breaker for me. I will not be a third wheel, you got it? By the way, do you walk?"

Now I know why the dating experts say to keep it short and sweet.

"Hey, you know what? I'm having trouble hearing you. Can we talk some other time?" I say.

"Yeah, when we go out, or if we start dating, I have to walk."

"Okay. I will keep that in mind. It was nice talking to you Craig. Good-bye."

"Good-bye."

Oh, my God. This is pure torture. Sometimes I think the gods are messing with me for pure amusement. I just want to cry uncle so they will leave me alone. I never talk to Craig again.

Late Night and Warm Milk

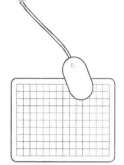

*A*s the months go on, I find myself growing restless. I often sleep with the television on, and I awake in the middle of the night to various shows. One night, I wake to *Cheaters*.

Seriously?

On *Cheaters*, a person believes his or her partner is cheating, so detectives follow the supposed cheater around. When the camera crew has gathered enough evidence, the host makes sure there is a confrontation. It doesn't matter if it's in a restaurant, a hotel room, or a bar, as long as it's public. A fight always ensues. Chaos erupts. Lights and cameras flash. Usually the "mistress," or "boy toy" has no idea what's going on. However, at the end of some of these shows, some of the couples reunite and are smiling and holding hands and vowing to work things out. Hmmmm…

Lo and behold, a website for *Cheaters* exists, and you can put your personal ad up; I just don't know if I can utter the words, "We met each other on the *Cheaters* website." I decide not to put a profile up; I'm tempted though. What do I have to lose? Then I decide, oh so much.

I can just imagine myself confronting a lover who has wronged me. He would look me in the eye and say, "What did you expect? Look how we met."

After waking up many a night to screams from the victims on the show, I change the channel to *I Love Lucy* and fall back asleep. I wake the next night to the MTV show, *Next*. When a person has to degrade themselves on national TV to get a date, you know we have hit the bowels of society. After watching a man dressed as a giant baby crawling around on the floor to get a kiss, I change the channel again. I think I have a nightmare about that when I fall back asleep.

The next time I awake in the middle of the night it's to "Jessie," a beautiful, seductive blonde who is preparing to go on a date with her telephone. What? My hand gropes in the darkness for my glasses, so I can see what Jessie is up to. Jessie is about to call a dating hotline service and meet the man of her dreams.

Dazzling us with her smile, she picks up the phone, looks right at the camera, and says in a very low husky voice, "I'm dialing, are you?"

For $3.99 a minute, I'm not about to find out if her male counterpart looks just as good as her.

It's time to actively continue my quest. Each day is supposed to bring me closer to him…but each day I feel like I'm moving farther and farther away.

I restlessly fall asleep one night in September, and I wake up in October.

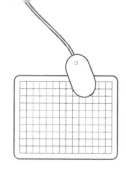

The 40ish-Year-Old Virgin

*M*ike and I connect immediately when we first start talking on the phone. The first time we talk, it's very brief. We talk a little bit about our jobs and what we like to do for fun. I can tell that he is shy. I'm also trying to keep it brief instead of talking non-stop for hours on end. I don't want to open up about everything during our first conversation. "Can I call you during the week?" I tell him yes, and a few days later he calls me.

Our second conversation is much longer and more informative.

I think he and I are beginning to feel comfortable talking to each other. While talking on the phone that night, I ask him, "What is the one thing you wouldn't want me to know about you until the 'honeymoon' period of the relationship is over?" I don't think that is too personal.

Besides, nothing can floor me after meeting the men I have met.

He coughs, "Well, I do have one thing I want you to know about me before our first date."

I brace myself. Sweat begins to roll down my face. My cat jumps off of my lap because I squeeze her so hard. She gives me a dirty look and storms off.

He continues, "I have been in a few relationships; however, I'm a virgin."

"Really, I didn't know any of those still existed." I say trying to lighten the mood. Is that all? I was waiting for him to tell me he has just been released from prison for killing his ex-girlfriend. We talk a little bit more about that, and I don't really think anything of it at this time.

We set a time and a place to meet, and I'm actually looking forward to it.

When I meet Mike, I study him more intently than I have other men I have gone out with. Why is he still a virgin? Is he gay? Has he just not found the right one? How far has he gotten with a woman? These are the politically incorrect questions I have for him. He is a nice man. He has this innocence about him. He is older than me, but he still has that "wide-eyed little boy" look.

Everything he does fascinates me. I become obsessed to find out why he's still a virgin. He says he can't explain it; he just hasn't found the one he wants to give himself to. That just sounds too simple to me.

After seeing a movie, we decide to get dinner. It's there where I uncover one of the reasons why he is still a virgin. Toward the end of dinner, Mike starts licking his fingers. I'm not talking about just putting one finger in his mouth because he drops some sauce on it and doesn't have a napkin handy. He puts one finger at a time in his mouth and sucks on them. He begins making this horrid smacking sound that goes with it. SLURRRRPPPP, SLURRRPPPP, smack…smack…smack… I shudder still as I write this.

"Is it bad that I do that?" he asks.

"Oh…no," I say. Come on, what else was I going to say? "Yes, and that is why you are a virgin"? I shrug it off. If we get closer and this progresses, that will be one habit that he has to change.

After dinner, he walks me to my car and says, "Do you want to do this again?"

Finally, a man who doesn't screw around. Literally! I like when a man takes the initiative right then and there and asks me out again.

On our next date, we go for a hike at Rancho San Antonio. It's a perfect autumn day. The leaves are beginning to fall, and the grass is turning from a rich green to a warm wheat color. We laugh and joke around, huffing and puffing up the steep inclines. About halfway through the hike, he takes my hand.

Afterwards, we grab a bite to eat at In-N-Out Burger. He is a really funny guy. His wit matches mine. We banter back and forth and see who can have the quickest comebacks. Apart from his sucking on his fingers, I still can't figure out why he's still a virgin. He seems to be very comfortable around the opposite sex, and he is not inhibited by public displays of affection.

This is becoming an obsession with me, I think because I'm a very curious person by nature, and I love to study people. But, when I get something stuck in my head, I can't let it go. This is one trait that isn't necessarily a good thing.

"So, do you want to come over and cook dinner with me on Friday night?" Mike asks. "Hello? Are you listening to me?"

Coming out of my trance, I say, "Yes, that would be great."

I'm starting to get a little nervous. What if I'm the one to de-virginize Mike? That is a lot of pressure. I'm not saying that this is going to happen on the third date, but if the third date leads to another, and another, well eventually something is going to happen, right? What if I traumatize him so much that he vows to be celibate his whole life? What if I don't train him properly? Hell, do I even have the ability to train someone? I could do some serious damage to this poor man.

Yet, there is another part of me that is starting to feel invincible. Now that the first and second dates are over, I can even start to let my guard down a little. I am really trying to have fun while doing this, but sometimes this just takes a toll on my psyche. In every stage of a relationship there's the "honeymoon" period. However, over time, signs of our true selves begin to peek through. I even start to get a little cocky.

Then reality sets in, and more often than not, I'm knocked on my ass again.

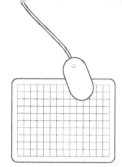

Crunch, Snap, Frump

*C*arrying a box of strawberry shortcake, I ring the doorbell, and Mike opens the door, pulls me into his arms, and kisses me.

"Hey. You found me. I'm really glad to see you."

Smiling, "Well, it's good to be here. Thank you so much for..." I stop in mid-sentence because I just stepped in to the biggest hell-hole you can ever imagine. There are clothes everywhere. The floor is sticky and two pizza boxes lie on top of the garbage, which probably hasn't been taken out since the Reagan years. The dust on the coffee table is so thick I could easily write my book on it. A strange odor lingers in the air. I just stand there, a little shell shocked, with a smile frozen on my face.

"Sorry the place is such a mess," Mike says. "My roommate is a complete slob. I thought I would have time to clean up, but the day got away from me."

I kick an empty beer can out of the way, and it goes flying into the popcorn bag that is lying on the floor as I make a path to the kitchen. Every step I take, I hear crunch, snap, frump. Okay, I didn't really hear frump, but I needed another sound!

Trying to hide my utter horror, I say, "Is it safe to eat in here?"

He laughs hysterically. "Of course." He pulls me into his arms. "I will make sure we get a maid." He kisses me lightly on the mouth.

Okay, I have to admit that's a great line. He scores points with that one. I begrudgingly look beyond the mess around me, for the moment.

We cook dinner, and I use the same path I created to the kitchen to make my way back to the couch. We eat our dinner and watch a movie. There isn't a lot of interaction between us. We just sit and watch the movie.

As the credits roll, we begin to clean up our mess (which is kind of ironic when you think about it). He excuses himself and retreats to his bedroom. After I put the dishes in the sink, I make my way back to the couch. When Mike comes back, he is chewing a piece of gum. A slight scent of spearmint hangs in the air. He pulls me into his arms, and we begin to watch the news.

During the news, he begins to kiss me. The kissing is really nice at first, until I open my eyes. While kissing me, Mike is watching TV. He is kissing me, but his eyes are open, and he is completely focused on the news clip about dogs who like to swim. The news—I'm losing out to the ten o'clock news?

I pull away and look at him.

"What? I always watch the ten o'clock news," he says.

My mind begins to flashback to all of the images of our dates—the finger licking, the dirty clothes, the fact that he is a virgin, and the overall state of his apartment are just too much. I have reached my limit.

I stand up and say, "I think I better get going. It's late." I'm afraid to ask the next question, but I really have to. "Could I use your bathroom before I go?"

He smiles, "Sure. I actually did clean that up. But the toilet doesn't flush unless you lift the lid and jiggle the wire inside."

This is ridiculous. I look at him and smile, "I think I'll wait until I get home. Thanks again for dinner."

I give him a quick hug and bolt out the door. As I walk to my car, I wonder how long it will take for Mike to meet a woman he can be with whole-heartedly. I wish them both well.

Got Bones?

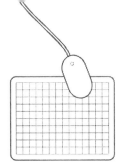

*A*round October 15th, I start talking to Ken. Ken is a bonehead. No wait, he is just really into "bones". I think that is a Freudian slip.

To: Kenpickingupbones@Kenpickingupbones.com
From: Dianne@dontdoitatall.com
Dear Ken:
    I liked your profile. Now, I have been ice skating before, and it was a complete disaster. I knew I was doing something wrong when my friend told me, "You are supposed to be in an upright position." Anyway, how do you like your personal trainer? I have a love/hate relationship with mine. Do you play tennis?
Dianne

Ken responds a couple of hours later. He says that he likes his trainer, and he loves to play hockey. He also says something that causes my brow to furrow for a moment, "I've never played tennis. I've always thought of it as a thin person's sport. It turns out that hockey is, too, but I didn't know that when I started."

Later, he writes me that his online dating experiences have been mostly disappointing and occasionally humiliating.

```
To: Dianne@dontdoitatall.com
From: Kenpickingupbones@Kenpickingupbones.
com
Subject: Food in the Box
        I haven't had any of the usual bad
experiences that you hear about. It's
also a bit confusing. For weeks no one
replied to or contacted me. Then, in one
week, four or five women got in touch.
Did you all get together and plan that?
Was it 'Throw Ken a Bone Week?' Has that
ever happened to you? One last thing,
I don't cook. The good people at Weight
Watchers and Lean Cuisine cook my dinner
for me. I'm not fat. I just don't eat
food that doesn't come from a box.
Ken
```

I'm not sure what he means by that, "…doesn't come from a box." Do cows come in a box? What about fruit? Do cans count? Is a fresh salad out of the question?

Ken and I decide to talk on the phone. I like to think I can weed out a lot of strange people that way, but as you have read, I'm not having too much luck with that screening process. Some phone calls can be pure torture.

Ken and I play phone tag a couple of times. I email him and try to nail down a specific time to chit-chat. He tells me that he's going to the gym later that night, but his phone will be by his side. So I can call him then. Wait! What? He can run on a treadmill, do a bicep curl with one arm, and talk to me with the other? Didn't Cameron Diaz do something like that in *Charlie's Angels?*

I'm not really looking forward to talking to Ken anymore. His emails are pleasant, and his candor is refreshing. However, it shouldn't take this much work to try and set up a phone conversation with someone. If it does, then that should immediately send up red flags.

I also should not pursue someone who is constantly, "picking up bones"—a phrase Ken uses to refer to women he communicates with or just women in general. A phrase I will come to loathe. After many emails and missed calls, we finally connect. Our phone tag game has ended. I'm it.

"Hey, Deanne, it's Ken."

"Hi Ken. It's Dianne, actually."

"Oh, my bad."

"How long have you been doing online dating?" I ask.

"A little while. It has been a busy week. There are bones everywhere."

"Hmmmm," I say.

"Anyway, today was a great day. I got my bonus that I told you about. I'm using part of it to bring my mom out here."

Racking my brain, I don't recall him ever mentioning a bonus. However, I go with it. "Yeah, that's great."

"Yeah, I can't leave her alone in Pennsylvania. Isn't it weird that we both grew up in Pennsylvania?"

Okay, now I have known myself all my life, and I know I didn't grow up in Pennsylvania. So I say, "Ummm, no, that isn't me. It must be some other woman you are talking to."

"Oh yeah. You're right. Remember, this has been a big bone week."

At this point, I'm not sure what to think. I mean most of us pretend like we aren't talking to anyone else, but who are we kidding? I think, more than anything, it's his constant reference to bones that is irritating. At the end of our conversation, he doesn't suggest we meet, and I'm not about to do it. I have chased enough men in my life. If he is into me, then he will set something up. However, I think I will have to decline. We say good-bye. No more tag—he is not it.

Later that week, Ken emails me and asks me out for coffee. He tells me I'm now the front runner. He has tossed all the other bones back. I respond with a polite thanks, but no thanks.

Got Boobs?

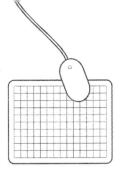

Dan doesn't mention anything about bones when I start talking to him. Thank God! However, I do learn that he is a "boob" man, or he is just a boob.

There is a "secret" test that men use on women. It's one of the many lessons that they learn in *A Bronx Tale*, a coming of age movie for most men. I call it the door test. In talking to many men about dating and being in relationships, they all seem either to have used this test or know of it. I have never heard of this, but when I asked a few different men about it, they all seem to know it.

The Test

"*I've been doing this one since I stole my first car back when I was 14. The 'door' test basically boils down to this: When you take a girl out for the first time, lock the door on your side of the car, open her door first, walk around the back, and see if she unlocks the door for you. If she does, she's a keeper. If she doesn't, she's [selfish] and*

*you should consider yourself lucky to have recognized
that early on." Mario-A Bronx Tale*

Women have many tests, too. One of the tests that
we often use to see if a man is into us is the "movie" test.
When a man and a woman first meet, or when they are just
getting to know each other, a night at the movies is always
a safe bet. While watching the movie, if a woman feels a
connection with a man, and wants to know if he feels a
connection with her, she will often lean toward her date and
press part of her arm against his. If his arm stays there, it's
often an indication that he is interested in her. If he moves
away, doubt creeps in.

Dan fails my test miserably, which really means I'm
the one who receives the F.

Dan and I decide to see *Resurrecting the Champ*. A
mistake on my part from the beginning; I can tell that Dan
doesn't want to see this movie. He actually looks annoyed
that we are sitting there watching it. On the screen, the "Joe
Cat," the mascot for the theater, is dancing around. I'm not
sure why the company chose a cat, but they bring in billions
of dollars in revenue, so they must be doing something right.
"Joe Cat," dressed in a tux, is twirling around another cat in
an evening gown that has a very low neckline. She has the
biggest knockers I have ever seen on a cat, or a woman for
that matter. I joke, "Wow, that cat has the biggest boobs I
have ever seen."

Dan leans over and says, "Jealous?"

Whoa, hold the phone. Did he seriously just say
that to me? I'm not jealous of the cat with huge knockers,

and I'm taken aback by that question. I don't think I need to get implants to make myself more enhanced. I struggle every day with trying to keep weight off. Why the heck would I spend thousands of dollars to make any part of my body look bigger? However, a few minutes later I realize that it's something that Dan admires in a woman. I cannot fault Dan for this—isn't there a multi-million dollar business in breast implants? I can, however, fault him for his poor manners.

Watching the previews for the movie, Dan sighs in his chair. I lean over to make another joke, "Okay, before this begins, I'm sorry." The previews are for chick flicks.

Dan leans into me and says, "You can always tell what the upcoming movie is going to be about because of the previews. There are no guns or battle scenes or women with big boobs in these previews." To make sure that I understand his fascination with big boobs, he holds his hands in front of his chest, simulating them. Yeah, I get it: You want big boobs. Please note that "must have big boobs" does not appear once in his profile. Trying to lighten the mood, I ask if he would like some gummy worms. He looks at me and says, "No thanks, I'm not twelve."

It's my turn to sigh now. You are probably wondering why I even do the test on Dan. Call it a social experiment. I'm bored. I'm not into him, but I begin to think of ways to entertain myself. I start to become annoyed with all of these men. Can't they see I'm a good catch?

I try the test on Dan two times, and each time he moves his arm away from mine. I'm actually worried that he is going to move one seat over, so I will stop crowding him.

Once I realize he is crouched into his corner of the seat, I move away from the center arm rest, so he can at least sit in a more upright position. I'm not sure at this point why I continue to push the envelope. I think I want to see what will happen if I do. I admit it; I'm playing games. I also want to see if he has a pulse.

Every date must come to an end, but we all know how awkward the last few minutes of a first date can be if there is no chemistry. Dan walks me to my car, and we continue to make small talk. He actually uses the last remaining minutes we have together to tell me how much he hated the movie. "That was so stupid. Worst movie I have ever seen. I should get my money back."

I just look at him and nod my head in agreement. When we arrive at my car, we just stand there looking at each other. "Well, this was fun," I say. *Liar.*

"Yeah, it was." *Liar, liar.*

All of a sudden, he leans in and pats me on the back. Yes, that's right; he pats me on the back as if I'm his crazy aunt who makes him hug her at every family gathering. So what can I do? I pat him on the back, too. There we are patting each other, or possibly consoling each other on another lousy date. I pull back and thank him again. I get into my car, and he walks to his.

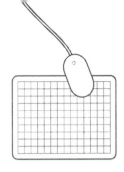

Who Says Men and Women Can't Be Friends?

*A*fter many of my dates, I talk to my friend, Tim. He helps me put the date into perspective before I begin to write about it. On the way home, I dial Tim's number, and in his usual fashion, he answers with, "Talk to me."

I begin to tell him about the date and my test.

"Okay, well maybe he was just getting comfortable," Tim says with a laugh.

"Two times?" I ask.

He laughs again, "Okay, well, I don't know what to tell ya. But you do know it's only 7:32 on a Saturday night don't you?"

I look at the clock and sigh. It's only 7:32, and I'm headed home.

I think about Ken out there digging up bones, James eating at a Subway, and John SCUBA diving, and wonder what the man of my dreams is doing right now.

Match Made in Heaven?

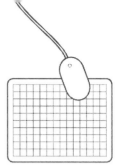

*T*here is one website that drives me crazy. As soon as my membership ends, I will not be renewing it. For me, this experiment is beginning to feel like a race against the clock. However, I think I'm racing for all the wrong reasons. Often times, I race home to check my emails. I race to make sure that I close initial contact first. I race to make sure I send the Dear John letter first. I need to slow down. I think I rush because I would rather be the first person to pull away, than be pushed away. I feel like I'm in control that way. But really it's just to protect myself from getting hurt. It drives me crazy when I receive the following message, "This person has decided to stop communicating with you," or in other words, "Thanks, but no thanks."

What the heck does that mean? It doesn't matter though. Half of the time I can't get past the first round of questions. If we are compatible on all of these different levels, and the only thing we have to go on is our pictures, does that mean we are judging each other by the picture and not on whether we match spiritually or emotionally? Is that why there are so many divorces today? Are we a society that is so hung up on looks that we ignore the potential for an everlasting love that will remain when our looks have faded? As many of us know, there are a series of questions that we must answer before exchanging emails.

Johnny is the first person with whom I begin emailing, but there are a few things that don't add up in his profile, or in his pictures. He has three completely different photos. When we begin talking, I ask him which picture is the most recent, and I ask him to clarify a couple of things he has written in his profile.

```
To:  Dianne@dontdoitatall.com
From: JohnnybeGood@JohnnybeGood.com
Subject:  Hey Dianne
Hi Dianne,
    How are you?  The most recent picture
isn't actually on the website.  I have
attached it.  The climbing pics were
taken about 5 years ago.  The graduation
pic is the oldest about 10 years. If you
would like to learn more about me, don't
hesitate to ask.  Take care and God Bless.
God works in mysterious ways, and he holds
the key to the Kingdom.
P.S.  As for my profile, I didn't write it.
My friend did.
Johnny
```

The picture he attached is completely different from the others. The most "recent" picture is of a man who looks like he is 5'8", maybe 5'9" on a good day, with a 44" waist—not that that is a deal breaker for me–wearing a thick, gold chain with a huge cross on it. Frustrated, I re-read his email. I'm more spiritual than religious, but some of my good friends are very religious (they don't, however, impose their religion on others). I'm annoyed by the way he closed his email. I can't explain it. I ask Tim, and his wife, Andrea, if I'm being too critical. Andrea, who never holds back when she has an opinion, a trait I regard highly, says, "I don't think you are; you did put that you were more spiritual than religious. But that doesn't really matter. He still doesn't know your religious beliefs, and for some people it's a very important part of their life. How does he know that you are not an atheist, or that you weren't raised Jewish?"

With that, I write Johnny a quick email and tell him that it's awesome that religion plays an important role in his life, but I just don't think we're that compatible.

Within two minutes, I receive the following message:

```
To:  Dianne@dontdoitatall.com
From: JohnnybeGood@JohnnybeGood.com
Subject:  Hey Dianne
Dianne
    I will pray for your soul.
Johnny
```

I'm seething, but I check myself and don't respond. Oh, how I want to though! My restraint ought to score me a few points with the big guy upstairs, right?

Frogs in Cyberspace

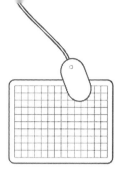

 am sends me these questions to answer.

1. If you were to stay home for the evening what would you tend to do?

A. This one is funny. I would play on my computer, write, and watch TV all at the same time…or if I was with that special someone, hopefully, none of the above.

2. What marriage issues do you fear the most?

A. I have a fear of someone trying to chain me down or turning me into someone I'm not.

3. On a Friday night, what would you like to do?

A. Grab a bite to eat at a hole in the wall, go to the movies, or over to Santa Cruz.

4. If you went out to eat with a friend, which of the following would you prefer Mexican, Italian, Chinese, or Thai?

A. It depends on what mood I'm in. Can I go out with four different friends, four different nights and choose a different one each night?

After reading my answers, Sam stops emailing me. I send the following email to Art.

```
To: Art58585858@Art58585858.com
From: Dianne@dontdoitatall.com
Subject:  Your Profile
Hello
    You emailed me recently, but I realized
that I hadn't responded to you. I attached
my photo, so you would remember which
one I am in the sea of faces. How are you
doing? I look forward to talking to you.
Dianne
```

I never hear back from Art.

Now, it's my turn to ask Eric questions.

1. Where have you traveled to, and where do you want to go?

A. I like to travel, but haven't been to very many places. I really want to go to Eurpoe and Australia. I have been to Phoenix, Wyoming, and Idaho. Nothing spectacular. ☹

2. How long ago was your last long-term committed relationship, and what did you learn from it?

A. 6 year relationship that ended almost 2 years ago. I have had others since, but none as that serious. We lived together for 5 of those years. No kids - 2 English bulldogs that she kept - i miss on of them dearly :(lot of reasons it ended - was for the best; she moved to Phoenix and is living with a guy now; she calls about every 3 months to let me know how the dog is doing. Money was part of the problem. She started spending more and working less; that forced me to work more hours to makeup for the difference - then she would get mad that i was working so many hours. she had lots of self image issues and gained lots of weight and had gastric bypass surgery then didn't lose as much weight as she thought she should and got more depressed. Long story—I have no problem explaining, but running out of typing space

3. Are you emotionally available? Do you have clean socks? ;)

A. Let me check..... yes, clean socks are on - only have 3 pair - JK emotionally available?

Yes, I'm not hung up on any past relationships, nor they on me. I'm looking for that special person, but don't feel rushed to do so.

For some reason Eric and I stop communicating. It's almost like we are zombies, just going through the motions without putting any thought or feeling into our answers. Neither of us email each other again. I wonder what ever happened to him.

I love when I get mail from dating websites that tell me that somebody's got his eye on me. In a way, it's a little creepy. I know it's supposed to be flattering, but it reminds me of the popular 80s song *Every Breath You Take*. When that song debuted it was number one for quite a few weeks. Everybody loved it. But have you ever really listened to the lyrics? "Every move you make, every breath you take, every smile you fake, I'll be watching you." I don't know if I want someone to be that infatuated with me. But, for right now, a fan is a fan. The following two men have had their eye on me for quite a long time.

Man Seeking Woman

41

Champaign, Illinois

So that's my problem, I'm in the wrong state. Thank God, I have another stalker.

Man Seeking Woman

38

Odessa, Ukraine

Or in the wrong country.

Later that week, I get an email from Jay... or is it Jy?

```
To: Dianne@dontdoitatall.com
From: Jay123456789@Jay123456789.com
Subject: You and I
Hi Dine,
      I don't match what you're looking for,
not exactly. I'm 5'8", and that's with shoes
on. More like 5'7". And, my two daughters
```

live with me full time, ages 13 and 10.
But, you know what? I speak the truth,
and I'm not mean about it. And, I'm always
getting in trouble. Or, at least, on the
verge of gettin in trouble. Even though
I'm a peaceful and docile character (I
have to be to raise these girls right),
inside, in the creative mind category
where I'm highly Influenced by my heart
and desires, I'm a wild and crazy guy.
Like no other. Hard to handle, but in a
fun way...if you know what I mean?
JayManiac

Maybe my reply should say…

To: Jay123456789@Jay123456789.com
From: Dianne@dontdoitatall.com
Subject: uz and i
Dear Jy
    I is wikd too. Crazy u betcha
lets live a longgggggggggg and hapy lif
together, or Yo Yo ….I thinks wez mke
a grate coupe. U wana hang ut wid me
somtim? Tht be awesome. Cal me. K?
Dine

I try to find someone named Dine to forward this to,
but I have no luck.

The next person is just as charming as the last one.
However, his email has got to be the longest sentence I have
ever read outside of a Faulkner novel.

To: Dianne@dontdoitatall.com
From: Lovewalking@Lovewalking.com
Subject: Hey Dianea
i enjoy all walks of life from motorcycle
racing to going to the lake and fishing
or going camping with friends i consider
myself a spontanous person who is up
for just about anything my friends would
describe me as their personal comedian
I'm easy going how ever i dont like games
I HAVE LEARNED A FEW OTHER THINGS LATELY
I'm finding out I'm looking for someone who
enjoys spending Time together on a regular
bases cause thats the only way you truely
get to know someone communication is a
must cant hide inside so if you want to
know more drop me a line.

Okay, fair is fair. I make mistakes, too.

To: Dianne@dontdoitatall.com
From: Lucas23232323@Lucas23232323.com
Subject: Your Mistakes
    Hi. Neat profile. Interesting, you're
behind something in every photo except
two. Was that intentional, or is it a
metaphor for the small wall you put
up when you meet people? :)..btw (and
apologies for being forward, but I usually
appreciate it when my friends point it out
for me), you have a typo in your
description. In particular: compliment
should be complement.

```
Cheers
-Lucas
```

Thanks, Lucas, my editor or I should have caught that one. I can just imagine us on a date together. That was great, but next time you need to...

```
To: Dianne@dontdoitatall.com
From: Bucky3333@Bucky3333.com
Subject:
Dear Diane
        Let's see what can I say. I could
tell you about me or better yet, have my
friends say a little bit about me: ...a
good man, romantic, appreciates a woman
and wants to find that special one... You
know the "one" that makes your heart skip
a beat, the one that when I smell her
fragrance I get lost for a moment. ...treat
you better than you've ever been treated...
You know the way you've always wanted to
be, but maybe just didn't believe it
could happen to you. For whatever reason
that may be... I appreciate you taking the
time to respond to my profile.  I make
it a point to respond back.  It's just
curterous.
Bucky
```

Finally, a guy who takes a couple of minutes to respond...I email him, but never get a reply back. Wait, he never actually says it's just "courteous". He says it's just "curterous". Maybe that's Latin for "it's just not going to happen."

Every week without fail, the dating websites send me my top results for the week. Usually there is a "top pick" of the week. I think it's nice that they are looking after me so carefully.

This man is my top pick for the week: "Are you more than just a pretty face? I'm a romantic, good natured guy with a good sense of humor. I could list a bunch of attributes like a lot of men do on this site."

Had this been a stranger, I probably would have sent him an email, but I've learned my lesson and delete this email. This is the second dating website that has tried to tell me Nick is my number one match. However, I'm not going to fall for that again. I block his ad, so he won't show up again.

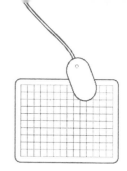

Mr. Right Now U Have 2 Leave

ater on in the week, I receive an email from Mr. Racer. Mr. Racer asks me to look him up on instant messenger, so I do. I soon regret it.

> Racer: So how are you today?
>
> Me: I'm great, and you? How has your experience with online dating been?
>
> Racer: good and bad.
>
> Me: That sounds equitable. Do you like living in Tracy?
>
> Racer: Yea close to everything. BTW- I'm open and easy going. You can ask me anything. Even personal questions....Wink....Wink...

Oh, please.

Me: Hmmm, why aren't you in a relationship... and what are you looking for....

Racer: It doesn't matter, you can ask what ever you are prepared to have answered. I was engaged for 4 years.

Me: Wow, that is way too long...lol

Racer: Yea.

Me: I would have kicked your ass to the curb long ago...lol...if you made me wait that long.

Racer: First I'm looking for a friend to hang out and do things. If things go well it could lead to more.

Me: What is your ideal woman?

Racer: Is there such a thing?

Me: I would hope for you, yes ☺.

Racer: First has to be easy going, smart, active. Open to new things and ideas.

Me: Like what? New things? Do tell?

Racer: Affectionate. Don't have a specific example. Just like an open mind. I tend to think way, way outside the box. In everything that happens when in a relationship.

Wink...Wink...

Me: How old are you?

Racer: 36. It's ok to be a bad girl.

Sigh!

Me: When was the last time you were intimate with someone?

Racer: Last week. And you?

Me: Hmmm, now if I say last century that is going to make me look bad. Was it a one night stand or are you seeing her on a regular basis?

Racer: A friend, not really a regular basis. Friends with sex....

Me: Ahhh....

Racer: More friend with a side of sex. Went out a few times but just wasn't a real click. But ended up being friends.

Me: Well, something must have clicked.

Racer: Well the sex was good but not enough for a relationship. I think I made it good.

Someone kill me; kill me now.

> Racer: Hard to explain.
>
> Me: So, what do you find attractive in a woman...
>
> Racer: The way she moves, her confidence. Love a sexy woman but not to be confused with the public's idea of sexy. Like a woman that can keep me on my toes. Smart enough to keep up with me. Everything's relative. I need sex to live.

Oh man, if that were true for me, I would have been dead long ago.

> Racer: How about coffee sometime?
>
> Me: Maybe...however, I do like to do the "phone thing" it weeds out a lot of people.

We never do get that cup of coffee.

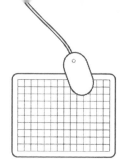

This Can't Be My Destiny

*E*ven with my current dating rut, I can always depend on the Internet to look out for me.

Clicking through my spam today, I realize that I have been on the wrong dating websites this whole time. Well, now I know the next website to try: *"Search and date 1000's of NAUGHTY girls and guys who are ready and willing to go on a date with you. All singles are lonely and tired of the clubbing scene and want a date tonite!"*

Ugh, I think I need to take a break from all of this and go play some online games. However, the world of Internet dating isn't going to let me off the hook that easily.

While I'm playing an interactive slot machine game, one of my online girlfriends asks me how my dating adventures are coming along. I tell her it's great, but I've been in a real dating rut lately, and just can't shake myself out of it. Well, this comment gives way to every single man or married man playing the room tonight. All of a sudden,

I'm bombarded by instant messages. One man in particular IMs me and says, "One date with me, and your rut would be over." You know that line is too good to pass up. I just have to follow my gut instinct and write back.

Me: So how do you meet women? Do you stalk them on various gaming sites?

LRH2MSP: What do you mean stalk? I usually bowl them over with my good looks. How long have you been on the dating websites?

Me: A few months. Went out with about 5 or 6 men.

LRH2MSP: That is not bad, anyone all that great? Any fun? We could have some fun.

Me: What in cyberspace? I mean come on what is going to materialize in cyberspace? Oh wait, are you talking cybersex? Do people still do that?

LRH2MSP: I didn't mean cybersex...just explore your inner fantasies with me...

Me: What I'm supposed to type them out? How romantic...

LRH2MSP: Well, I'm just a phone call away.

Me: Oh, you are talking phone sex....I'm dense...do people still do that, too?

> **LRH2MSP:** Wink wink....It would be worth your while.. I have a great voice. I want us to do a little more than play bingo—what is it you are up for?

Do you see what I do for material for this book?

> **Me:** I don't know....I mean I guess I should be honored that you chose me out of all the people in the game room...but...
>
> **LRH2MSP:** We could talk, chat, q and a...that is always fun. What are you wearing?
>
> Playing teasing...exciting, and what are you up for?.... Where do you draw the line?..If you don't like to type, how do you like to do it?... wink wink..... I could tell you exactly how I like it, baby.
>
> **Me:** You don't even know what I look like, I could be a man pretending to be a woman; I could be a 90-year-old woman.
>
> **LRH2MSP:** In my mind, you are hot and are wearing three inch heels.

You know, I don't actually own a pair of those. I do have a great pair of boots though.

Well, what can I say? In my mind, he is a lonely, lonely man. I gently tell him that it will be a cold day in hell before I succumb to cybersex. I mean, if I'm not in an intimate relationship, my computer certainly isn't going to be in one. As I'm leaving the game room, he begins chatting up

Kittylovr345. I wish them all the happiness in the world… or cyberspace.

Chucky?

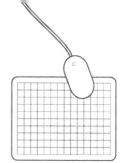

A few years ago, I would have never given men I met online my phone number. I wanted to be in control of the situation. However, I realize now that that isn't necessarily the right thing do to. I don't want to be responsible for making the first move anymore. I want them to pursue me. So, this time around, I have been giving men my phone number. I mean, if the guy is a psychotic mass murderer, he can't kill me over the phone lines. Right? I have given my number to a couple of men with whom I have been chatting, but I haven't heard from them. Oh well. Their loss, right? Anyway, I figure, if they want to call, they will call.

My telephone rings in the dark night. I jump up and start groping around for it. What time is it? I reach for my glasses but, as usual, I have already knocked them off the bed. I fumble for my cell phone and knock over a glass of water. I grab my cell phone and realize that it's 12:45 a.m. For a moment, I panic because I think maybe someone I care about has been hurt or in an accident.

"Hello?"

"Is this Dianne?" a voice says, rather suave.

"Yes, it is."

"How the hell are ya? This is Shucky."

"Chucky?" I say, confused. I remembered emailing my number to a Steve, but who was this person calling?

"No, Shucky. Shhh…Shhh…My friends call me that because I shuck and jive. My real name is Steve."

"Ah, okay. I'm fine. How are you?" I say still a little groggy.

"Just getting back from the bar scene. You party?" he asks.

"Ah, you still go to the bars, eh?" I say, already knowing that Chucky…oh wait, Shucky….well…forget it…I'm at a loss for what to write. Just read the rest of the conversation, and you will feel my pain.

"Yeah, I like to stay out and party all night."

"How old are you again?"

"Well, here is the thing. I took this test that tells you what your real age is according to how you treat your body."

"Uh huh."

"And my age is 39.6."

"Hmmm, so what age are you according to the calendar?"

"I'm 48. But really age is just a number. I'm going to another bar. Do you want to meet me for a drink?"

Just as he says that, one of our cell phones drops the call. Did I accidently hang up? Only my cell phone and I know the truth. Neither one of us bother to ring back.

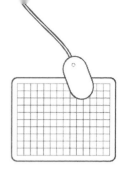

Ghosts, Goblins, and Witches- Oh My!

*A*s I'm driving to work early one morning, a full moon peers portentously over the mountain tops. The fall season is upon us. This is my favorite time of year. Halloween is one of the best holidays. Children, teens, and adults all over the United States get to take a break from their day-to-day routine and their structured lives to transform into a Power Ranger, a witch, a French maid, Jason or Michael from their favorite horror films. It's a night of make-believe. It's a night of fantasy. It's the one night of the year where we don't have to worry about who we are—we only have to focus on the person we have created in our minds and for the outside world to see.

We can escape.

Later that night, the children laugh as they run through the streets, seeking candy. Men and women attend parties and mingle. A ballerina twirls down the street, a clown laughs, and Freddy Krueger slides his razorblade fingers up and down the back of his girlfriend, who is dressed as a sexy cheerleader. The moon illuminates the night and closes October with the sound of witches cackling in the distance.

I think that Halloween is an apt metaphor for Internet dating. Masked suitors come calling—looking for treats—and often pull tricks.

Adam

I'm surrounded by the most amazing men and women in my life. Long ago, I don't think I had a lot of respect for myself, so I would just cling on to anyone who gave me the time of day. Now, I realize that I only want to be around people who value me and respect me. One of those people is my friend, Adam. He is an important man in my life.

During dinner tonight, Adam makes me realize something about myself, and from that moment on, I have kept his words of wisdom near and dear.

"I have got to break this one date curse I'm on," I say to him as I'm diving into my gelato.

"Sweens, you know you are a good person right? I hope you aren't defining yourself by the relationships you are in or not in."

I think about that for a moment. "I don't think I am."

"Okay, I just want to make sure that you surround yourself with people who value you and want good things for you. Take Nick, for example. You give that guy a lot of credit for someone who you just spent a couple of nights together with, but what's he done since then?"

I just look at Adam.

"Sure you trusted him enough to be with him, but men will take from you whatever you give them. If they think they can get away with it, they will take even more and not even give you a second thought. Trust me, I'm a man."

As if a light suddenly goes on, I am stunned. I have reverted to the little girl waiting to be shown how to ride a bike. Afraid to surrender her training wheels.

I look at Adam and say, "No, you're right. I do give Nick too much credit. The real Nick is not very nice or respectful. I wanted so badly to believe he was my knight in shining armor that I created an image of him that never existed.

Now I just worry because if I don't know what love is, and everything I thought it was never existed, then what is love? How will I know when I find it? What does it mean to be "head over heels," in love? Is it possible to go through your whole life and never find that one person that you truly can't live without? Do we hold onto what we find because we think that there may never be another? Why do we just settle? Are we that afraid of being alone? Is it really that bad to say *I'm single.*

Adam responds, "There are a lot of broken people out there. There are a lot of people who settle and end up more miserable than you can possibly imagine. But you don't have to be one of them. You need to make sure you value yourself and surround yourself with people who love you and respect you; if they don't then they are not worth your time. Who cares if you are single? Write, vacation, live your life. If you meet someone, great, if you don't, it doesn't mean there is anything wrong with you. Just don't settle for anything less than what you are worth."

"I totally hear what you are saying." I really do, too.

"The last thing I will say before I get off my soapbox," he says with a smile. "Are you getting anything out of the relationships you are in with these various people? If not, then are they worth the time and emotional energy you spend on them? You know the answers to all of these questions I'm asking you. You just need to listen to yourself."

"This is all very depressing. Do they have gummy worms for my gelato?" I say half-jokingly.

Seriously though, I pass these words on to all of you—except the bit about the gummy worms—in the hopes that you fall in love with yourself first, and only then give yourself to someone who loves you just as much as you love yourself. How many of us have ever dated ourselves first?

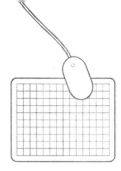

Houston, We Have a Problem

*E*very astronaut must eventually return to earth. I think it's time to leave cyberspace and venture out into the real world. During the month of November, I'm going to "hang out" and "prowl" at coffee shops, book stores, and street corners. Well, maybe not street corners. I'm also going to spend time being in a relationship with myself. I'm even going to take one of my profiles down.

Stop! I Want off This Roller Coaster

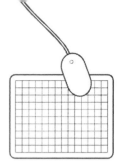

*U*nfortunately, trying to cancel a membership to one particular site is difficult. I have not enjoyed myself there, and I'm not enjoying my attempts to sign off. I'm at the end of my subscription, and I'm not going to renew it. However, they aren't about to let me go so easily.

To: Dianne@dontdoitatall.com
From: DatingExperts123@DatingExperts123.com
Subject: Give Us Money Now
Dear Dianne,
    This email is to notify you that on November 15th, your subscription to our most amazing website was renewed. Your new subscription will expire on December 15th. The first payment for $49.99 for your new 1-month subscription was charged to the payment method we have on file.
Sincerely,
The Dating Experts

Wait, no, no, no. I don't want to continue with this website. I want this canceled. I write to them that very day.

To: DatingExperts123@DatingExperts123.com
From: Dianne@dontdoitatall.com
Subject: No, I don't.
Dear Dating Uhhhh Experts:
    Please cancel my account. I don't want another month with your website. I don't like it.
Thanks,
Dianne Sweeney

To: Dianne@dontdoitatall.com
From: DatingExperts123@DatingExperts123.com
Subject: A Little Tip
Dear Valued Customer,
Thank you for contacting Customer Care.
    I can understand your frustration, but we are still unable to process your refund request. If you would like to send a comment regarding our refund policy, please send a letter to our Customer Relations Department.
    Also, I looked at your profile and might I suggest widening your religious beliefs. I'm not advocating you change your beliefs in anyway. However, if you would put your potential match could be Christian or other denomination, you may get a wider selection of men.
I wish you the best.

```
Sincerely,
Anthony
The Dating Experts
```

On this site you have to cancel on the very day your subscription expires, or they charge you for the next month. Your only other option is to cancel your membership at the moment you decide, and forego the rest of the month. No wonder they have thousands of people on their website—no one can figure out how the hell to get off of it.

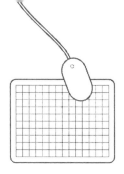

Game, Set, No Match

*J*ason may not be my perfect match; however, he does like to play tennis. After passing each other on the tennis court a few times, Jason and I decide to meet for a game of tennis of our own. Before arriving at the tennis courts, I stop to purchase two bottles of water. It's a warm day, and I want to stay hydrated. Shortly after, I meet Jason at the park. We greet each other and then prepare to take to the courts. I pull out my bottles of water and he says, "Hey, thanks for bringing me one."

I smile and hand him one, "Oh, sure. I thought you might get thirsty."

Okay, I have no problem sharing my water. He probably thinks I'm a super nice person, or does he? We step onto the court. We rally for a while and then decide to take a break. As we are sitting on the bench, a man with an ice cream cart comes strolling by, ringing his bell.

"Hey, ice cream sounds good. Do you want one?" he asks.

"Yeah, I could go for a popsicle," I answer, smiling.

"Great. I left my wallet in the car. Do you have any money?"

"Uhh, sure. Here's a couple of dollars."

After we finish playing tennis, he says, "Hey, are you hungry? We can grab a bite at that Taco Bell." He points to the fast food restaurant across the street.

"I'm not really hungry, but I could go for a Diet Pepsi and maybe a taco." He grabs his wallet out of the car (thank God), and we walk over there. We stand in line, and he orders a number one combo with a Sprite. He ends his order with, "That will do."

"$4.73, please."

After paying her, he turns to me and says, "Oh, did you want something?" I just stare at him in disbelief. I ask for a cup of water and tell him good-bye.

Game, Set, No Match. Okay, so meeting someone in the real world hasn't worked out any better than meeting someone on the World Wide Web.

Baby Steps

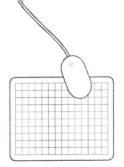

*N*ick and I haven't really talked to each other since he sent his email to me about online dating. Today, when I get home, I find the following email from him:

> To: Dianne@dontdoitatall.com
> From: Nick@Nick.com
> Subject: Hey Dianne
> Hey Dianne
>   I thought we could get together and have coffee or go to a movie or something? I'm just talking movies or coffee, don't get the wrong idea, I'm not that kind of person. ;).
> Nick

Oh how I want to respond with HELL YEAH. But, I think about my conversation with Adam, and I think about my conversations with Tim. I send this to Tim, who is a self-reformed Lothario.

To: Tman@Tman.com
From: Dianne@Dontdoitatall.com
Subject: T Read This!
T-man

   What the hell is this??????? I got this
yesterday....I'm kind of annoyed about the
just talking about a coffee or movie....It
makes it seem like he is warning me not to
expect anything....am I right?
D

To: Dianne@dontdoitatall.com
From: Tman@Tman.com
Subject: DO NOT DO IT!
D-

   Without question I would NOT do
this....I repeat, do NOT do this...it's all
a game...he is saying that so that YOU will
respond with something like "Yeah, I'm
not that easy either..." Then you'll get
together for a movie, he'll bring it up in
what he thinks is a subtle way, like "See,
I told you it would just be for a movie...
unless, of course, you wanted to go back
to my place..." TYPICAL maneuver, I used to
do it all the time with ex-girlfriends, do
NOT do this!!!!!!!!!!!

   Oh, and every time I did it, it WORKED!
So don't do it!
T

I want so badly to prove Tim wrong. But I know he is right. I write to Nick and thank him for the invite but tell him I don't think it would be a good idea to see each other. I haven't heard from him since. It's a really good feeling. No…it's a great feeling.

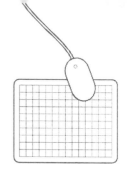

I'm Too Old for
the Bar Scene

*S*itting in the bar area of the local brewery, I glance from side to side at all the people in the room. Single men and women sneak glances at each other, hoping to catch someone's eye or a smile.

Co-workers gather to close the end of the work week, or to celebrate a job well done. Men sitting with men, women sitting with women, and a few lonely people sitting at the bar with their shields in hand. One woman is reading a book; one man is rifling through folders.

Jenna and I sit in the middle of it all. Jenna is one of my co-workers who is going through a divorce and for the present time has sworn off all men. I glance at some of the men, but there aren't too many who appeal to me. Don't get me wrong, there are a lot of good-looking men in here tonight, but I just am not in the mood to be on the prowl. Glancing around the room, my eyes rest on two women. Both of them are dressed in business casual attire.

I turn to Jenna, "Oh, my God, that woman's underwear is showing."

Jenna glances over at her.

"Do you see why bars don't work for me? How am I supposed to compete with that?" I say, exasperated. "I'm not going to sit here with half of my underwear hanging out to entice a man to approach me."

At that point, I look over at the woman, and, with a quick gesture, she reaches her hand behind her back and pushes her pants down a little further.

"Did you see that?" Jenna asks, laughing.

"Yeah, I saw it. I don't think I can do the whole thong sticking out of my pants thing. Actually, what is the fascination with the thong? Half of the time, I feel like someone is just giving me an atomic wedgie."

Jenna laughs really loud and says, "Don't knock it until you try it. They are really comfortable."

"So you are saying that I won't be able to attract a man if my Spanx are sticking out of my pants?"

"No, granny underwear does not send a man running toward you; it sends him running in that direction. Right into the arms of Thong Woman," she says, pointing her finger in the direction of the two ladies.

I spin around on my bar stool and watch them interact with two men who have approached them. Thong Woman is looking at them and smiling; they are glancing at her underwear and smiling, too.

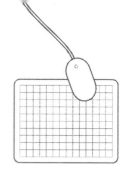

Cyber World vs. Spiritual World

*F*or fun, my sister and I decide to visit a psychic who has received rave reviews. I have been to a few psychics before, done the Tarot cards, and had my palm read. I take all that with a grain of salt, of course.

Heidi is supposed to be an amazing psychic. I need someone amazing, so I walk through the curtains to meet her.

"I have been expecting you," she says.

Of course she has! She is a psychic after all. But it could have been the bell that went off when the door opened, too.

I sit down. "I only really want to know one thing. What does the future hold for me when it comes to relationships?"

She begins to shuffle her Tarot cards and tells me to cut them. I do.

After a few minutes, she makes a pattern with the cards. There are three cards in the middle and one on the top and the bottom. She then turns to me and says, "How long do you want me to talk for?"

Puzzled, I say, "Until you are done?"

"Well, I charge by a certain number of minutes. Some people want me to read for fifteen minutes, and others want me to read for an hour and a half."

An hour and a half? Will it take that long?

I say, "Why don't we do a fifteen minute session, and if we need more time, we will go from there."

She sets her timer and begins.

"Do you have any specific questions?"

"Yes, I have just started dating again, and I want to know what the future holds for me in terms of relationships."

Doesn't everybody?

She takes quite a few minutes to study the Tarot cards and asks for my hand. I give it to her. She leans back and closes her eyes. "Oh yes, I see a man behind you in the distance."

I turn slightly and look over my shoulder. For a second, I think, damn, she's good. Then I realize she is speaking metaphorically.

"He has great eyes, and he smiles all the time. He should be coming into your life within the next one to six months."

"Well, maybe we could speed up this process? Do you have an exact address?" I ask her.

She opens one eye and looks at me, "No, it doesn't work that way. However, there is a man that is going to be coming into your life that I'm not too sure about. You need to be on your guard and listen to your instincts."

BEEP. BEEP. BEEP. The timer goes off.

Wait, wait, wait! Is she seriously going to send me off into the world on that last piece of advice? I can't trust my instincts. For the most part, I actually think I have good instincts, but I only use them when it's convenient. Otherwise, that annoying little pit at the bottom of my stomach that I get when something isn't right, I usually attribute to ulcers!

Okay, I'm going to turn my attention to men who have eyes and smile, but I'm going to stay away from all others because they could be potentially dangerous. No Cyclops, no men without teeth, or who do not have a good dental plan. That should be easy, right?

I thank Heidi for her sound advice; I pay my $50.00 and walk out.

As my sister and I are driving away from Heidi's, we see a sign in front of her business that says, "Thank You for Healing With Us."

Right after that, there is a temporary electronic sign on the side of the road that says, "Caution Rough Road Ahead." I suddenly get a strange feeling in the bottom of my stomach, I turn to my sister and say, "I don't think the breakfast I ate this morning agrees with my stomach."

"Hmmmmmm," she says.

We continue driving out of the canyon, down the windy road.

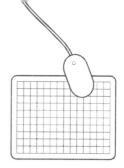

On a Quest for Him...or Me?

One of the hardest things for me to do is to sit back and let things take their natural course. I want to push things. I want to know if there is going to be another date. In the end, though, the only thing I push away is the man. As I wait for Matthew to ask me out for a third date, my mind begins to scrutinize our second date. I've been trying to remain true to myself. At the end of the date, he had walked me to my car, and given me a kiss good-night.

Uh-oh, what is that? I catch my breath as he leans in to say good-bye, and my stomach does flip-flops. I stand there, waiting for the, "I can't wait to see you again," or "Let's get together soon." Nothing. The clear blue water is turning murky. There is an uneasy feeling in the pit of my stomach. Trust your instincts. This feels good, but it doesn't feel right.

There could be something there, but I don't know. Practicing what I preach is a nightmare. When I'm unsure of my feelings, I will just hang in there and try and force them, but that is why I'm thirty-five and single. Even if there are red flags all over the place, I still grab on and I don't let go. These thoughts have been plaguing my mind for the last few hours.

I have to admit that all of these thoughts are causing me to have a bit of a meltdown. You can laugh or cry at these various situations, and for the most part I have chosen to laugh, but every once in awhile it's okay to cry. After Matthew and I decide not to see each other again, I become frustrated.

I turn to the two women in my life whom I most admire and adore. After talking to them, being real with them, and crying to them, I feel a lot better. Normally, I would call Adam, or even Tim, but I need my girlfriends. I need to be vulnerable with them. It has been a long time since either one of them has seen me cry. The crying isn't about Matthew, it isn't about Nick or John, and it isn't about anyone I have met so far, nor is it about the uncertainty of the beginning of a possible relationship. It's about the uncertainty of who I have been as a woman and who I'm now becoming. It's about the person to whom I have turned a deaf ear. It's about finally learning how to love the woman I am. When I look in the mirror, I smile. I see the woman I want my man to see. No more schemes, no more games. No more uncertainty about who I am.

My tears are washing away the woman I was. My tears are cleansing my soul as this journey comes to an end and a new one begins. Like the first rainstorm of the season, my tears are settling the dust and removing the grime that has been built up over the years. I don't exactly know when I got lost in the shuffle and began playing different roles, but it feels good to be the leading lady in my life again. Yet, I would be lying if I told you that I'm not afraid that I will never meet my leading man. I'm learning to trust my gut instincts more. To not get so wrapped up in a man who is only "a date." If anything, each man I meet will hopefully bring me closer to the right one. I turn to Jennifer during my meltdown.

Jennifer and I met last year. She had just been married, and she met her husband on one of these dating websites. She knows exactly what I'm going through because she has gone through it herself. Jennifer and I hit it off right away.

She listens to me, lets me cry, and then tells me, "Get over it."

"Huh?" Where is the sympathy?

Without missing a beat, she continues, "You are fabulous. If it doesn't happen with this guy, if it doesn't happen with Wifeless, if it doesn't happen with the guy who screams in movie theaters, then screw them. They're the ones missing out."

Jennifer and Adam are right. Why would I waste my valuable time on any guy who isn't going to make me feel secure in myself, or let me know that he wants to date me again? As long as I'm true to myself, that's all that matters.

She continues, "If there is not a second date, if there is not a third date, then thank God you weren't tied up for too long, because there is someone out there who is waiting for you. Who is searching for you. You may not find him in two months or in two years. You will find him, though. Don't waste your time with these men who don't know how great you are."

My tears dissipate and I throw out all of the soaking wet tissues that are surrounding me. I take a deep breath and realize that no matter what happens things are going to be okay.

Mr. Ironman

I have a confession to make. I'm afraid of getting hurt. Do you know how many years of therapy I could have saved had I written this book sooner? I'm not afraid of being in an intimate relationship; that is what I dream about. However, I'm terrified of the process. What if I show my potential mate my true colors, and he rejects me?

I have thought about this question a lot lately. Then I ask myself a better question—what if you don't show a person your true colors, and he rejects you anyway? Aren't I just deceiving that person or worse yet, myself? Am I sarcastic or jaded sometimes as a defense mechanism? Do I always say what is on my mind because I have to get the last word in? Do I close matches down quickly on the various sites so I can "beat them to the punch?" Yes, I do.

It's exhausting playing two, three, or sometimes even four different roles. The bricks that I have been chiseling away at are becoming smaller and smaller, and tonight I punch a hole through that wall.

Tonight, I do something that I have not done in a long time. I go on a date without my shield, without any armor on at all. Mr. Ironman, for better or worse, is going to see me for who I am. In the past, if a man were to tell me, "I love to bowl," my response would automatically be, "I love bowling." That would have been a lie. I like to bowl, but I do not love it. If a man says to me, "I love gin and tonic, do you?"

"Yes." Another lie.

I hate gin, and what the hell is tonic? I drink two or three drinks, if that. Pretending to be someone I want the other person to think I am has been a horrendous experience and has not gotten me anywhere.

Mr. Ironman has no idea who I really am; he knows of me only from a few pictures and some emails we have exchanged. I make the decision that I'm not going to pretend to be someone I'm not.

When he opens the car door for me, I lean over and unlock his door, not because I know about the "car-test," but because I want to unlock the door for him. Casually, we chat about some of the rock groups he enjoys listening to, and I don't cry out, "I love those guys!" If I'm not familiar with their music, I tell him so. This actually makes our conversations more real and down to earth.

Later in the evening, while sitting in a dimly lit bar, I would normally be looking for hints or clues to see if this person is into me, regardless of whether or not I'm into him. I do not do that tonight. We are going to see the movie, *30 Days of Night*. However, we are two hours early. This might get painful. It's up to us to figure out how to pass the time.

Lucky for us, there is a bar right next to the movie theater. We sit down and order drinks, and the minutes fly by.

As Mr. Ironman and I bounce from topic to topic, there are a few times where I actually utter the words, "I normally don't tell people this…" I don't preface my conversation with that to show him that I can be vulnerable. Actually, I find myself drawn to our conversation. Because of this, I find myself opening up more and more. There are things I would not tell anyone about my life until well into our relationship, or I would never speak of at all. However, during our conversation, we happen upon our families.

My family puts the "fun" in dysfunctional. We were not, and are not to this day, huggy, happy-go-lucky, "Brady Bunch" types. It's not a flaw, but sometimes people associate the family that a person comes from with the person he or she has become. I don't think this is fair, and that is one of the reasons why I don't talk about my family often. The apple can fall from the tree and roll a few feet away. Even if what I say about my family might make him look at me differently or send up a red flag, I say it anyway. Being seen as different isn't necessarily a bad thing. I don't pretend that there is a family reunion right around the corner, or that we gather around the piano and sing Christmas carols. Normally, during this time I still would be trying to figure out if he is into me. Should I touch his arm to see if he moves away? Instead, I focus on getting to know him and being present. Living in the now, and not thinking about the, "what ifs," and "oh nos".

It's one of the best dates I've been on in awhile. I don't know if there will be a second date. If there is, I'm going to continue to live in the present, not the past, and not even worry about the future—just yet. I want to focus on the process and get to know who he is and let him see exactly who I am. There will be no more role-playing with him or anybody else I may encounter along this journey. Didn't someone once say, "Our lessons come from the journey, not the destination."? That person was right.

I only care about right now. Three years ago, I would never have thought I would be writing a book. I don't know what will happen in three more years. All I can do is take life day by day and continue to evolve. Tonight, I went out with a great guy, but I met a fabulous woman.

December and Amy

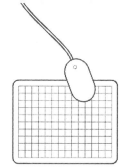

*G*od, I love my friend Amy. She is amazing and has been one of my best friends since she and I started teaching together. Funny, talkative and imaginative are just a few words that can only begin to describe her. She has the best laugh in the world. She and I could talk for hours about anything.

As I read her my piece on Mr. Ironman, she listens intently but also is dealing with Ben, her two-month-old baby. Dramatically, I begin reading. I get to the part where, "I punch a hole through the wall," and Amy pauses.

"Oh, my God. You punched a hole in your wall?" Amy exclaims.

I pause. Look at her, "Ummm, no I was speaking metaphorically, hon."

We laugh our heads off. I then continue to read, pausing slightly once in a while to make sure she is really with me.

At the end, I read with gusto, "Tonight, I went out with a great guy, but I met a fabulous woman."

I look up. She is staring at me, not really saying anything. I stare back at her; then, I break the silence, "You know I'm talking about me, right? I'm not becoming a lesbian."

We start laughing all over again.

What is That Noise?

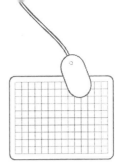

The voices in my head have disappeared. I may hear some whispering once in a while, but I'm learning to replace the whispers with Jennifer's words, Adam's profound advice, and mine and Christy's laughter. I will be okay. Whether there is a third date, a fourth date, or a fifth, with any man that comes into my life. When one match closes, I'm just going to click on my next potential match until I eventually click on the button that says, "Are you sure you want to cancel your account with us?"

Then, I will click *yes*, with confidence. I will shut my computer down, get up, walk over to "him," and kiss him, so *my* stomach does flip-flops.

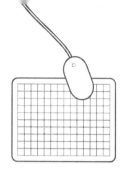

The Merry-Go-Round of Life

*I*s life a never ending circle? Do we ever really learn from our mistakes? If we don't learn from our mistakes, are we doomed to repeat them? Maybe. Is there a person out there who is just right for us, or are there thousands of men and women out there who are perfect for us? I don't know. However, I do know that I'm fabulous, smart, and sexy. When the right man comes along, I will know it. When the wrong man comes along, I will trust my instincts and let him go, even if there is a brief fluttering of butterflies. I'm not going to waste time on someone who makes me feel like I'm not worthy of his affection. I'm worth more than that. I have made some pretty stupid mistakes in my life when it comes to men, but I have learned to get past John, get past Nick, and any other "ghosts" who have haunted my thoughts.

As the merry-go-round continues to spin, I realize that I may get dizzy from time to time. I may want to throw up. I may get bucked off now and again, and I may get sick of this never ending circle, but eventually it will stop. All I can do is lean back, and enjoy the ride.

Besides, I can't get off this merry-go-round; I just got a free membership. And here-we-go…again.